D

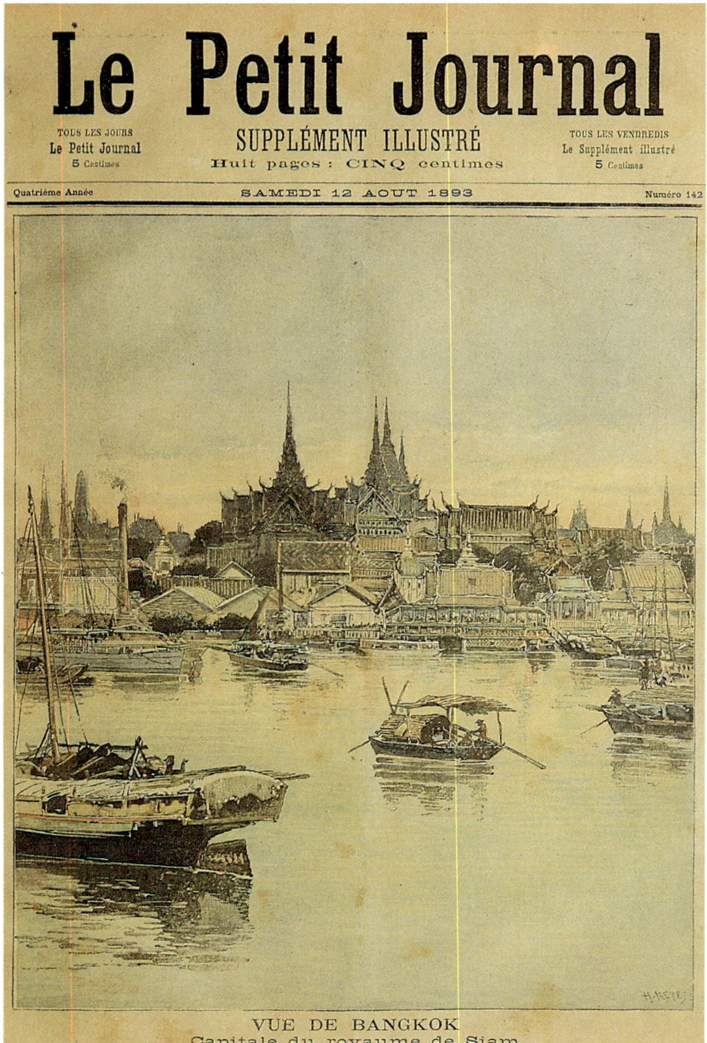

The Grand Palace seen from the river, from the cover of *Le Petit Journal*, Paris, 12 August 1893.

Descriptions of Old Siam

Compiled and Introduced by
MICHAEL SMITHIES

KUALA LUMPUR
OXFORD UNIVERSITY PRESS
OXFORD SINGAPORE NEW YORK
1995

Oxford University Press
Oxford New York
Athens Auckland Bangkok Bombay
Calcutta Cape Town Dar es Salaam Delhi
Florence Hong Kong Istanbul Karachi
Madras Madrid Melbourne Mexico City
Nairobi Paris Shah Alam Singapore
Taipei Tokyo Toronto

and associated companies in
Berlin Ibadan

Oxford is a trade mark of Oxford University Press

Published in the United States
by Oxford University Press, New York

First published 1995

British Library Cataloguing in Publication Data
Data available

Library of Congress Cataloging-in-Publication Data

Descriptions of old Siam/compiled and introduced by Michael Smithies.
p. cm.—(Oxford in Asia paperbacks)
Includes bibliographical references.
ISBN 967 65 3083 2 (paper)
1. Thailand. I. Smithies, Michael, II. Series.
DS561.5.D47 1995
959.3—dc20
94-45559
CIP

Typeset by Indah Photosetting Centre Sdn. Bhd., Malaysia
Printed by KHL Printing Co. Ptd. Ltd., Singapore
Published by the South-East Asian Publishing Unit,
a division of Penerbit Fajar Bakti Sdn. Bhd.,
under licence from Oxford University Press,
4 Jalan U1/15, Seksyen U1, 40000 Shah Alam,
Selangor Darul Ehsan, Malaysia

Preface and Acknowledgements

THE present volume of extracts is meant to follow a pattern in a series relating to South-East Asia, though clearly there are bound to be differences between one country and another. Thailand, formerly Siam, is and always was a highly centralized state, with the focal point being the king and his court until the abolition of the absolute monarchy in 1932. In spite of countless coups and the introduction of numerous constitutions since that date, the throne remains the most powerful symbol of unity in the country and the reverence accorded to it is often little understood by outsiders.

It is the continuities as well as the changes which these passages seek to reflect. If there are very few examples of twentieth-century writing, it is for two reasons: one, aesthetic, is that, with a country with such a long recorded past as Thailand's, the continuities and changes in this century are relatively less interesting and less marked, and, let it be said, modern travellers or residents often have little new to say that earlier visitors did not say better; the other, purely practical, is that obtaining permissions for reproduction is time-consuming, sometimes fruitless, and often costly.

The other lacuna is the absence of texts from other than Western sources. This is due largely to their absence, or at least, their lack of accessibility in a European language. Only one non-Western text is represented, a fascinating account of a Persian embassy at the close of the seventeenth century.

The spelling of Thai proper names is a vexed question on which much ink has been spilt. Authors quoted have been allowed to keep their chosen forms, though they may not conform to current notions of Thai transliteration.

The Compiler and the Publishers would like to thank the following for granting permission to use texts:

Lindeboom Inor: Cornelis van Neijenrode and Gijsbert Heeck
The Siam Society: Jeremias van Vliet

Hong Kong University Press: Father de Bèze
Routledge and Kegan Paul: Ibn Muhammad Ibrahim
William Carey Library: Dr Dan Beach Bradley
W. Heffer and Sons: Reginald Le May
Dr M. G. and Mr A. G. Smith: Malcolm Smith
Souvenir Press: W. A. R. Wood
J. M. Dent and Sons: James Kirkup

The Compiler has made every effort to discover which passage included here is subject to copyright and believes he has traced them all; if there are any lapses, the Compiler and Publishers offer their apologies to the copyright holders, trusting they will accept the intention for the act.

The Compiler, who has translated some passages into English for the first time, would also like to thank various persons who have helped in his quest for information, particularly Professor Dirk van der Cruysse, Dr Michel Jacq-Hergoualc'h, Dr John Villiers, and Mrs Genevieve Weiler.

Bua Yai
1994 MICHAEL SMITHIES

Contents

Introduction

MICHAEL SMITHIES

THIS collection of the written impressions of Siam left by overseas residents and visitors to the country spans four centuries, but in some respects unevenly. Although the presence of the Chinese in the country has been long and continuous, few, if any, seem to have left accounts of their stay, and certainly none of the thoroughness of Chou Ta-kuan, whose record of Cambodia at the end of the thirteenth century remains a classic. The reason for this lack of Chinese records may well be because the Chinese who came simply stayed. Chou Ta-kuan says in his section on immigrants in *The Customs of Cambodia*: 'Chinese sailors coming to the country note with pleasure that it is not necessary to wear clothes, and, since rice is easily had, women easily persuaded, houses easily run, furniture easily come by, and trade easily carried on, a great many sailors desert to take up permanent residence.'

The Chinese in Siam likewise assimilated, probably for similar reasons, and saw no need to write about their adopted country for the benefit of their countrymen they had left behind. There were periods when Chinese who left the Middle Kingdom were considered as outcasts by the imperial regime they had abandoned, and so there was good reason for keeping quiet in their adopted country. Furthermore, many were what would now be called low-status economic migrants and few of these could muster literary skills or even literacy. Certainly, the comparatively small numbers of Japanese who came in the seventeenth century were forced to remain when Japan shut itself off from the world, and as many had escaped religious persecution in Japan, they saw no point in attempting to return, and had no alternative to assimilation.

All these accounts therefore (with the single exception of a Persian text), are from Westerners, who first came to the country in the sixteenth century. The Portuguese conquest in 1511 of Malacca, nominally a dependency of Siam, profoundly disrupted trading patterns and traditional allegiances in the region, and the Portuguese at once sent an emissary to Ayutthaya, the capital of Siam (by which name both the city and the country were usually known), to be assured of the friendship of the king. He was well received and he and his entourage, with their strange clothes and beards, caused a great sensation.

Only the Portuguese and those in their wake seem to have made contact with Siam at this early period. The Dutch and English followed in the seventeenth century, along with the Japanese and Makassarese (Bugis) from the Celebes (though no firm date is known for their arrival, it is unlikely that the Bugis settled in any number before the country itself was stable at the end of the struggles with Burma in the sixteenth century). The object of all was trade: Siam was a great entrepôt centre in a period when sailing through the turbulent and pirate-infested waters of the Strait of Malacca in minute and flimsy boats was very dangerous; the longer and arduous overland route through Mergui and Tenasserim, Siamese territory on the Bay of Bengal, to Ayutthaya, and then usually in a Chinese junk to southern China or sometimes overland again, was a good deal safer. The accounts of this period, of Joost Schouten and Jeremias van Vliet, among others, were essentially concerned with possibilities and terms of trade.

The French did not appear until the second half of the seventeenth century and initially were less interested in trade in goods than in souls. Their encouragement was due to the presence on the throne of a remarkable monarch, Narai, intellectually curious and open-minded, a keen politician desirous of the best. He employed a Persian and a Greek as ministers, and he tried to play off one foreign power against another (so establishing a pattern for events in the nineteenth century). The French presence between 1685 and 1688 was overpowering and inevitably led to a reaction. These three years were the source of countless detailed accounts in French of the country, the most famous being that of Simon de La Loubère, which continued to be published until well into the next century.

From the very beginning, travellers were fascinated by Siamese elephants, and more particularly the veneration accorded to the white elephant. Accounts of these had become so frequent by the mid-seventeenth century that Nicolas Gervaise pointedly spared his readers details about them. Not so the chatterbox Abbé de Choisy, who had many pages devoted to elephant hunts organized by King Narai, and details of methods of catching wild elephants.

The death of Narai in 1688, the seizure of the throne by the usurper Petracha, the murder of the favourite Constance Phaulkon, and the ignominious retreat of the French troops from their ceded ports of Bangkok and Mergui, began a period in which Siam, previously so open to outside influences, became a hermit kingdom in a similar fashion to Japan which had earlier closed itself off from the outside world, though to a less marked degree. Embassies were still received, though to little purpose, the Dutch continued to trade, the French missionaries were, though under constraints, allowed to remain, and sea captains called on Siamese shores. The destruction of Ayutthaya by the Burmese in 1767, the re-establishment of the kingdom under Taksin, his madness, and the foundation in 1782 of a new dynasty were all accomplished with very few foreign observers of the scene, and fewer participants.

The cession of Penang to the East India Company by the Sultan of Kedah, a nominal subject of Siam, in 1785, and the Sultan's later contacts with Burma, together with Sir Thomas Stamford Raffles's establishment of Singapore in 1819, inevitably drew Siam into the world around more closely than before. Apart from trading concerns, there were problems over the legality of the acquisition of Penang, and the British occupation of Lower Burma in 1826, after the quick war that subdued Siam's traditional enemy, forced the court at Bangkok to look more closely to its frontiers and its allegiances. John Crawfurd's mission of 1822 was a total failure, apart from obtaining assurances that Siam recognized British rights to Penang. But by the time the better prepared Henry Burney went to Siam in 1826, the tide seemed to be passing to the British, and he succeeded in obtaining some concessions for trading, though little of substance. Of the two, Crawfurd's account, supplemented by that of his surgeon, George Finlayson, is the more accessible. Then came the first Protestant missionaries, particularly the Americans, who were to leave numerous accounts, the American diplomatic mission led by Edmund Roberts, and Frederick Arthur Neale's curious relation of his stay during the last years of Phra Nangklao (Rama III) seen through thoroughly unadaptable eyes. Whereas most sixteenth- and seventeenth-century visitors were simply curious and sometimes astonished spectators, early nineteenth-century accounts begin to exhibit signs of supposed Western superiority towards Orientals, and a sometimes irritating note of disdain creeps into many texts.

From the accession of King Mongkut in 1851, an entirely new era in the country began. The doors were thrown wide open to outside influences. Mongkut realized through his contacts with Westerners, before ascending the throne, the futility of resisting technological advances and saw that he must help the country adapt to a changed geopolitical situation. His friends, Bishop Pallegoix and Sir John Bowring, both left excellent accounts of the country. The king became more accessible, and foreigners regularly began to be received. John Thomson and the Marquis de Beauvoir both departed leaving delightful (and delighted) accounts of their reception in the palace; Anna Leonowens less so.

In the seventeenth century, few visitors ventured outside the capital (or Lopburi during Narai's reign), apart from taking the overland route to it through Tenasserim. Missionaries in the nineteenth century began to travel further afield, and it was the French explorer, Henri Mouhot, who was one of the first to leave substantial accounts of anywhere in the country outside Bangkok, Ayutthaya, and Lopburi and the routes thereto.

The long reign of King Chulalongkorn saw a great increase in foreign residents in the country, many in the employ of the Siamese government, and many more simply visitors to the country. Published accounts of their impressions flowed. Most continued to see the land as fertile, the society feudal, the people unusual, and the customs extraordinary. Explorers like the Norwegian Carl Bock followed in the steps of Mouhot. The residents continued into the twentieth century to write books about Siam, but a note of tired repetition can be detected in some of these texts. By the end of the century, the novelty was wearing off and the triumph of Western technology seemed to assure a colonial mentality.

With an increasing foreign trading presence in the country came the establishment of foreign consuls, the opening of legations, converted after the Second World War by diplomatic inflation to embassies, accounts of Siam became legion. After the fall of the absolute monarchy in 1932, there are so many that few will be quoted here. Although Siam remained exotic until the advent of mass tourism, it had long ceased to be a closed kingdom (as this book shows, it never was) and the realm of the unknown. A guidebook for tourists was produced in 1928 by Erik Seidenfaden for the State Railways, describing the sights of the capital and the places to see up-country. With that, one can reckon that Siam entered the mainstream of international developments, which the advent of jet aeroplanes some forty years later made absolute.

The Earliest Accounts (Sixteenth Century)

1
Ordering the Waters to Go Down

DIOGO DO COUTO

The honour for the first outside account of Siam which can be clearly identified, but which since the late eighteenth century was no longer a part of the kingdom, goes to the Venetian merchant, Nicolo di Conti. He spent twenty-five years travelling in Asia, returning in 1444, when he beseeched the pardon of Pope Eugenius IV for renouncing Christianity and embracing Islam, which he did in order to save his life. He was pardoned on condition he gave an account of his travels to the Pope's secretary, Bracciolini, who wrote down his recollections. Between 1425 and 1430, di Conti visited Mergui and Tenasserim, which was 'found at the mouth of a river of this name and all the countryside around is rich in elephants and sapan wood'.

More substantial and frequent accounts of Siam come from the Portuguese, who sent a delegation led by Duarte Fernandes to Ayutthaya immediately after the capture of Malacca in 1511. The most important Portuguese accounts are those of Tomé Pires, Duarte Barbosa, Mendez Pinto, and Gaspar de Cruz. The principal Spanish sources of the sixteenth and seventeenth century are Gabriel Quiroga de San Antonio and Marcelo de Ribadaneira. The Comentários *of Alfonso de Albuqueque and the chronicles of Fernão Lopes de Castanheda, Gaspar Correia, Fernão Guerreiro, and Antonio Bocarro also contain information about Siam. The great Portuguese poet, Luis de Camoẽs (1524–80), in his* Os Lusíadas *(1572), has references to Siam and the Menam Chao Phraya:*

Olha o rio Menaõ que se derame
Do grande lago que Chiamai se chama
(The Meinam now behold, whose waters take
Their sources in the great Chiamai lake)
Translation by Sir John Bowring of Lus. *X.cxxv)*

and in the tenth canto refers to the mouth of the Mekong, where he had the misfortune to be shipwrecked.

The Décadas, *started by João de Barros and continued by Diogo do Couto (1542–1616), state that there were nine kingdoms subject to the monarchs of Siam, but only in Autthaya and Chaumua (Chiangmai) was Siamese spoken. Diogo do Couto gives details of the Burmese invasion of Siam in 1543, and describes the banks of the Chao Phraya in terms, according to Sir John Bowring (the source of this information), similar to its condition in the mid-nineteenth century. Diogo do Couto, incidentally, gives an early description of Angkor.*

Here is do Couto's description, in Sir John Bowring's translation, of the ceremony to mark the end of the rainy season, when the king orders the water to recede.

THE King comes out of the city, accompanied by the whole of the nobility, in barges richly gilded and covered with ornaments, with great display and noise of musical instruments. They proclaim that the King is about to order the waters to disperse; and this is the great festival of the year. A mast is raised in the middle of the stream, adorned with silken flags, and a prize suspended for the best rower. All the contending boats put themselves in trim, and at a given signal start, with such cries, and shouting, and tumults, as if the world was being destroyed; the first who arrives carrying off the prize. But in the contest there is terrible confusion—boats running against and swamping one another, oars tangled and disentangled in a disorder admirable to look at from around. So that the people are not so barbarous, but that they imitate the ancient Trojans (as in the same manner, Eneas, when he arrived in Sicily, had the festival of his galleys, giving precious prizes to the most alert); and when these Siamese have won the prize, they return to the city with such rejoicings, shoutings, and tumultuous music, that the noise shakes both the waters and the land. Then the King having returned to the city, the people say he has driven back the waters, because these heathens attribute to their Kings all the attributes of God, and believe they are the source of all good.

Quoted in Sir John Bowring, *The Kingdom and People of Siam*, London, Parker and Sons, 1857, Vol. 1, pp. 101–2.

2
The Extent, Wealth, and Organization of the Kingdom

FERNÃO MENDEZ PINTO

Fernão Mendez Pinto travelled for twenty-one years throughout the East before returning to Portugal in 1558, dying there in 1583. His huge Peregrinação *was published in 1614 based on his memory in honourable retirement. He devotes nine chapters (181–9) to the 'Empire of Sornau, which the people of the country ordinarily call Siam' where he lived in the 1540s, taking part in the wars of King Chairacha (r. 1534–47) against the Burmese. He relates the poisoning of the king (his successor, in fact, Yot Fa) by his queen, the usurpation of the throne by her lover, Ok Khun Chinnarat Worawongs, in 1548, the accession of Chairacha's half-brother, Thienracha Chakkraphat, and the seige of Ayutthaya by the Burmese in 1549. Much of what Pinto wrote has been disputed. Certainly, he confuses facts and muddles dates, but a Portuguese Jesuit, Cardim, who lived in Ayutthaya from 1626 to 1629, wrote that 'Although the book of Pinto, the* Peregrinação, *is considered apocryphal, it is correct in what he wrote about Siam.'*

Pinto's last section on Siam, Chapter 189,[1] *'On the great fertility of the Kingdom of Siam, and of many other particularities concerning this country', is perhaps the most interesting, and is given here in full.*

HAVING written previously of the success of this incursion of the Burmese king to the Kingdom of Siam, and of the uprising in the Kingdom of Pegu, it seems to me to be relevant to speak briefly here of the situation, extent, abundance, wealth and fertility which I saw in this Kingdom of Siam and of this Empire of Sornau, to show that its conquest would have been much more useful than are today all the states which we possess in the Indies, especially considering that it could have been acquired with far less outlay.

This kingdom as can be seen from the map, is some 700[2] leagues in length and 60[3] in breadth in the interior. Most of it consists of broad plains, where can be seen many fields and fresh water rivers, on account of which this country is extremely fertile, and provided with an abundance of cattle and victuals. In its upland regions there are dense forests of *angelin* [teak?], which can be used to make thousands of boats of all kinds; there are several silver, iron, steel, lead, tin, saltpetre and sulphur mines, as well as silk, eaglewood, benzoin, lacquer, indigo, cotton, rubies, sapphires, ivory, gold, all in great abundance. In the forests are also much Brazil and ebony wood, which fill every year more than one hundred junks to carry it to China, Hainan, Lequois [?], Cambodia, and Champa, without mentioning wax, honey and sugar which are gathered in different places.

The king normally receives as his dues twelve millions of gold [*sic*], apart from the numerous presents which the lords of the country offer him. In the jurisdiction of his lands he has 2,600 boroughs which they call *prodon*, like our cities and towns, not to mention the small hamlets and villages of which I

[1]In the 1645 French edition, this actually appears as Chapter 188, but this is in error, as there are two chapters numbered 187.

[2]Robert Viale's 1991 translation from Portuguese into French (Paris, La Différence) gives the more likely figure of seventy.

[3]In Viale's text, 160.

Map of the Kingdom of Siam, from Simon de La Loubère, *A New Historical Relation of the Kingdom of Siam*, London, 1693.

take no account. Most of these towns have no other fortifications or walls to their boroughs than wooden pallisades, thus making it very easy to whoever attacked them to make himself master of them. Furthermore, the inhabitants of these towns are naturally passive, they are not used to carrying offensive weapons.

The coast of this kingdom touches the two seas of the north and the south; that of the Indies by Junkceylon [Phuket] and Tenassarim, and that of China by Monpolocata, Cuy, [Kuiburi], Lugor [Nakorn Srithammaraj], Chintabu [Chantaburi?], and Berdio [Bandol or Pattalung?]. The capital of all this empire is the town of Odiaa [Ayutthaya], about which I have spoken before. It is fortified by brick and mortar walls, and peopled, according to some, by 400,000 hearths, including 100,000 foreigners from diverse countries of the world. For, since this kingdom is very rich, and has much trade, there is never a year in which all the provinces and islands of Java, Bali, Madura, Angenio [Ambon?], Borneo, and Solor [Sulu?] do not send less than 10,000 junks[4] without counting the other smaller vessels, which constantly fill all the rivers and all the ports.

The king has not in his nature a disposition to tyranny. The customs dues of the entire kingdom are destined charitably for the upkeep of certain pagodas, so the taxes needed to be paid are very low. For as the persons of religion are forbidden to use money, they only ask of merchants who genuinely wish to give alms. There are in the country twelve gentile sects, as in the Kingdom of Pegu, and the king is given the supreme title of *Prechau Saleu*,[5] which in our language means 'Holy Member of God'. He is only seen by his people twice a year, but does so with great pomp and majesty which show his importance and power. Nevertheless, for all that I have said, he still allows himself to be called a vassal, and sends tribute to the King of China, so that by this means the junks of his subjects can land at the port of Combay [Canton?], where they ordinarily conduct their commerce.

[4]One thousand in Viale.

[5]Usually *Prachau Paendin* or *Prachau Chiwit*, 'Lord of the Land' or 'Lord of Life'.

There is furthermore in this kingdom a great quantity of pepper, ginger, cinnamon, camphor, alum, senna, tamarind, cardamom, to the extent that one can affirm without lying, what I have often heard said in these lands, that this kingdom is one of the best in the whole world, and easier to seize than any other province, however small it might be.

I could relate here many strange things I have seen in the town of Odiaa alone, which I have not discussed in relation to the whole kingdom, but I am not permitted to mention them, in order not to cause those who read me here the same grief which I have for the losses which we have suffered for our sins, and the gain which we would have acquired in conquering this kingdom.

Les Voyages Adventureux de Fernand Mendez Pinto fidèlement traduits de Portugais en François par le Sieur Bernard Figuier Gentilhomme Portugais, Paris, Arnold Continet et Jean Roger, 1645, pp. 844–6.

3
The Monarch and His Elephants

JACQUES DE COUTRE

Jacques de Coutre was a merchant from Bruges, whose Life *was written down by his son Esteban in Spanish, and published in Madrid in 1640 in the year of his death. De Coutre left Bruges in 1591, when fourteen, for Lisbon, whence he departed for the Indies with his brother Joseph. He spent thirty years in Asia, where he amassed and lost great wealth. He was captured and sold almost as many times as Pinto, and spent eight months in Siam in 1596 during the reign of Naresuan (1590–1605), who re-established Siamese independence from Burma in the decisive battle of Nong Sarai in 1593. De Coutre was in Siam at a period before contacts were established on a regular basis with the Dutch and the English under the reign of Ekathotsarot (1605–11); the only Westerners known in Siam at the time were the Portuguese.*

De Coutre formed part of a delegation from the Portuguese Governor of Malacca sent at the request of the King of Siam. Naresuan was so impressed by the promises of the mission at their solemn audience that he decided to send an embassy to the King of Portugal. De Coutre was worried by these false promises, and admitted them to one of the king's concubines, who informed the king. The mission was cancelled and de Coutre and his friends were summoned to the palace, taking the customary presents, and prostrating themselves. The king heard them and granted them and any other Portuguese who wished to leave permission to return to Malacca with trade goods.

Worried that they might be 'fried like sardines', the head of the mission, Father da Motta, and the Envoy, Pereira de Abreu, then revealed that the captain of their junk, Luis de Freitas, had stolen some gilded Buddha statues. Naresuan was furious, had about fifteen 'mandarins' executed for not revealing the Portuguese machinations, and went off on an elephant hunt, forbidding the departure of the Portuguese. Jacques de Coutre joined the hunt, hoping to escape the country at the first opportunity. He was not able to, but finally received permission to leave for Malacca, on his return with the king to Ayutthaya.

De Coutre was deported to Spain in 1623 when the King of Spain (also the ruler of Portugal from 1580 to 1640) ordered all aliens to leave Spanish and Portuguese colonies in Asia. He died in Saragossa in 1640.

The capital city and its royal palace and pagodas are all carefully described by de Coutre, but he was particularly impressed by the treatment of the royal elephants. As this is the first such description, it follows in extenso. *One has to treat de Coutre's text with caution, as there is virtually no means of checking its veracity (though van Vliet bears out King Naresuan's alleged cruelty), and he wrote or dictated his memoirs more than forty years after his stay in Siam. However, he would have needed a keen imagination to evoke in such detail places which are recognizable from other descriptions.*

De Coutre's account is little known in Siam. A Dutch translation appeared in 1988, and parts of it appeared in French in Dirk van der Cruysse's Louis XIV et le Siam *in 1991. In the same year, Stols, Teensma, and Werberckmoes published in*

Madrid, with the title Andanzas asiáticas, *the original Spanish text, which has not at the time of writing yet been published in English.*

WHEN the king goes forth, he does so with great pomp and accompanied by all his guards in two rows. He goes quite naked, apart from a small piece of cloth covering his secret parts, but with no other robe. On his head he wears a mitre like a bishop's, fluted at the top and all in gold, and inserted with numerous precious stones and other jewels. Seated on an elephant with two golden hooks in his hands, he guides the beast.... His brother follows on another elephant, his hands joined and raised above his head and very low as though receiving a blessing. Around them marches all the trumpets, the horn players and drummers.... Four huge umbrellas, signs of royal rank, were carried. Everything took place in total silence and we met no one in the streets.... People were warned when he left his palace and by which roads he would pass. At that moment, one met not a soul, not even a dog. Not even barking was heard, for the dog and its owner would have been killed in the cruellest fashion on earth.

The palace is surrounded by stables where live the favourite elephants ridden by the king when he goes out. I went to see them out of curiosity. They were in great number, and two among them were particularly valued and pampered. The sumptuosity of their treatment deserves to be mentioned. Each one had its silk cushion, and they slept on it as if they were small dogs. It is easy to imagine the size of cushions made for elephants of six yards and more. They were fastened with chains as heavy as door-chains, plated with gold. Since I thought them to be made of solid gold, curiosity made me go nearer, and I found out that they were worn away in some places and gold-plated. Even the tassels were of silk, and each one of them had six very large bowls of gold. It is obvious that they had to be huge; their thickness was that of a four reál piece. Some contained oil to grease their skins; others were filled with water for sprinkling; others served for eating, others for drinking, others for urinating and defecating. The elephants were indeed so well trained that they got up

The king seated on an elephant, from Guy Tachard, *Voyage de Siam des Pères Jésuites envoyés par le Roi aux Indies et à la Chine*, Paris, Seneuze et Horthemels, 1686.

from their beds when they felt the urge to urinate or defecate. Their attendants understood at once and handed them the bowls. And they kept their lodgings always very sweet-smelling and fumigated with benzoin and other fragrant substances. Thus they lived in great luxury. I would not have believed it if I had not actually seen it.

On the day of the death [of a royal elephant], the king was overcome with grief, and said that his own father had passed away. He ordered the people and all the dignitaries of his realm to worship the elephant. For that reason they carried the elephant outside the city to the other bank of the river and placed it in front of a pagoda.... They built a huge canopy of blue damask over the elephant, opened his belly and removed the viscera. They annointed him with many sweet-smelling aromatics and put on top a great quantity of flowers and roses. And to keep the belly wide open, they inserted several gilded poles, and four talapoins (who are their priests) went inside and sat down, dressed in yellow robes with strings of beads in their hands (they call them *ganitra*); many wax candles were lit. A few more [talapoins] entered, others left after a while. After this they built a huge gallery of gilded and painted wood around the elephant, with five flights of stairs reaching the ground and balustrades all around. It took them less than one and a half days to make the whole thing. One could smell the elephant from more than half a league away. Then all the dignitaries and lords came to worship him from the gallery or cloister, where a great number of candles were lighted on the balustrades all around, and then they worshipped the beast on their knees. These barbarities went on for eight days, during which there were, all the time, day and night, dances and infernal music with bells, kettledrums, pans and other instruments worthy of Pandora. Many men were dressed as tigers, devils and white horses all made of paper. And there were birds [*kinnari*], made of yellow painted wood, looking like ostriches the size of horses. The talapoins sat on them, one talapoin on each. They placed on all sides painted pots containing all sorts of food; the openings were painted and sealed. The barbarians said that they were for the animal to eat in the afterlife. When the eight days had come to an end, the talapoins covered him with large and small pieces of wood. Then the king came, walked three times around the elephant, and kindled the fire. When the cremation was over he ordered the ashes to be collected in gold urns, and they stored them with the urns of his ancestors and predecessors.

After the storing of the urns, two men, former servants or attendants of the elephant, presented themselves before the king. They told him that since the elephant, their master, was dead, they wished to go and serve him in the other world. The king thanked them profusely, drew his sword, cut them in two, and had them cremated with much honour.... So ended the barbarian ceremonies for the [dead] elephant.

Jacques de Coutre, *Vida de Iaqves de Covttre, Natvral de la Civdad de Brvgas,* Madrid, 1640, Book I, Ch. 10, p. 62; Ch. 13. pp. 85–6; Ch. 14, pp. 97–101. This text and the details relating to Jacques de Coutre were kindly supplied by Professor Dirk van der Cruysse, who gave permission to quote from his paper on de Coutre presented at the Fifth International Conference on Thai Studies, SOAS, London, 1993.

The Dutch Traders (Early Seventeenth Century)

4
A Land of Plenty, Magnificence, and Charity

CORNELIS VAN NEIJENRODE

Cornelis van Neijenrode was a VOC (Dutch East Indies Company) official of some importance. He became a director in 1617 after spending two years in Ayutthaya and Pattani and five in Nakorn Srithammaraj. He went on to stay ten years in the VOC post at Hirado in Japan. His Account of the Kingdom of Siam, *probably written in 1621, was not published until the nineteenth century, but it was the earliest Dutch account of the country. Van Neijenrode writes, according to Brummelhuis, 'with honest amazement' that the Siamese should tolerate all religions, that children are rarely beaten but grow up obedient, that people wash frequently each day, and that flattery is not esteemed.*

ALL in all, [the Siamese is] well supplied with all manner of livestock and animals. Sugar, salt, plants yielding oil-seed, green vegetables, fruit and a thousand other products of the soil abound, sufficing for man's subsistence—milk and honey are plentiful—so that in time of necessity he can supply his needs, indeed lavishly so, without the aid of other countries....

The Emperor or King of Siam maintains as magnificent pomp and ceremony as any king in the whole of the Indies. He never sets foot on the earth; wherever he wishes to go he is carried, sitting on a golden throne, and appears before his lords and nobles at his court once each day with a magnificence exceeding that of any Christian king ... all in all, with a pomp and grandeur not to be imagined or credited by anyone who had not seen it, yet although I have seen it many times, both at court and elsewhere and have been invited to visit His Majesty, I cannot fully describe it....

[The monks'] food, clothing and needs are supplied very finely, richly and abundantly by all, both great and small, who take great care of their scholars or priests (and more than those in our countries do of their teachers), and it is a cause of great amazement to our nation to see the heathens display such great love for one another.

Quoted in Han ten Brummelhuis, *Merchant, Courtier and Diplomat: A History of the Contacts between the Netherlands and Thailand*, Lochem, Uitgeversmaatschappij De Tijdstroom BV, 1987, p. 16.

5
Impressions of the Country

JOOST SCHOUTEN

Joost Schouten was born in Rotterdam, but little else is known about his early life. He was living in Batavia by 1628 and was a person of rank in the VOC, the Dutch East Indies Company. He was an ambassador from the Prince of Orange to King Prasart Thong in Ayutthaya in that year, and lived for some years in Japan. Schouten went again to Siam as resident overseer of the Dutch factory, and was received by the king in February 1634. He made several journeys between Batavia and Siam, and for a short while returned to the Netherlands. In 1644, this loyal servant of the VOC was accused in Batavia of the 'filthy and vile sodomitish Sin', which habit he admitted to having started in Siam, was condemned to death by strangulation at the stake, after which his body was burned, the ashes scattered, and all his considerable property confiscated.

Schouten wrote his account of Siam in 1636, and it was published in The Hague two years later. From 1646 it was invariably added to the account, also written in 1636, of Japan by François Caron, another employee of the VOC. Both first appeared in English in The Voyages and Travels of J. Albert de Medelslo ... *in 1662. Roger Manley's classic (though not always accurate) translation of* A True Description of the Mighty Kingdoms of Japan and Siam *first appeared the following year.*

Schouten's account of Siam is brief, coming to only thirty-two pages of duodecimo in the 1671 edition followed here. He first of all describes the extent of the country, the court, the royal revenues, the system of justice, the armed forces, and the wars with Burma. There is then an extensive section on capturing elephants, followed by comments on the practice of religion, marriage customs, and the foreign communities of Ayutthaya. Schouten concludes with a section on the Dutch contacts and trade with the country.

ONCE every year, about the moneth of October, the King of Siam shews himself by water and land in state to his people, going to the principal Temple of the Gods, to offer there for the welfare of his Person and Kingdom, the manner follows: When he goes by land, the procession is led by two hundred Elephants, each attended with three armed men; these are followed by many Musitians with Gomnies [trumpets?], Pipes and Drums, and a thousand men richly armed, and provided with Banners: Then march the great Lords of the Kingdom on horse-back, many of them wearing Crowns of Gold upon their heads; and every one waited upon by sixty, eighty, or an hundred men on foot: Two hundred Japan Souldiers follow these with bright Arms and rich Colours, and much noise of Instruments, then comes the Lifeguard with the King's Horses and Elephants, richly adorned with precious Stones and Gold furniture; which is followed by many Servants loaden with fruits and presents for the Sacrifice, accompanied with a sweet consort of Musick: These are again followed by many of the great Ones on foot, with folded hands; as also some Crowned Grandees, whereof one carrieth the gilded Standard, and the other the Sword of

Justice; his Majesty follows next in person in his royal Robes, sitting upon an Elephant, or else a gilded Throne, carried upon mens shoulders, and waited upon by many Lords and Courtiers; the Prince, or Heir of the Kingdom, followeth him; and then in order the Kings Wives and Concubins, seated upon Elephants in little enclosed Cabinets: lastly the ordinary Courtiers follow; the whole provision consisting of fifteen or sixteen thousand persons, having its rear brought up by six hundred armed men. But if the King go by water, then two hundred Lords, each in his Barge, seated in a gilded Cabinet, with eighty or ninety Rowers, led the van; these are followed by ten extraordinary rich figured Praws, or Barges, the which, as also the Oars, are all gilded, each having ninety or an hundred Watermen: The King is in the richest of them, sitting like an Idol upon a golden Throne, with his Lords in their humblest posture at his feet: the royal Banner is born by one of these Grandees, at the head of the Barge, in state. The King's Brother followeth next with his Train; and after him his Majesties Wives and Concubins, in gilded Cabinets and Tents, each in their Barges apart: lastly the Gentry, Courtiers, Guards, and other Attendants follow, the whole amounting to five or six and twenty thousand persons. The River is bordered on both sides with Boats, and an infinite number of People, who reverence and adore their King in his passage, with bended heads and folded hands.

A white Elephant (esteemed by the Indians a wonder in Nature) hath been found in Siam, and no other known Land; it is esteemed by the inhabitants as the Prince of the Elephants, and hath been so treated by the Kings of this Country, who have had of them in the Palaces many times, and caused them to be served in state, often visited them, and honoured their Vassals with more than ordinary respect. These white Elephants have formerly occasioned great wars betwixt the Siammers and their Neighbours; and some sixty years since against the King of Pegu, who proving victorious, did not only take the white Elephant prisoner, but obliged the King of Siam to become his Tributary; which yoke the following Princes did not only cast off, but gloriously revenge their Predecessours misfortunes. During my first residence in Siam, the then King took two young white Elephants, but both died shortly after

The sacred elephant of Siam, from Marquis de Beauvoir, *A Week in Siam, January 1867*, Bangkok, Siam Society, 1986.

to his great grief. This Nation believes somewhat more then humane nature of this creature, alledging they do not only respect him for his whiteness, but for his divine understanding; which appears in his pride and glorying when he is treated in state, and of his melancholy and sorrow when those honours are denied him, or that the black Elephant refuses him his obeisance.

The Siammers, as also the Neighbouring Nations, are all Idolaters and Heathens, so that they have every where great and little Temples and Cloysters for the service of their Gods; and the dwellings of their Priests. These Edifices are builded of Wood and Stone very Artificial and sumptuous, with gilded Towers and Pyramids; each of the Temples and Cloysters being filled with an incredible number of Idols, of divers materials and greatness, gilded adorned and beautified very rich and admirable; some of the Idols are four, six, eight, and ten fathoms long; amongst the rest there is one of an unimaginable greatness, being one hundred and twenty foot high. In these Temples and Cloysters there are many Priests and religious Men disciplined, and very obedient to their superiours, being all subject to the Arch Flamin [High Priest], or Prior of the great Temple of Judica [Ayutthaya], whose spiritual power is vastly great, though subordinate to the Kings. All the Clergy (whereof there are in Judica alone at least thirty thousand) are clothed, without any remarkable difference, in yellow linnen clothes, having their heads all shorn. The learnedst amongst these are professed Priests, out of which the Regents of their Temples are chosen (who are held in great esteem and reverence by the People), preaching, teaching, and offering upon their Feasts and Holy-dayes. These are prohibited the natural use of Women, upon pain of being burned; but they may alwayes, and at pleasure, upon declaration of their frailty or weakness, quit their frocks, and betake themselves to another life, which happens often amongst them. They have their morning and evening Song, Readings and other Services, celebrated in their Cloysters every day, and frequented by their society. They live upon the Alms and bounty of the King and great Ones, as also on the fruit which their Church Lands bring forth; but principally out of the sweet [sweat] and labours of the Commonalty, who unanimously share with them, they sending every morning some Priests and Clerks out of their Cloysters, with begging bags to receive these donations and charity: Besides these Priests, there are a sort of old Nuns shorn, lodged in Chappels near the greatest Temples, who assist very devoutly in all their preachings, singings, ceremonies, and other Church services, but all voluntary, being tied to no rules or prescriptions. These Heathens do generally believe (however differing in many particulars), that there is one upper God, with many lesser Deities in Heaven, who created all things: that the Souls of Men are immortal, and shall be rewarded or punished according to their merits and actions; the good dwelling with the God in bliss, whilest the wicked are tormented by the Devils that seduced them.... The Priests carry themselves very moderately to those of a contrary Religion, condemning no opinions, but believe that all, though of differing tenets, living vertuously, may be saved, all services which are performed with zeal being acceptable to the great God, especially theirs, they being convinced of its truth and innocency. This constancy of theirs makes them not easily to be drawn to any other perswasion, which hath been sufficiently attempted by the Portugals; whose industrious Priests omitted nothing for their conversion, and by the Mahometans who are no less zealous in their way, though with little or no success by either of them, and yet the Christians, as also the Mahometans, are both permitted the free exercise of their Religions in their Countrey....

The people of the Countrey are reasonably well proportioned, brown and tawny; they are none of the best Souldiers, though proud and insolent in their victories; they are modest enough in their civil conversation, though naturally light, fearful, incredulous, dissimuled, deceitful, and very lying. The men are lazy and slow, insomuch that the women, with their slaves, are forced (contrary to the customs of other Nations) to labour the earth, & do most of their husbands work, besides taking care for their families & houses, whilst the men follow their pleasure & divertisements abroad. They cloath themselves (both men & women) thin, according to the hot climat they live in; both sexes wear painted petticoats, the men covering their upper parts with a short shirt with half-sleeves, and the women with a thin cloth, both ends hanging over their shoulders to hide their brests: They wear for ornaments gold pins in their hair, and rings of the same mettal on their fingers: This is the ordinary wear, high & low being all of a fashion, & not distinguishable but by the richness of their vestments, & the greatness of their trains, which they much glory in: The Gentry & Nobles have many slaves attending them when they go abroad, some ten, twenty, thirty, or more, according to their abilities and greatness; and not a Citizen or his Wife stirs in the streets without one or two of these slaves to wait upon them. Their houses are builded according to the fashion in India, of wood and reeds, and covered with Coco leaves, or tiles; the floors are raised three or four foot high, their apparte-ments being commodious, though but slenderly furnished, only for sleeping, and dressing what is necessary for their refection. Their diet is but mean, as rice, fish, and herbs; they drink water, though on Feast-dayes they indulge more the common people, drinking ordinarily Arak, or Brandy-Wine....

The Siammers, who live in Towns and populous places, are either Courtiers, Officers, Merchants, Watermen, Fishermen, Tradesmen, or Artificers, each one containing himself in his vocation: The Country people brew, till, plant, and bring up swarms of Cattel, as Horses, Klne, Swine, Deer; and domestick Fowl, as Geese, Peacocks, Ducks, Hens, Pigeons, and other tame creatures, insomuch that provision is very cheap, not withstanding the abundance of it which is sent into the neighbouring Provinces for their supply and use: They have Brick, Lime, Wood, and all materials for building of Churches, Forts, Houses, Ships, Prawes, Jonks, and other vessels in great quantities.

François Caron and Joost Schouten, *A True Description of the Mighty Kingdoms of Japan and Siam*, London, 1671, pp. 128–30, 139–46, 147–8.

6
The Character of the Reigning Monarch, Prasart Thong

JEREMIAS VAN VLIET

Jeremias van Vliet was born in 1602 in Schiedam, joined the VOC in Rotterdam, and arrived in Batavia in 1629. From 1633 to 1636, he was Joost Schouten's deputy at the Dutch factory in Ayutthaya, and succeeded him as director in 1636. He returned to Batavia in 1641, and became director of the trading post at Malacca. From 1647 to his death in 1663, he remained in Schiedam, where he became an alderman. Van Vliet was often in conflict with the king, Prasart Thong (r. 1629–56), and his Phra Klang (chief minister), largely on the issue of whether the Siamese could require the Dutch to observe Siamese customs. In one incident, the king was ready to have two Dutch prisoners tied to stakes to be trampled to death by elephants, but relented on the intercession of van Vliet through the intermediary of a Muslim trader and a Chinese.

Van Vliet wrote a detailed Description of the Kingdom of Siam, *similar to the accounts of Cornelis van Neijenrode and Joost Schouten, again for the Governor-General in Batavia, and* The Short History of the Kings of Ayutthaya, *much of the information in which must have come from Siamese chronicles and from personal questioning. The extract which follows deals with Prasart Thong, with whom van Vliet was obliged to have several personal and not always comfortable dealings.*

Phra-ong Si Thammarachathirat [Prasart Thong, r. 1629–56], Twenty-fifth King of Siam, Has been Ruling Eleven Years.

AFTER the death of the young prince, the provisionally-crowned king Okya Kalahom … was declared sole and absolute king and crowned when he was thirty years old. He was called Phra-ong Si Thammarachathirat. This king and the two murdered kings were close relatives because the father of the two murdered princes and the present king were children of a sister and brother.… The present king was very majestic in the beginning of his rule and was merciful toward his mandarins [the *khunnang*, or nobility] and lesser subjects. He was also very considerate; if any complaints came before His Majesty, he did not condemn nor judge the guilty hastily but commissioned the impartial to investigate the disputed matter, with orders that the examiners should not be swayed by the individual on trial but by the gods, the king, and by justice. But debauchery and vainglory so corrupted his former nature and understanding that the more powerful he became on the throne, the quicker he became in passing judgment.

In the beginning of his reign, he waged war against Lakhon [Lampang] (a city bordering Lan Chang) and Ligor [Nakorn Srithammaraj], which cities had broken away from the crown during the troubles. However, he conquered Lakhon and again bound it to the kingdom. He expelled the Japanese living in Siam who had served him during the usurpation, but he recalled them within a short time. His Majesty also dealt with the Portuguese in a hostile fashion and treated them as if they were prisoners. After that, however, he sent ambassadors to Malacca and letters to Manila to offer peace to the Portuguese and the Spanish. His Majesty was reconciled with the Portuguese but no answer came from Manila. He sent emissaries to the Kings of Acheh and Arakan to establish firm peace with their majesties. These kings, especially the King of Acheh, did not oppose it, but it subsequently proved to be a friendship of words without any real substance behind it.

The Kingdom of Patani refused to pay homage, and so in the fifth year of his reign, His Majesty sent a powerful army there. His armies, however, were repulsed. Thus His Majesty had all the war galleys repaired and new ones built in order to attack Patani once again. But through the mediation of the king of Kedah and Siamese monks, a treaty and a peace finally resulted. In the third year of his reign he had two young princes killed, one seven years and the other five years old, both sons of the great king[1] and brothers of the young murdered king. The mandarins who opposed his plans suffered injuries at his own hands and had their houses and properties pillaged.

In the third year of his reign the golden tower of the Nopphathat [Wat Mahathat] suddenly collapsed without a

[1]This appears to be Song Tham, r. *c.*1611–28.

cross-wind, thunder or lightning. He had it quickly erected again, but before this tower was totally restored, the scaffolding (beautifully and durably made of bamboo) also collapsed unexpectedly during a rainstorm. As a consequence, strange omens were seen but were kept secret by the soothsayers.

In the fourth year of his reign the white elephant born during the reign of the young king died. In that same year a round-tailed elephant was born in the environs of the city of Ayudhya. There are many stories told about the death of the white elephant and the birth of the round-tailed elephant, but these are heathen fables; therefore, I beg to be excused from relating them.

In the seventh year of his reign he had Okya Phitsanulok put to death under some trumped-up charge, despite the fact that the latter had helped him in gaining his royal office and in setting the crown on his head. He survived the 1000th year,[2] which was considered to bring great fortune. In this year he also renewed the great feastdays which were introduced by the fortune-fated King Phrachao Ramathibodi. This act was held in great respect by the mandarins and the monks.

He was the first who made the mandarins so slavish that they come to court every single day and are allowed to visit each other in their houses or sequestered places but not permitted to speak to one another except in a public meeting place. It is said that he had the walls of Ayudhya wholly renovated and the palace and city greatly improved. He has built, renewed and repaired more temples, towers, and pyramids than any of his predecessors. In order to reach the end of this story, I will note his nature in brief. He is warlike in the Siamese fashion, of great wisdom, eloquent and friendly of speech, very religious and devout, and has great love for the monks and especially the learned. He is a lover of foreign nations, and in order to attract them to him, he has lightened many of their burdens, and improved, renewed, and corrected the ordinances introduced by the eleventh king [Ramathipodi, r. 1491–1529] and continued by the twenty-first king [Ekathotsarot, r. 1605–10/11]. But he is proud, haughty, glorious, beautiful in his raiments, colorful, and although quick to judge, is quickly transformed from anger to mercy so

[2]The Siamese Era Chulasakaraj 1000 (AD 1638).

that few are put to death by the law. He is inclined toward drink and excesses. After he became king he took his wife's mother and sister for his wives and had children by all three of them. He is more feared than any other king before him. No one dares contradict him, not even the monks who have always been outspoken with previous kings. He is more avaricious than any other former Siamese king. He had temples torn down and their foundations dug up to search for gold and silver. The king called No Phutthangkun [Borommaracha IV, r. 1529–33] introduced the practice that for every ten measured lands which the mandarins owned, they had to pay a tical's weight in gold to His Majesty at their death. The King Phra Anuchathirat Phra Ramesuan introduced the practice in which one-third of the mandarin's personal possessions would go to His Majesty at their death. But this king wants everything. If a mandarin dies, his wives and children are taken into custody. One mandarin will often spy on another in order to discover whether anything is being concealed. Widows and orphans show great gratitide whenever the king extends to them a small section of their properties. It appears that His Majesty cannot consider himself rich until he has gathered all the treasures into his own treasury and has had everything squeezed out of the community.

Previously I mentioned that Phra Chaiyaracha [r. 1534–47], thirteenth King of Siam, built the temple Phra Chi Chiang, from which place many miraculous things are reported to have occurred. Since these tales are too fabulous, I beg to be excused from relating them. This temple was at one time the largest and the highest of the entire kingdom, but it has been knocked down as a result of lightning and thunderstorms through the years. Many kings undertook to rebuild this temple, but as soon as work began, they had to abandon it because the foremen and laborers were struck by numerous illnesses and died pitifully. It was also said that the brahmans and the monks have a prophecy that this temple can only be repaired by a king who is descended from the old, pure family and rightful line of the Siamese kings. A few months ago the ruling king demolished the temple to its very base and had a large copper heathen image which was located there pulled back several rods so that another temple like the last could be built over the image. There are various opinions concerning the re-doing of this temple. Many people say that the king will complete this work, and scrupulously give as a reason that His Majesty is like the first founder of the Siamese kingdom in so many ways. This is acceptable, but it is not intended so by the Siamese people since the former builder of the temple ruled the kingdom as a guardian, killed the young king [Woraratsadathirat, r. 1533–4] of five years (after the child had ruled five months) and usurped the crown. However, the brahmans say that they have seen in the signs in the heavens, that His Majesty would not complete the newly-begun temple but would die before its completion, principally because the rebuilding was not begun out of pure devotion but out of His Majesty's hope of finding great treasures in the demolition of the former temple. But what will come of this, only time will tell. The king has now ruled ten years and seven months, but his reign has never seen a prosperous time. On the contrary, it has been troublesome times, and the soothsayers remark that this will continue till the end of his life.

My Lord, there are still many worthwhile things to write about, such as the sickness of the great king, the expelling of the prince, His Majesty's brother, the succession and the death of the young kings, as well as the usurpation of the crown. During my presence here, I have investigated almost all the particulars and have put part of them down on paper. But circumspection prevents me from completing what I have begun. However, permit me to present this to you as a beginning. If I should have the undeserved honor of receiving your Lordship's pleasure with this my unworthy work, I would industriously put everything in order and compile it succinctly and truthfully. Meanwhile I humbly request that your Lordship be so kind as to accept this in a kindly manner from he who is and remains,

In Ayudhya in the Siam Comptoir, 8th February 1640
Your Lordship's humble servant
Jeremias van Vliet.

Jeremias van Vliet, *The Short History of the Kings of Ayutthaya*, edited by David K. Wyatt, translated by Leonard Andaya, Bangkok, Siam Society, 1975, pp. 94–7.

7
The Dutch 'Factory' at Ayutthaya

GIJSBERT HEECK

The Dutch were undoubtedly the most important traders in Siam. They built a warehouse below Bangkok called Amsterdam, traces of which could still be seen a few years back, but their godown in the capital was more impressive, far more substantial than those occupied by the English and French. Gijsbert Heeck was a surgeon working for the VOC who visited Ayutthaya in 1655, and left an extremely detailed account of the Dutch lodge, of which no trace remains apart from a plaque marking the spot.

THE lodge lies a musket shot below the city of Ayutthaya, directly opposite the Portuguese and Japanese quarters. It is a strong and excellent building, fairly large and tall with airy lofts and spacious and admirable warehouses below. It has two white brick façades, with many apertures for doors and windows, most of which are protected with bars. The walls are built entirely of brick and plastered with good lime. All the woodwork is teak, well polished and very durable, not much different from oak.

The internal plan is as follows: on the ground floor there is a wide corridor running the length of the building, with storerooms on either side. A double staircase with about 20 steps leads up to the dining room on the first floor. On either side of it are various other rooms: to the right are those where the director resides and to the left those of his deputy. At the front are the quarters of the sub-merchants and the principal assistants, each room being furnished according to the resident's rank and position. Downstairs, behind the main building, there are various brick-built quarters on separate foundations along the canal which are occupied by the rest of the assistants, the surgeon, steward, cook, trumpeter, sculptor, carpenters, two smiths and a few other sailors including a bookbinder, a baker and an ostler.

The lodge is entirely surrounded by a bamboo fence in the form of a rectangle. Against this stand the various quarters to which I have referred, the brick-built food-store, kitchen and prison and a bamboo stable with room for about eight horses. On the other side there are one or two smaller stables, a sheep-pen and accommodation for goats, chickens, geese, ducks, pigeons and cranes, of which there were five or six wandering about. There were ten or twelve horses in the stables, which the gentlemen use to go out riding in the dry season.

The whole complex is surrounded by a moat, with a gate and a wide bridge, and along the moat there are railings and banks suitable for barques and other vessels to moor alongside and to load and discharge cargo. Behind the lodge there is another warehouse where rice and planks are stored, which is about the same size as the *Amsterdam* warehouse downriver. The residence is roofed with Siamese tiles, and the stables and other buildings with atap [nipa palm].

As you approach it from the river, you see to your right, on the square, a fine brick-built pavilion which is light and airy on account of its many windows which can be opened on all sides, with a *troktafel* (a type of billiard table) inside for the recreation of the junior ranks. In the fence there is a little bamboo gate leading to a plank across the moat which provides access to the Company's garden. The garden is small and contains a number of pomegranate, orange and lime trees. When I saw it, it was wild and untended. There were also two pyramids in it, under which the last director, Mr Crayer, and some of Mr Rijk's children were buried. Next to the garden was the Dutch cemetery, where both high and low have traditionally been buried without distinction.

To the left of the residence, in a corner beside the stable, there is another door with a wide bridge leading to Jau Soet's house (Jau Soet was the ex-wife of Van Meerwijck, Van Vliet and Van Muijden). She has often been very helpful to the Company's servants in their trade in Siam, has gradually gained a good deal of experience of it, and still supplies the Company with all its wax and with other goods which it needs each year. In reward for her good services and because the King has confiscated all her privately acquired property on a number of occasions, she keeps this back door open at all times so as to be able to remove her possessions quickly to the safety of the Company's compound and to pay regular visits for a neighbourly chat.

Gijsbert Heeck [1655], 'Derde Voijage van Gijsbert Heecq Naer Oost Indijen', edited by S. P. l'Honoré Naber, *Marineblad*, Vol. 25, 1910–11, pp. 422–50, quoted in Han ten Brummelhuis, *Merchant, Courtier and Diplomat: A History of the Contacts between the Netherlands and Thailand*, Lochem, Uitgeversmaatschappij De Tijdstroom BV, 1987, pp. 25, 28.

The French Offensive (1662–1688)

8
Religious Tolerance

JACQUES DE BOURGES

Jacques de Bourges was the author of the first account in French concerning Siam, published in 1666, two decades before the massive outpourings which the later French near invasion caused, and before most of the Dutch texts (with the exception of Joost Schouten) were published.

He was born in Paris about 1630, ordained about 1655, and joined the newly founded Société des Missions Etrangères. He was chosen to accompany Mgr. Lambert de la Motte, appointed by Pope Alexander VI as Bishop to the non-existent see of Béryte (Beirut), and given the additional title of Apostolic Vicar, on his overland journey (to avoid conflict with the Portuguese on the coasts) to South-East Asia. De Bourges was in Siam for a year and a half, from April 1662 (but not reaching the capital until August) to October 1663.

De Bourges has four chapters on Siam, covering its geography and economy, its fruits, the manners and customs of the Siamese, and religion. Extracts of his views of the last subject are given here. Nowhere does it occur to him (nor did it to most of his contemporaries) that the religious tolerance which prevailed in Siam was not reflected in his own attitudes or in his own country. He does not mention the Buddha or Buddhism, and merely saw the images of the Buddha as idols which were worshipped. He also appears to be unaware of the belief in metempsychosis, which was to fascinate later French clerics to the country. But he does praise the Siamese for their charity and their manner of making funerals light-hearted affairs.

De Bourges returned to Siam briefly in 1669 to go on to do missionary work in Tongking. He returned again to Ayutthaya to be consecrated Bishop of Auren and Apostolic Vicar of west Tongking by the Bishop of Metellopolis, Mgr. Laneau, in 1682. He remained in Tongking until 1713, when he and his seminarians were expelled. He came once more to Ayutthaya, where he died the following year, aged about eighty-four.

I do not believe there is a country in the world where there are more religions and where their practice is more [freely] permitted than in Siam. The Gentiles, Christians, Mahometans, who are all divided into different sects, have complete liberty to follow whichever cult they think best. The Portuguese, the English, the Dutch, the Chinese, the Japanese, the Peguans, the people of Cambodia, Malacca, Cochinchina, Champa and several other places along the north coast have their establishments in Siam. There are nearly 2,000 Catholics, mostly Portuguese, who come from various parts of the Indies, from where they have been expelled, and have come to take refuge in Siam, where they have a separate quarter which is a suburb of the city....

[The Siamese] say that heaven is like a great palace to which several paths lead, some are shorter, some more frequented, some more difficult, but that all in the end arrive at the palace of bliss which men seek; that it would be something too difficult to determine in deciding which of these paths is the best, the more so that the number of religions being great, the examination of them all would be very irksome, and all one's life would be consumed in this research before being able to decide. And given that they believe in the plurality of gods, they add that as they are all great lords, they require of men different forms of worship and desire to be honoured in divers fashions.

Those who have observed more carefully the opinions of the Siamese concerning religion maintain that their indifference on this point is one of the most established maxims and the most approved by their learned men. The gentleness of their character, the presence and frequentation of so many foreigners, the prudent affability that they are obliged to show them, has committed them in this pernicious opinion, which means that, despairing of finding the truth, they do not concern themselves with seeking it. This indifference is one of the greatest obstacles to their conversion, for when learned Christians expound our holy faith to them, and explain the reasons which prove its truth, they do not contradict; and, agreeing that the Christian religion is good, they merely maintain that it is bold to dismiss other religions, and since they have the object of adoring the gods, one must believe that they are happy with this state. This is the way the Siamese reason, in which they reveal their blindness; since their indifference to religion only proceeds from an ignorance of the unity of God, who cannot be worshipped by contrary and opposing forms. . . .

The Siamese are idolaters. They have a great number of idols and their multiplicity is no less strange than their appearance and size. You can see on an altar up to 50 or 60 idols more than 40 feet high; they are made of brick and stone, and gilded on the outside. In the houses of the priests can be seen galleries where there are 300 or 400 idols of different shapes and sizes, all gilded and shining brightly.

The temples they build for these idols are most sumptuous. One could say that the Siamese only have skill and wealth for these constructions, and as much as they are moderate in their expenditure in that it concerns them, so they are extravagant in the accommodation of their temples. These buildings are solid, and constructed rather like our churches ... they also have cloisters similar to those of our religion, all around which are arranged statues of humans. In the middle of the cloister is a pyramid [a stupa] of great height, brilliantly gilded, so well applied to the brick that the inclemency of the weather never diminishes its sparkle. The custom is to enclose beneath these pyramids the ashes of some great lord.

The ordinary people and the talapoins (who are their priests) assemble on certain feast days in the temples to render homage to their idols. As they believe it is a sin to kill animals, they sacrifice nothing which has life, but only present and lay before the idols the products of the land, rice, and cloth, which, after they have been exposed some time in front of the idols, are used by the talapoins. It is indeed a compassionate sight to see these deluded people render so much honour to masses of stone. I was surprised to see their outward devotion, the signs of respect they display and the religious confidence they award these idols....

This is what we have reasonably divined by means of our Christian intermediaries on the occasions when we sought to enter into discussion with the talapoins. I shall introduce here an example. When the Right Reverend Bishop of Béryte was in Tenasserim, he went to visit one of the chief priests of that place, with a Portuguese to serve as an interpreter. In order not to surprise the old man, he questioned him as though he wished to learn about his faith from him. This man began his discourse by telling us that it was necessary to start with the principle that there were seven gods, that their dwelling was in heaven, which was a delightful place full of pleasures which one inevitably reached after death. Mgr. de Béryte gave for his part the articles of his belief, without bothering to refute his extravagances, and he appeared to listen with satisfaction, confessing in the end that he believed the Christian religion was very good, and that the God of the Christians and his were brothers, that his was older and more powerful than the younger; this was seen, he said, in the difference they had together, which having obliged them to defend themselves, the younger had been overcome, seized and put to death for his revolt. This is the musing which this learned man recounted to us, which shows clearly how much these people are removed from the knowledge of the real God....

The Siamese being so little decided in their own religion do not have particular views concerning the future life; one cannot say that they believe in the immortality of the soul, because they affirm nothing in this respect. They also do not say that it finishes with the body; on the contrary, they are of the opinion that it survives it. This is why in their lifetime they are careful to prepare themselves for the needs of another life; they accumulate money, they save all they can and hide it in some concealed place with as much secrecy as possible....

The precepts which the religion of the Siamese prescribes for moral conduct are in conformity with the natural law which God has granted the souls of men for the conduct of their actions. These precepts can be reduced to two which subsume all the others: to avoid evil and practise good deeds. As for the observation of the first, the Siamese detest injustice, and are neither malicious, nor cruel, nor deceitful; and for the second they are very much inclined to observe it, displaying charity to everyone, especially to strangers, passers-by, animals and the dead....

The talapoins who are their priests benefit by their charity more than all others. Although they are poor by profession, they are the best provided in the abundance of alms which are daily given them. They are rarely given money, but they receive liberally of things that grow in the country so that there remains enough to give others; and myself, when passing before a house of the talapoins in Tenasserim on my journey from Siam, benefited from their charity. They housed me and provided me with their usual presents, which are rice, fruits and other refreshments. To gather alms they sent into the town the young talapoins, who go seeking them from door to door. There are festivals when the devout people have the piety to take them themselves [to the temple], especially when they go on a pilgrimage....

The Siamese also practise charity to the dead, and are most scrupulous in the celebration of their funerals; this is what they spend most on. They sometimes spend a whole year in preparation, deciding on a convenient place to receive the ashes of the dead person, and they have a particular skill in embalming bodies.... The pyres are surrounded by many square towers, made of cypress wood[1] and decorated with sheets of rough paper painted in many colours contrived with art and pleasing to behold. They place many fireworks on the top of the towers. When everything is ready, some of the talapoins who take part in the ceremony go to the location of the funeral, and some go to collect the body from its resting place; it is closed in a bier or gilded coffin over which is raised a pyramid decorated with various decorative pieces of carpentrywork similarly gilded ... while [the body] is being consumed by the flames, the fireworks are set off to which is added the noise of several musical instruments. After the body is burnt the ashes are interred beneath a pyramid. Thus

[1]Not so, since cypress does not grow in Siam; any precious wood.

these people have learned to remove from funerals their lugubrious aspect, and by the pomp of the ceremonies which accompany them, they are less an occasion of mourning than an agreeable spectacle to diminish the horror of death and entertain the participants.

Jacques de Bourges, *Relation du voyage de Monseigneur l'Evêque de Béryte, Vicaire Apostolique du Royaume de la Cochinchine, par la Turquie, la Perse, les Indes, etc., jusqu'au Royaume de Siam et autres lieux, par M. de Bourges, prêtre, missionaire apostolique*, Paris, Denys Bechet, 1666. A copy of extracts of the first edition was kindly made available by Professor Dirk van der Cruysse, University of Antwerp.

9
Men's Clothes and Women's Ornaments

NICOLAS GERVAISE

Nicolas Gervaise was born in Paris about 1662 and was ordained a priest before he was twenty. He joined the Société des Missions Etrangères, and in 1683 was sent as a missionary to Siam with the Bishop of Heliopolis, Mgr. Pallu. He returned to France about 1686, became a curé in Brittany, and then moved to Tours, where he wrote his Histoire Naturelle et Politique du Royaume de Siam, *the* Description Historique du Royaume de Macaçar *(it is not known if he ever went to Makassar, but he did bring the two sons of the Sultan of Gowa with him to France), and a life of St. Martin. He went to Rome in 1724, was made titular Bishop of Horren, and went to what is now Venezuela with a group of missionaries, where he was killed by Carib Indians in 1729.*

His book on Siam was, after that of Simon de La Loubère, the most authoritative on the country at the time. It was first published in 1688, by which time two French embassies had gone to that distant country to convert King Narai, seek trade advantages, and even take over territory, and the much publicized Siamese embassy to France led by Kosa Pan from 1686 to 1687 had taken place. Siam was in the fashion, and he specifically avoided mentioning its wild elephants about which he considered sufficient had already been written. Gervaise divided his book into four parts. The first dealt with its situation and products; this contains a long description of the palace in Ayutthaya, and the towns of Lopburi and Bangkok. The second covered Siamese manners, laws, and customs; the third, their religion (a remarkably fair account); and the fourth, the present king, Narai, the royal family, and the court. Given here is an extract from the second part.

IN the kingdom of Siam there is no trade more unprofitable than that of tailor, for the common people have no need of such a man. The whole dress of a man consists of two pieces of silk or cotton material. With one piece, which is about two ells long and three-quarters of an ell wide, they cover their shoulders as with a scarf, and with the other, which is of about the same length and breadth, they encircle the waist, and then tuck in the two ends very neatly at the rear, thus making of it a kind of breeches which reach down to just below the knees. This garment is called in Siamese, *Pa-nonc* [p'anung], and in common parlance, *Panne* or *Pagne*. A Mandarin's *Pagne* is much more ample and richer than others. It is usually made of cloth of gold and silver, or else from those beautiful hand-painted cloths of the Indies, commonly known as Chit of Masulipatam. Underneath, these gentlemen wear short trousers of some good material which reach down below the knees, and the bottoms of which are artistically embroidered with gold or silver. In the hot season the only jacket they wear is of muslin, cut like a dressing-gown, which does not extend below their trousers. But in the North Winds Season they wear a close-fitting garment made of Chinese brocade, or of some fine European cloth, which closes up in the front by means of ten or twelve filigreed buttons of gold or silver, placed at a distance from one another. The sleeves which are very wide, are buttoned like our old doublets used to be, and above this garment they wear in the form of a scarf (after the manner of our knights), a piece of gold or silver brocade, or a piece of painted cloth as beautiful as can be found in the country. In Siam shoemakers are scarcely any more necessary than tailors. Everyone walks barefooted, with the exception of the mandarins, who sometimes use slippers of a Moorish pattern. Also, they go bareheaded, as the rest do, unless, on certain days, they are obliged to appear in ceremonial dress before the King: for then, they wear a pointed hat made after the style of our sugar-loaf. At other times they content themselves with having their slaves carry behind them a hat (which resembles those in fashion in France during the last century), and also, their sword and their boussette (a small gold or silver box in which they keep their betel).

The dress of the women does not vary much from that of the men. Their *p'anung* (it bears the same name) seemed to me a little larger. They let it hang down almost to the ground like a petticoat. Its colour is generally black, the colour which they regard as being the most beautiful and worthy, and it is often embroidered in gold and silver. A small piece of muslin covers the bosom, and the rest of the body is bare. The better-class ladies are distinguished, amongst them as amongst us, by a certain grace that demands the respect of all who see them. Their fingers are laden with rings, diamonds and various precious stones. They are usually fairer in complexion than those of lower birth, because they go outside less often. But the better-class men, who are as dark as the rest, attribute this difference to the merit acquired by the good works they did in their former lives. Moreover, these ladies are very clean, although they always walk about barefooted. They go bareheaded and wear their hair as short as the men do. In order to make it more glossy, they rub it with an oil called *Naman hom*, that is to say, 'oil of sweet smell'. The men, as well as the women, use it, for there is no discourtesy equal to that committed should a husband go to see his wife, or a wife her husband, or a child his father and mother, without having first perfumed the hair with this sweet smelling oil. Men having a flat nose or flat feet are most welcome by the ladies, for they believe that these men must be worthy, since in their deformity they resemble their great God, *Sommonokodom* [Buddha]. Like the men, the women are medium-sized, and among them there are found hunchbacks, although it seems that they are all deformed. It is a pity to see such scanty care bestowed by parents upon their children. As soon as a child comes into the world, they go and wash it in the river, after which, without a single swaddling cloth, it is placed in a little

Siamese women, from Henri Mouhot, *Travels in the Central Parts of Indo-China (Siam), Cambodia, and Laos*..., London, John Murray, 1864.

bed where it remains until it is six months old, when it is weaned. It is then taught how to eat rice. Many children, who cannot get accustomed at so early an age to this Spartan code of life, die within a few days or months after their birth, and it is by great luck that, of every ten or twelve born, two or three are saved. At their birth they are given by their parents a name altogether different from their family name, and no-one but the King has the right to alter it, as he does do when he elevates them to some government post which demands distinction. The names given to them by their parents are usually ridiculous. These, for example, are thought to be the prettiest: *Ceou*, that is to say, Crystal; *Boune*, which signifies 'he who has made merit'; *Pet*, precious stones; *Thon*, meaning 'gold'. The Siamese ladies cannot bear to see our white teeth, for they believe that the devil has white teeth, and that it is shameful for a man to have teeth like those of beasts. Scarcely have the men and women reached the age of fourteen or fifteen years than they set about making their teeth black and shiny, and this is how they do it. The person whom they have chosen to do them this service, causes them to lie down on their back, and keeps them in this position for the three days during which the operation lasts. First of all, he cleans the teeth with lemon juice and afterwards rubs them with a certain fluid which makes them red. On the top of this he puts a coat of powder made from burnt cocoanut which blackens them. But the teeth are so weakened by the application of these drugs that they could be extracted painlessly, and would fall out if the owner risked eating anything solid. During these three days, the patient lives on cold broths only, which may flow gently down the throat without touching the teeth: the least breeze may hinder the effect of this operation. That is why those who undergo it, keep abed and take care to cover themselves, until it is felt that the operation has come to a fortunate conclusion by the hardening of the gums and the stopping of the swelling of the mouth which assumes normal proportions. The same fluid that is first used for the reddening of the teeth is also used for reddening the nail of the little finger on each hand. It is only for high-class people to wear large finger nails and to redden that of the little finger. Working people cut them and are thereby distinguished. The modesty of our most humble houses does not equal that of theirs, for in the rooms of their finest palaces they have neither table, chair, nor tapestry. The only things to be seen are a few Chinese cabinets, some badly arranged pieces of porcelain, along with a few Persian carpets covering the floor; and several small pillows made of silk material are in the corners of the room with mats of rushes or rice-straw. One of these mats serves as a bed when they stretch it out, and they cover themselves with a *p'anung*. During the night they sleep with all their clothes on, as in daytime, unless they think they may soil them; for, then, they change them, and take others not so valuable. Sheets are not used by them, and those who are cleanest and tidiest, have only a light mattress of cotton on a small bed of rushes, along with a bed-net of muslin.

Nicolas Gervaise, *The Natural and Political History of the Kingdom of Siam A.D. 1688*, translated by Herbert Stanley O'Neill, Bangkok, Siam Observer Press, 1928, pp. 45–7.

10
The Ambassador's Arrival and Sundry Observations

CHEVALIER DE CHAUMONT

The Chevalier de Chaumont (c.1640–1710) came from a distinguished Huguenot family, converted to Catholicism, and served as ship's captain in the navy and major-general in the army. He was pious to a degree, unbending, and very concerned with his rank. On account of his conversion, he was considered appropriate to lead Louis XIV's first embassy to King Narai in 1685, since his mission was to convert the king. His rather disordered account of his embassy is far less interesting than that of the Abbé de Choisy, but contains a journal of events and factual material meant to inform the Secretary of State for the Navy, the Marquis de Seignelay, about the state and importance of the country. Like all visitors, he gives a detailed account of the capturing of wild elephants and the importance of white elephants. He also was apparently impressed by the number of foreigners living at peace in Siam.

THE river of Siam, called the Menan, is very fine and very broad; it has at least four fathoms of water, sometimes seven or eight. It is edged by very fine trees. But three or four months each year its banks are flooded, which is why the houses one sees are built on piles, and made of bamboo. This is the wood the Siamese use as much for foundations and floors as for the upper parts of their houses; they also use it for what they need within the house, even to lighting the fire with it, using it like a flint, so that they only have to pare this wood a little and then to rub it against another piece, and it ignites.

All the people in these parts have small canals and boats to go from house to house to conduct their trade. One usually only sees women working, the men being more often employed in the king's service, which they perform like slaves. The same honours were accorded me as those given to the King of Siam when he goes on the river. Everyone was in barges, prostrate, their hands joined together in front of their foreheads. In front of the houses and the villages there was a sort of parapet raised seven or eight feet above the height of the water, made of rushes. The Siamese respect their king so much that they dare not raise their eyes to look on him.

All the mandarins who had come to receive me on the river continued to accompany me. The first were the gentlemen of the bedchamber, and the others, who came after, were always even more important than those who had come before. Finally, the princes came last. These mandarins all have very decent barges, in the middle of which there is a kind of throne on which they sit. They normally travel one in each barge; their arms are beside them, including sabres, lances, swords, arrows, breastplates and even pitchforks. They are all dressed in the same manner I have already described. A Portuguese whom the king had put in command of the troops in Bangkok always accompanied me, and gave orders for everything. There were fifty or sixty barges following me, many of which were from fifty to eighty feet long, with rowers numbering from twenty to a hundred. They do not row in our fashion, because there are two seats to each bench, one on one side and one on the other, their heads are turned to the direction they are going, and they hold in their hands an oar they call a *pagai*, about four feet long, and need much bodily strength to move. These rowers work hard, but are content to eat cooked rice and water, and when they have a piece of fish, they think they are feasting. They eat a leaf they call *betel* which is like ivy, and a sort of oak bark, which they call *areca*, putting lime on the leaf, which gives it some taste. They eat local tobacco which is very strong. All that blackens their teeth, which they consider most handsome. A man can live in this manner for fifteen or twenty sous a month, for the Siamese ordinarily only drink water. They make a kind of very strong aquavit with areca and rice.

On the 30th [October 1685] I went to the palace to see the pagoda or family temple of the King of Siam. In the courtyard of the palace there was a fight, or rather, a kind of fight, between elephants, for the animals were fastened by their two rear legs, and on each two men were mounted, holding in their hands a hook with which they controlled them as a bridle does a horse. They gave them several blows to encourage them, and the elephants would have fought indeed if they had been free, but they just adminstered a few blows at each other with their teeth and their trunks. The king was present, but I did not see him.

We passed from this courtyard into many others and then we went to the pagoda. The doorway appeared very old and of good workmanship, the building quite fine and constructed in the shape of our churches in Europe. We saw there several gilded bronze statues, which seemed to pay homage to a huge idol all of gold about forty feet high. Beside this enormous idol there were several others, smaller, some of which in gold had lamps lit from top to bottom. At the end of the pagoda was a very large idol on a mausoleum of inestimable value. I then went to another pagoda right by the first, and passed through a vault in the shape of a cloister, where there were idols on all sides every two feet, all gilded, each of which had in front a lamp which the talapoins, who are the priests of the Siamese, light every evening. In this pagoda, I saw the mausoleum to the queen who had died four or five years ago; it is passing magnificent, and behind this mausoleum was that of a King of Siam represented lying on one side and dressed like the kings are on ceremonial occasions.[1] This statue was perhaps some twenty-five feet in length, and was of gilded copper. I then went into other places, where there were many golden and silver statues. Many have very fine diamonds and rubies on their fingers. I had never seen so many idols and so much gold. The whole

[1]Chaumont is probably referring to a sleeping Buddha.

was but fine because of the display of wealth.

I went to see next the elephants; there was quite a number and their size prodigious. I saw a cannon cast in Siam eighteen feet long, fourteen inches in diameter at the mouth and designed for balls about three hundred pounds. There are many cannons cast in Siam which the Siamese make themselves.

The King of Siam has a great number of Malays in his states who are Mahometans, and good soldiers, but there is some difference between their religion and that of the Moors. The Peguans [Mons] are almost as numerous as the Siamese born in the country. The Laos are very numerous, especially in the north.

There are in this state eight or nine true Portuguese families, but those called mixed race more than a thousand, having been born of a Portuguese and a Siamese mother. The Dutch have only a factory. The English the same. The French likewise.

The Cochin Chinese number about 100 families, mostly Christian. Among the Tonkinese are seven or eight Christian families.

The Malays are quite numerous, but most are slaves, and consequently are not bodyguards. The Makassarese and many peoples of the Island of Java are established here, likewise the Moors. Included in the latter are Turks, Persians, Mogols, Golcondans, and Bengalis.

The Armenians are separate and number fifteen or sixteen families, all Christian and Catholic, most of them are horsemen in the king's guard....

In this great kingdom are many Peguans who were taken prisoner of war. They are more active than the Siamese and usually stronger. There is great freedom among their women and their conversation is perilous. Those Lao who live in the Kingdom of Siam constitute a quarter [of the population], and as they are half-Chinese, they have their disposition, their dexterity, and their ability to steal with finesse; their women are white and beautiful, very bold, and in consequence dangerous....

There is no city in the Orient where one sees so many different nationalities as in the capital city of Siam and where one speaks so many different languages. It is two leagues around and half a league broad, and very populous, even though it is nearly always flooded, so that it seems more like an island than a town on dry land. Only the Moors, the Chinese, the French and the English live in the city, all the other nationalities dwell in the suburbs in sectors; that is to say, each is together. If they were all put together they would constitute as big an area as the city.

Relation de l'Ambassade de Mr le Chevalier de Chaumont à la Cour du Roi de Siam, Paris, 1686, pp. 42–6, 74–7, 127–31, 167.

11
The Audience of Reception and the Palace of King Narai

ABBÉ DE CHOISY

François-Timoléon de Choisy (1644–1724) was one of the most colourful characters of the late seventeenth century: he was, in his time, a transvestite abbé with a passion for seducing young girls (whom he dressed as men), a gambler who lost fortunes at the gaming tables of Venice, a secretary to the Cardinal de Bouillon at the election of Pope Innocent XI, coadjudant Ambassador to the King of Siam in 1685–6, a member of the French Academy (from 1687) and later its Dean, a post he still held at his death, and throughout his life in close contact with the mightiest in the land, including Monsieur, the Duke of Orleans, the king's younger brother, Turenne, the Marshal of France, the Duke of La Rochefoucauld, Madame de Lafayette, the Duke of Saint-Aignan, Madame de Maintenon, the king's secret wife, and many others. Many of these appear in the pages of his incomplete and posthumous Mémoires pour servir à l'Histoire de Louis XIV.

The Abbé de Choisy was an incontinent scribbler (among other writings, he produced an eleven-volume Histoire de l'Eglise*), but it is his* Journal du Voyage de Siam fait en 1685 et 1686, *first published in 1687, which is one of his most enduring works, if one discounts the notorious posthumous publication* *of what became known as the* Memoirs of the Abbé de Choisy Disguised as a Woman. *Recently translated into English, the Siamese journey is described with verve and a keen eye for detail. During it, Choisy finally took holy orders in Lopburi, and on many occasions has some pangs of conscience over his past conduct, which a serious illness in 1683 caused him, with the aid of the Abbé de Dangeau (another future academician and close friend), to reform. Neither religious vows nor reform stopped him from placing bets, with porcelain pieces given by King Narai as wagers, on the return journey as to when the ship would reach particular points* en route.

Extracted here is Choisy's detailed account of the presentation of Louis XIV's letter and the audience of reception which took place on 18 October in Ayutthaya.

THAT'S an important event over; the entrance and the audience. There are a thousand curious things to note, and I propose giving you a formal account when I know the names and ranks of all those taking part. I want all the same to say something about it today.

In the early morning, the Ambassador himself placed the King's letter in a golden box, and this box in a gold cup, and the cup on a saucer likewise of gold, and then displayed it on the table. Then came two Oyas, Dukes and Peers of the Kingdom of Siam, followed by forty important mandarins, who after having greeted His Excellency prostrated themselves in front of the letter. After that, they went on board their barges and went in the direction of the city.

Then the Ambassador took the King's letter, and placed it in my hands. We walked towards the river, I always keeping to his left. He took the letter again, and placed it in a gilded barge, where even the King's son cannot enter. The barge with the letter followed the barges in which were the presents [from Louis XIV] and was accompanied by eight escort barges. The Ambassador followed alone in his barge. I followed him in one of the King's barges all alone. I wore a black satin cassock, a surplice, and a great mantle on top. We also had to the right and the left escort barges. Then came four barges with the gentlemen our King had placed in the Ambassador's suite, with his secretary; and in other barges were the household staff, *maîtres d'hôtel,* butlers, valets, all

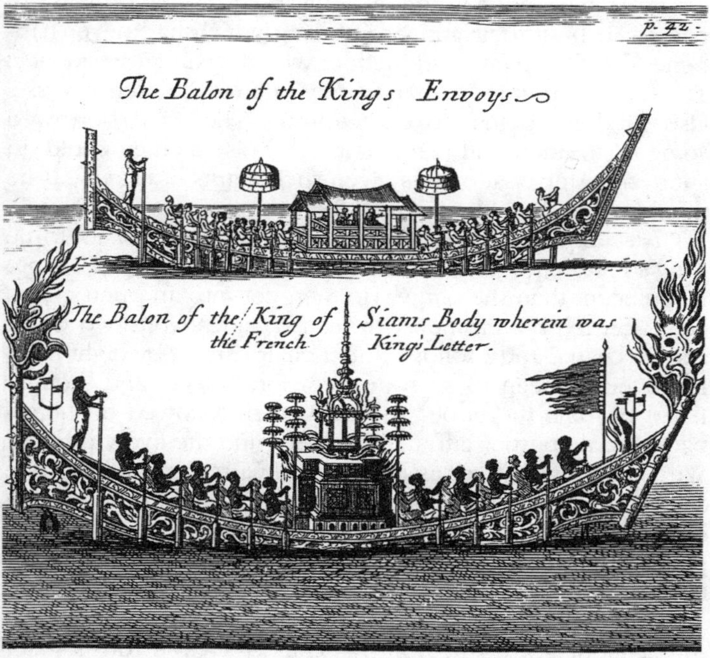

The barges bearing the letter from King Louis XIV to King Narai, from Simon de La Loubère, *A New Historical Relation of the Kingdom of Siam*, London, 1693.

very clean; and finally the trumpets and twenty persons in livery. The livery was very fine, and something the Siamese found most beautiful. They have often seen gilded jerkins; the small European merchants have them here; even the locksmiths wear silk. The Ambassador has four or five cloth-of-gold costumes: that would be many for London or Madrid, but they say here one has to change them every day.

Finally the procession ended with the barges of all the different nations. This was a march over the water, which is something quite special. All the King's barges were gilded, and had intricately carved and heavily gilded spires. There were sixty men on each side with small gilded oars, which all struck and rose from the water in unison; in the sunlight it made a most impressive sight.

The Dutch godown and an English ship saluted us as we passed with all their guns, something which had never happened in the capital of a kingdom with the King in residence. The fortress fired more than twenty salutes; the French vessel also fired more than twenty rounds. They had borrowed some quarrymen and made as much noise as they could. In short, the Ambassador was given such marks of esteem as he would never dared have asked for.

On setting foot on the ground, the Ambassador took the King's letter, and placed it on a triumphal carriage still more magnificent than the barge. He then got into an open gilded chair, carried by ten men. On his two sides were two Oyas, also in chairs; and I followed in a chair carried by eight men. I had never been to such an occasion before, and thought I had become the Pope. The gentlemen followed on horseback; the domestic staff, the trumpets, and the livery on foot. We walked in a street as long as but narrower than the Rue Saint Honoré, between two double rows of soldiers wearing helmets and carrying gilded shields. Some had sabres, others pikes. From time to time there were war elephants lining our route.

Everyone stopped at the outer gate of the palace. The Ambassador got down from his chair, took the King's letter from the triumphal carriage, and entered the palace carrying the letter; then he placed it in my hands. We walked solemnly, the gentlemen ahead, the Oyas to the right and left. We passed through three or four courtyards. In the first, there was a regiment of 1,000 men with helmets and gilded shields. They were squatting on their heels, their muskets in front of them stuck in the ground. That is very fine to look at, but frankly I think fifty musketeers would easily beat them.

In the second courtyard there was a squadron of perhaps 300 horses. The horses are rather fine but badly trained. But, something one does not see in any place on earth, there were also elephants, much bigger than those outside. We saw at least eighty, among others the famous white elephant, which in the wars with Pegu cost the lives of 500,000 or 600,000 men. It is fairly big, very old, wrinkled, and has screwed up eyes. There are always four mandarins around him with fans to keep him cool, greenery for keeping the flies at bay, and parasols to protect him from the sun when he walks about. He is only served in golden vessels, and I saw in front of him two golden vases, one for drinking, the other for eating. He is given water which has been kept for six months, the older being purer. It is said, but I have not seen it, that there is a small white elephant all ready to succeed the old one when his time comes to die. I have also seen the prince of the elephants, the biggest and cleverest of them all; this is the one the King rides. He is proud and uncontrollable for anyone else, but when the King appears, he gets down on his knees. I have been told that in Louvo [Lopburi] we shall see this performance.

Finally, in the last courtyard, we found the vast crowds of mandarins, their faces down to the ground, balanced on their elbows. We had to climb seven or eight steps to enter the audience chamber. The Ambassador stopped with Mr Constance [Phaulkon, the chief minister], to give time to the French gentlemen to enter the room, and to be seated on the carpets. It had been agreed that they would enter with the heads raised in the French manner, wearing their shoes, and they would be in their place before the King appeared on his throne; and that when he appeared, they would bow in the French manner without getting up. Meanwhile, the Ambassador and I were at the lowest step with the Barkalon [Phra Klang], who up to now we had not heard speak. He told His Excellency that at the news of his arrival at the bar, he desired to go there in person, but that affairs of state had prevented him.

As soon as the gentlemen were in position, we heard the trumpets and drums sound within: those outside replied. This was the signal that the King was going to be seated on the throne. Immediately Mr Constance, barefoot, that is to say with stockings but no shoes, climbed the stairs on all fours, as one does in Rome when going up the Scala Santa, but much more respectfully. The Ambassador followed him: I was on his left carrying the King's letter. His Excellency took off his hat at the topmost step, as soon as he saw the King, and after entering the audience hall, bowed deeply in the French manner. I was at his left, and did not bow, because I was carrying the King's letter. We walked to the middle of the chamber between two rows of important and prostrate mandarins.[1] Among them was a brother-in-law of the King of Cambodia. There the Ambassador bowed a second time, and moved to within earshot of the King's throne, to stand before the chair which had been prepared for him. He bowed a third time, and began his discourse standing bareheaded; but at the second word, sat down, and put his hat on again. I remained standing, still holding the King's letter.

He said that the King his master, so famous through so many victories, and by the peace which more than once he had granted his enemies while leading his armies, had commanded him to come to seek His Majesty at the extremity of the universe, to present him with the marks of his esteem and to assure him of his friendship. But that nothing was more likely to unite these two great monarchs than to live in the consciousness of the same belief, and that is what the King his master had particularly ordered him to indicate to His Majesty. He added that the King conjured him, by the interest he takes in his true glory, to think of that Supreme Majesty which he assumes on earth, that it can only come from the true God, that is to say, the all-powerful, eternal, and infinite God whom the Christians acknowledge and who alone allows Kings to reign and rule over the fortunes of all people; that it was to this God of heaven and earth to which all grandeur had to be subject, and not to the feeble divinities which are worshipped in the East, whose relative powerlessness His Majesty, who had so much illumination and penetration, could not but have noticed. He finished by saying that the most agreeable news which he could carry to the King his master would be that His Majesty, persuaded by the truth, would take instruction in the Christian religion, that this would cement forever the esteem and friendship between the two Kings, that the French would come to his states with greater eagerness and confidence, and that finally His Majesty could ensure by this means an everlasting happiness in paradise, after having reigned with such prosperity on earth.

The discourse over, the Ambassador, without getting up, and without taking off his hat, except when he spoke of the two Kings, showed His Majesty some of the presents which

[1]Forbin is less respectful: 'The posture of these mandarins with their beehives in each other's arses made all the French laugh.'

were in the chamber. He then did the honour of introducing me and next the gentlemen. Immediately, Mr Constance, who acted as interpreter, prostrated himself three times before speaking, and explained the discourse in Siamese,[2] with the Ambassador remaining seated and covered. After the interpretation was over, the Ambassador rose, took off his hat, turned towards me, respectfully acknowledged the King's letter, took it, and moved towards the throne.

I must here explain a very important incident. Mr Constance, in arranging everything, had greatly insisted on changing nothing in all the oriental customs, which is that kings do not receive letters from the hands of ambassadors: but His Excellency had been firm in wishing to give that from our King into the King's own hand. Mr Constance had proposed to put it in a cup at the end of a gold stick, so that the Ambassador could lift it up to the King's throne, but he had been told that either the throne had to be lowered, or a dais had to be built, so that His Excellency could personally give the letter to the King. Mr Constance had given assurances that this would be done. However, when we entered the room, we saw the King at a window at least six feet high. The Ambassador muttered to me, 'I cannot give him the letter at the end of a stick, and I shall never do it.' I must admit I was most embarrassed. I did not know what advice to give him. I thought of carrying the Ambassador's chair near to the throne, so that he could climb up on it, when, suddenly, after having finished his discourse, he made his decision. He moved proudly towards the throne, holding the golden cup in which was the letter, and presented the letter to the King without raising his elbow, as if the King were at the same low level as he. Mr Constance, who was crawling on the floor behind us, cried to the Ambassador, 'Lift it up, lift it up!' but he did no such thing, and the good King was obliged to lean half out the window to take the letter, which he did laughing. Here is the reason. The King had told Mr Constance, 'I leave you to arrange everything outside, do all that is possible to honour the Ambassador of France; I shall look after the inside.' He did not wish to lower his throne, or to build a dais, and had

[2]Duly omitting the more contentious passages concerning religion, which did not escape the Bishop of Metellopolis.

The Chevalier de Chaumont presents the letter from King Louis XIV to King Narai while Phaulkon prostrates before the king. Choisy is standing behind Chaumont, engraving attributed to Jean-Baptiste Nolin (1657–1725).

resolved, in case the Ambassador did not raise the letter to the height of his window, to lower himself to take it.

This action of the King of Siam calmed me; and I would have willingly embraced the Ambassador for the action he had just taken. But not only did this good King bend down so low to receive the King's letter; he lifted it up to be level with his head, which is the greatest honour he could ever show it. He then said that he received with great joy the King of France's marks of esteem and friendship, and that he was almost as happy to see the Ambassador as the King himself. He asked for news of the royal house, and news of peace and war. The Ambassador replied that the King, after having taken the stronghold of Luxemburg, had obliged the Spanish, the Dutch, the Emperor,[3] and all the German princes to sign a twenty-year truce with him. Finally the King expressed the wish that God in heaven would bring the Ambassador back to France as happily as He had brought him to the Kingdom of Siam.

I have forgotten to mention that the Bishop of Metellopolis and the Abbé de Lionne were in the chamber before us, and that after the Ambassador had delivered the King's letter, I also sat down on the carpet on his right hand side, the Bishop being to his left, the Abbé behind the Bishop, and Mr Constance a little in front of the Ambassador. The King remained some time without saying anything. After that, we heard trumpets and drums as before the audience; it was to warn those outside that His Majesty was going to descend from his throne. He withdrew gently and closed his little window. The Ambassador remained on his seat to give time to the gentlemen to leave with Mr Vachet, who by the express order of the King had led them in. The Bishop, the Abbé, and I followed, and a moment afterwards the Ambassador and Mr Constance.

As soon as the King withdrew, the Barkalon and all the important mandarins in the kingdom, who had prostrated themselves throughout the audience, sat up. Among these mandarins was the brother-in-law of the King of Cambodia and the sons of kings. I do not recall if I told you that at the palace gate a young Opra, a favourite of the King,[4] came to receive the Ambassador, and followed him into the audience. On leaving we found everything in the same order: the mandarins, the elephants, the troops. At the palace gate the Ambassador got into his chair again, and I in mine; the gentlemen followed on horseback, and the rest on foot. We had to board

[3]The Holy Roman Emperor, Leopold I.
[4]Probably Phra Pi.

the barges again to get to His Excellency's palace. We set foot on the ground again at the end of the street of the Chinamen, and then passed through the street of the Moors; these are the two best in the city of Siam. The houses are made of stone and brick; that means something in this country. The itinerary was just the same. We finally arrived at His Excellency's palace, surrounded by an unbelievable crowd of people; we could only see heads. The city is without doubt very populous, but it is not yet Paris.

The courtyard of our palace is big and very cheerful. To the right is a large, columned construction, which is magnificent and noble; the top is painted yellow, but appears golden; the walls are white, full of niches in which there are pieces of porcelain; the yellow, white, and blue mix very well together. In two days there will be a sparkling fountain; they are working day and night on a small reservoir which will provide the water. You can see from this if these people forget anything. To the left is the main building. The Ambassador has there an antechamber, a bedroom, dressing rooms, a gallery, and a very fine terrace. I have a very nice room there too. The chapel is big, and we have, they say, the consolation of seeing every day Christian turbans.

I must really feel affection for you to write so long, being as tired as I am. The honours cost dearly. I have carried the King's letter; the Siamese consider me with respect. But I carried it more than 300 paces in a golden vase which weighed 100 pounds, and I am worn out.

On returning, the Ambassador had 100 pistoles distributed in pieces of thirty sols to the barges which brought him from the bar, which took him to the audience, to the men who had carried him on their shoulders, and to those who served him while he was at the custom-house, the Tabanque. This generosity was rather excessive, and I do not think he escaped with less than 1,200 pistoles in presents. But how could he do otherwise? The other ambassadors do this. Should he discredit the King's name in a country where he passes for the greatest monarch on earth? Are there not occasions such as these when one has to give one's last penny?

Abbé de Choisy, *Journal of a Voyage to Siam 1685–1686*, translated and introduced by Michael Smithies, Kuala Lumpur, Oxford University Press, 1993, pp. 159–65.

12
Wat Phra Ram, Ayutthaya

GUY TACHARD

Guy Tachard was born in Marthon near Angoulême in 1648, and joined the Company of Jesus in 1668. About 1680 he went to the Antilles but was back in Paris in 1684, when he was named as one of the six Jesuit mathematicians, the leader of whom was Father de Fontaney, destined to go to China, and who accompanied the Chaumont–Choisy embassy of 1685–6 sent by Louis XIV. He managed to establish a close rapport with Phaulkon ('Mr Constance'), King Narai's chief minister, and returned to Europe instead of going on to China in order to supply twelve more mathematical Jesuits to satisfy the scientific whims of Narai. He went back to Siam with the La Loubère–Céberet embassy armed with secret instructions which he assumed placed him above the envoys, whose position he made as difficult as possible. He returned with La Loubère as Narai's envoy to the Pope and Louis XIV, and in France learnt of the death of Narai and Phaulkon and the assumption of power by Petracha. This did not stop him undertaking a third journey to Siam in 1690 (recorded by Robert Challe), and from Pondichéry attempting to gain admission to the country, writing frequently but in vain to Kosa Pan, formerly ambassador to France and now Phra Klang. In Pondichéry, he appears to have been engaged in illicit commerce, but instead of getting to Siam, he was taken along with other French hostages by the Dutch in 1693 and off-loaded in Dunkirk. He left again on his fourth journey to Siam in 1695, and was finally admitted to the court of Petracha in 1699, reaching Ayutthaya via Mergui, armed with a letter from Louis XIV originally destined for Narai and dating from 1687. His reception was cold and the letter he took back strictly formal. He returned to France in 1700, presented his letter, and set off on his fifth journey to the Indies. He was again in Pondichéry from 1702 to 1710 (managing to come into conflict this time with the Governor, Chevalier Hébert). He left in 1710 for Chandernagor in Bengal, near Calcutta, where he died in 1712.

Tachard comes out in the voluminous writings of the period as a very unsympathetic character, a paranoid schemer infiltrating himself everywhere and being in large measure responsible for the fiasco of the French adventure in Siam. The only person he seems to have established a rapport with was Phaulkon, who used him, inter alia, *as his secretary and for conveying orders to his cook.*

The writings of Tachard himself are numerous, but not all have been published. His account of his first journey, Voyage de Siam des Pères Jésuites envoyés par le Roi au Royaume de Siam *(1686), was an immediate success and translated into English in 1688. His* Second Voyage du Père Tachard et des Jésuites envoyés par le Roi au Royaume de Siam *(1689) tried to show himself in the best possible light, and has to be taken with some reservation.*

Here is an extract from his First Voyage ..., *a detailed description of what is generally agreed to be Wat Phra Ram in Ayutthaya.*

ABOUT an hundred paces South of the Palace there is a great Park walled in, in the middle whereof stands a vast and high Fabric built cross-ways in the manner of our Churches, having over it five solid gilt domes of Stone or Brick, and of extraordinary Architecture, the dome in the middle is far bigger than the rest, which are on the extremities and at the ends of the Cross. This Building rests upon several Bases or Pedistals, which are raised one over another, tapering and growing narrower towards the top. The way up to it on the four sides is only by narrow and steep Stairs of betwixt thirty and forty steps three hands broad apiece and all covered with gilt Calin or Tin like the Roof. The bottom of the great Stair-case is adorned on both sides with above twenty Statues bigger than the Life, some whereof are of Brass, and the rest of Calin and all gilt, but representing but sorrily the Persons and Animals for whom they have been made. This great Pile of Building is encompassed with forty four great Piramides of different form and well wrought, ranked orderly upon different Plat-forms. On the lowest Plat-form stand the four greatest at the four corners of it upon large bases. These Piramides end at the top in a long very slender Cone, extremely well gilt, and supporting a Needle or Arrow of Iron, that pierces through several Christal balls of an unequal bigness. The body of those great Piramides as well as of the rest, is of a kind of Architecture that comes pretty near ours; but it has too much Sculpture upon it, and wanting both the simplicity and proportions of ours, it comes short of its beauty, at least in the eyes of those that are not accustomed to it. If we have time we may give a more perfect Idea of that Architecture upon the second Plat-form, which is a little above the first, there are six and thirty other Piramides some what less than the former: making a square round the Pagod, nine on each side. They are of two different Figures, some taper into a point as the former did, and the rest are made round like a Bell on the top, after the manner of the domes which crown the Building; they are so mingled that there are not two together of the same form. Over these in the third Plat-form, are other four Piramides on the four corners of it, which terminate in a point. They are less indeed than the first, but bigger than the second. All the Fabrick and Piramides are inclosed in a kind of square Cloyster, above six-score common paces in length, about an hundred in breadth, and fifteen foot high. All the Galleries of the Cloyster are open towards the Pagod; the Cieling thereof is not ugly; for it is all painted and gilt after the Moresko way. Within the Galleries along the out Wall which is all close ranges along Pedestal breast high, on which stand above four hundred Statues, rarely well gilt, and placed in most excellent order. Though they be only of Brick gilt, yet they appear to be very well shaped, but they are so like one another, that if they were not unequal in bigness, one would think that they had been all cast in the same Mould. Amongst these Figures we reckoned twelve of a Gigantick Stature, one in the middle of each Gallery, and two at each Angle. These Figures, because of their height are fitting upon flat bases cross-leg'd, after the manner of the Country and of all the Orientals. We had the curiosity to measure one of their legs, which from the Toes to the Knee, was full six foot long, the Thumb of it was as big as an ordinary Arm, and the rest of the Body proportionably big and tall. Besides these which are of the first magnitude, there are about an hundred others that are as it were Demi-Giants, having the Leg from the extremity of the Foot to the Knee four foot long. In short between the first and second, we reckoned above three hundred, of which none are less than the life, and these stand upright. I mention not a great many other little Pagods no bigger than Puppets, which are mingled among the rest.

We never saw a Fabrick no not in France, where Symmetry is better observed, either for the body of the Building, or the Ornaments about it, than in this Pagod. The Cloister of it is flancked on the outside on each hand with sixteen great solid Piramids, rounded at the top in form of a Dome, above fourty foot high, and above twelve foot square, placed in a Line like a row of great Pillars, in the middle whereof there are larger niches filled with gilt Pagods. We were so long taken up with the sight of these things that we had not time to consider several other Temples close by the Post within the same compass of Walls. They judge of the Nobility of Families at Siam by the number of roofs that cover their Houses. This hath five one over another, and the Kings Apartment hath seven.

Guy Tachard, *A Relation of the Voyage to Siam Performed by Six Jesuits Sent by the French King to the Indies and China in the Year 1685, with their Astonomical Observations and their Remarks of Natural Philosophy, Geography, Hydrology and History*, London, A. Churchil [*sic*], 1688, pp. 181–4.

13
Travelling Overland from Bangkok to Mergui

CLAUDE CÉBERET DU BOULLAY

Claude Céberet du Boullay was born in Paris in 1647, and as a young man went as secretary to de Baas, Governor of the French islands in the Caribbean. He married there a relative of Madame de Maintenon, the secret wife of Louis XIV, and had one son. He returned to France from Martinique in the 1680s, and began his involvement in the affairs of the French Indies Company, of which he was made Director in 1685. He was sent with Simon de La Loubère (Passage 14), in 1687, as Envoy Extraordinary of Louis XIV to the King of Siam. La Loubère was charged with political and religious affairs, and Céberet with commercial matters. The mission was not a success, thanks to the extraordinary machinations of Father Tachard, who claimed he was the true ambassador, and who dealt directly with Phaulkon. If little of substance was agreed on the political front, and none on the religious, Céberet, who was accompanied by his son, aged about fifteen, managed to secure reasonable terms for the French Indies Company, and with these in his pocket left as soon as he could, taking the overland route to Mergui, then Siamese territory. He was made Intendant of the Company port of Port-Louis in 1689, a post he held until 1696, when he was made Naval Intendant at Dunkirk, where he died in 1702.

*Céberet's detailed journal of the embassy was only published in 1992 thanks to Michel Jacq-Hergoualc'h (*Etude historique et critique du 'Journal du Voyage de Siam de Claude Céberet' Envoyé Extraordinaire du Roi en 1687 et 1688, *Paris, L'Harmattan). It is long on the complex twists and turns to which Tachard and Phaulkon exposed the envoys, but rather reticent about his impressions of Siam. Here, however, is Céberet's account of his journey from Bangkok to Tenasserim and Mergui, whence he sailed with Forbin to Pondichéry, which was the only part of his record to be published before 1992, and that nearly 200 years after the journey in question.*

THE 17th December [1687] in the morning I embarked [at Bangkok] in the company of the Reverend Father d'Espagnac, one of the Jesuits, who was to accompany me to Mergui. Opra Vissiti Sompton [Kosa Pan] also embarked with me to accompany me to Mergui where he had to go with Mr de Brissy, the king's engineer, to make a plan of the island which had been granted to the Company.

I travelled all day with several attendant barges from the governors of the places I passed. Half-way from Bangkok, at Tachin, I found the governor of a big town called Rapry [Rajburi] followed by several barges; after greeting me, he went at the head of his escort, and the governor of Bangkok came to take leave of me to return.

It is to be noted that in each town or village there is a

mandarin who administers justice to the people, and carries out all the court's orders, and that when there is a fortress or a garrison in these towns or villages, the mandarin does not command the troops but another military person does, and they are everywhere foreigners.

Four or five leagues from Bangkok, I found 25 sailors whom I had summoned from Mergui, who were part of the crew of the *Président* to add to the king's crews, in particular those of the *Dromadaire* which could not have returned to France without this aid, having lost many of its crew *en route*.

A little distance from there, the river becomes narrow, so that it is no more than a small canal, with very little water; this is made up for by buffaloes which are placed at regular points to drag the barge over the mud until one finds sufficient water; this lasts for some two or three leagues, after which we continued our route to Tachin, where we arrived at five in the afternoon, after having crossed several streams which were linked with each other by canals traced in a straight line.

Tachin is a big village eight leagues from Bangkok, depending on the governor of Rapry, and situated on the banks of a pleasant stream up which ships of about 100 tons can go. There was a Chinese ship of this tonnage and several Malay ships there. I was received in a house built specially for me and furnished in the usual manner. There was no enclosure, only a small brick fort, with some curtain walls, about ten feet high, and neither moat nor terrace. There were only some battlements with cast-iron falconets which were fired when I arrived. There is very good water in this place.

The 18th I left Tachin to go to Meklong [Samut Songkram]. Half-way there was a part where, as on the previous day, the barges were drawn by buffaloes, but it was longer and more tiresome. I arrived in the evening at Meklong, ten leagues away from Tachin.

This town is bigger than Tachin, and is situated on the banks of a stream also called the Meklong, a league from the sea. The water is good here. The town has no walls, but is defended by a small square fort with four very small brick bastions. There is no moat, but it was flooded by the sea; the curtains were merely big posts placed in the ground with transoms from place to place.

I left the barges here and the following day, the 19th, went into a galley proper; other galleys and ships called *mirou* had been prepared to take my men and baggage. The governor of Rapry came to take me to the mouth of the stream, the Meklong, where he took his leave with his escort and went to rejoin me at the Pipely [Petchburi] River, four leagues away. The sea forms a fairly broad bay about four leagues wide and the Meklong River goes into it, flowing north to south. The Pipely River also flows into it, from south to north. When I was in the middle of the bay, I saw the tops of the masts of the king's ships opposite the mouth of the river of Siam [the Chao Phraya] six or seven leagues distance from this bay, and the vessels were to the east of us.

Having arrived in the Pipely River, I found the governor, a Turk from Bursa [near Istanbul], who was governor of Bangkok when the Chevalier de Chaumont came. He was at the head of his escort in a barge. He towed three galleys as far as Pipely which is eight leagues upstream. The entry to the river is entirely deserted, but after two leagues, one comes to very fine countryside stretching into plains on both sides, well cultivated and sown with rice. There was also some pasture full of animals.

The governor of Pipely, who had gone ahead, received me on land, to the sound of some cannons at the river's edge outside the town gates, and led me to the dwelling prepared for me, constructed and furnished like the others I had stayed in. From Meklong to Pipely is twelve leagues.

This town is one of the biggest in Siam, and formerly the kings stayed here. It is surrounded by a brick wall with some bastions, some of which are in good condition. The houses in the town are not handsome, being only made of bamboo. Only the pagodas are beautiful, and there is a large number of them, principally that near the landing-stage which is well built and much gilded. In the evening, the governor came to request me to delay my departure by a day for all the transport and the people he had ordered had not yet arrived, and he risked being chastised if I wished to leave before everything was ready. I did what I could to leave, being urged on by the time of the year, but seeing the governor so pained, and realizing I would lack many things, I promised to stay the whole of the following day.

The 20th some 40 carts each drawn by two buffaloes were brought before my dwelling; the carts are so narrow in the rear that none of the bales nor chests wider than a foot and a half can go in. At midday all my big pieces of baggage were loaded, and the rest, which filled 30 carts, I sent off in the evening. I only kept with me what I could not do without.

The 21st at daybreak I set off to go and sleep at Chaam. The governor came to take me at my dwelling, led me to my palanquin and excused himself for not firing cannons on my departure, but he was afraid the elephants might take fright at the sound of gunfire; he then got on his elephant at the head of 100 soldiers with two white taffeta standards. I followed on my palanquin. At my side was my son on horseback. I was followed by my elephant on which was a gilded seat covered with a kind of dome serving as an umbrella, upheld by four columns, the whole well gilded and decorated with carpets and cushions with gold brocade. The harness of the elephant was covered with scarlet cloth four fingers broad, decorated with silver nails of the same design and size as the studs on the bridles of horses in Europe. My elephant was followed by ten others, on each of which was a chair and a round covering like those on the barges of the *opra* [nobles], some were of red lacquer and others black and gilded overall. The ten elephants were mounted by people in my party and followed by 18 others with whole bamboo covers for my servants and liverymen. After these elephants came five palanquins in the manner of the country, covered with bamboo, and each carried by four men, with four more to relieve them. After came the necessary baggage for me and my party, the chapel, the kitchen and the pantry carried by 30 men walking in file. This parade was completed by some 50 soldiers and the ambassador [Kosa Pan] on his elephant and his chair of *opra*. My *maître d'hôtel*, on horseback, drew up behind.

We went through very fine countryside for two leagues, after which we found a house called Ponta de Serta, in Siamese Boakao, where I got down to eat. The governor excused himself from accompanying me further, saying he had received an order from the court to go there at once. I found in this place about 100 carts, 30 with my baggage, the rest carrying victuals and necessaries for the whole caravan, with more than 30 mandarins to give orders for everything.

After eating, I set off again. The governor accompanied me for about a league or two and then took leave of me, and returned to the town.

We arrived at Chaam after sunset, seven leagues from Ponta de Serta. This place has no enclosure and only consists of houses made of bamboo. I was lodged in a house built specially for me, as usual. Just before arriving at Chaam there is a very steep and quite high rock, though it is quite narrow in circumference, placed in the middle of the plain one finds after Ponta de Serta. In the middle of this mountain is a pagoda hollowed out into the rock which is reached by a stone staircase and the *talapoins* have created dwellings in the living rock. There are many white brick pyramids on this mountain; they serve as temple decorations. There is good water in this place. The Revd Fr. d'Espagnac and Mr Deslandes arrived at our dwelling very late at night. Their arrival relieved me of the concern that an accident might have befallen them on account of the tigers and wild elephants which are very numerous hereabouts.

The 22nd in the morning I set out again with the usual escort, apart from the soldiers from Pipely who returned, and those of Chaam who took their place. We went through a deserted land where we saw nothing apart occasionally from some cattle wandering around without keepers. We arrived in the evening at Praam [Pranburi], eleven and a half leagues from Chaam. This town is quite big. The houses and pagodas are all of bamboo. Its shape is an elongated square enclosed by upright stakes stuck in the ground, with four square towers at the four corners, built of bricks, twelve feet square or thereabouts, with some crenellations, without any moat or terrace, but inside the palissades bamboos were planted very close to each other, which form a stout and sound living hedge that was pleasant to see. I was lodged in a special dwelling as usual. There is a stream which flows around the enclosure of this town, two leagues from the sea, and ships can enter it. It was salty when I passed it because it was then the season of high tides and at the time there was no water to drink. I crossed this stream on a pontoon made of two barges on which planks had been laid transversally, which allowed the carts to pass, but the elephants were put in the water; they disappeared from time to time, walking on the river bottom, occasionally taking air with their trunks like a pipe raised above the water. The Siamese say that elephants can swim, but I could not see if they were swimming or walking on the bottom of the river.

The following day, the 23rd, I left Praam to go to Qouy [Kuiburi], nine leagues away. This town is more or less the same as Praam. There is a small stream in a deep valley around the town, which is built on an eminence. This stream goes into the sea a league and a half or thereabouts from here, and ships can come up to within three-quarters of a league of Qouy.

I went to sleep at Bahiron [?], six and a half leagues away. There is no other dwelling than that built on purpose to house me. It was in a wood, at the foot of a fairly steep mountain. There were thereabouts so many tigers that it was necessary to mount guard throughout the night, to light fires and fire muskets from time to time around the house, to frighten these animals which come in the night to surprise men and beasts. The ambassador told me that the Siamese who had been placed on guard during the night had to abandon post because the tigers came to attack them in bands. This made us take our precautions. At eleven at night I heard a confused sound of people's voices crying out in alarm. I had not yet retired and at first I thought it was tigers coming to visit us, but on going out I saw that fire had taken hold of the room of some of my men, who were then aroused. These dwellings are only made of bamboo, covered with straw, so I thought the whole place would go up in a moment. However, we got away with just being frightened. One of my liverymen who was asleep in the bed nearest the fire was burnt in a couple of places for not having got out smartly enough. There was a small barrel of powder underneath the mattress which had caught fire, without however any accident occurring.

The 24th I left at dawn to cross the mountain from which one can see both seas, that of Siam, on the east coast, and that of the Gulf of Bengal on the west. I went to dine at Nompaye [?], five leagues away, and in the evening slept at Sera [?] where there was no other house than that in which I stayed. From Nompaye to Sera is two leagues.

The 25th I went to dine at Meunam [?] which is a small

village in the mountains, four leagues from Sera. There was at this spot a stream before arriving in the village, which was close to its source where a small spring comes out of the rocks and the water of which is good and clear. We had not found any water since leaving Qouy. The water the ambassador had brought in the carts was drunk by the Siamese on the first day, so that without the precaution I had taken of carrying some in barrels, I would have suffered greatly on this journey in almost insupportable heat.

The governor of Meunam came to greet me, about two leagues before his village. He did me the honours, then he marched on foot before my elephant to the dwelling prepared for me, where, after arriving, he served me with many meats, fish and fruits in the manner of the country. I was surprised to see all the inhabitants of this place extremely thin and feeble; on asking the ambassador the reason, he told me that the air of the place was so unhealthy that no European or Siamese could live there, and that only the people who were born there would stay there, and they did not live to an old age and were in poor health. I noticed that what he said was true, for many of my men fell ill the same day, and had much difficulty in overcoming their weakness.

[The journey continued down the mountain, taking barges passing through waterfalls, before arriving at Tenasserim on 30th and at Mergui on 1st January 1688, where the party embarked on the *Président* for Pondichéry.]

Lucien Lanier, 'Voyage de Bangkok à Mergui par terre en 1687. Fragment du journal inédit de l'ambassadeur Céberet', *Revue de Géographie,* Vol. XIII, juillet–décembre 1883, pp. 415–27.

14
The King's Incidental Revenues and the Women of the Palace

SIMON DE LA LOUBÈRE

Simon de La Loubère (1642–1729) was born in Toulouse of a distinguished family and educated there, before going to Paris where he took part in salon and literary life. He became Secretary to the French Ambassador to Switzerland in 1676, and this led to his appointment by Louis XIV in 1687 as Envoy Extraordinary to King Narai of Siam, in tandem with Claude Céberet, a director of the French Indies Company, who was to cover the commercial aspects of the embassy.

The mission was more an expedition, accompanied by numerous troops, led by General Desfarges, who was to fortify and, if necessary, take by force Bangkok and the outpost of Mergui. The embassy was not a diplomatic success, largely on account of the machinations of the Jesuit Father Tachard, who maintained close links with Phaulkon, Narai's chief minister, and Father de la Chaize, Louis XIV's confessor. Because of Tachard, La Loubère was inevitably brought into conflict with Phaulkon, and his return journey with a paranoid Tachard in the next cabin accusing La Loubère of poking holes in the wall to read his papers was not pleasant. La Loubère consoled himself by passing money and books to the young musician in Tachard's company, Andre Cardinal-Destouches, and writing notes for his magisterial survey of Siam, one of the best accounts ever written of the country, which first appeared in French in 1691 and in English two years later.

La Loubère went on an equally unsuccessful mission to Spain a few years later, during which he was arrested. He was elected to the French Academy in 1693, and occupied himself with literary life and the revival of the old academy of Toulouse until his death.

His account of the country (in which he hardly mentions his own mission) is so detailed and extensive that a selection of the most interesting parts is difficult. Examples are given here of aspects of the country not hitherto covered by other visitors, namely, the king's sources of revenue through taxes, his income from trade, and the position of women at the king's court, notably his daughter.

After listing eleven different kinds of royal revenues, La Loubère continues to enumerate other benefits.

SIX Months service of every one of his Subjects per Annum: a Service which he or his Officers frequently extend much further, who alone discharges it from every thing, and from which there remains to him a good Increase. For in certain places this Service is converted into a payment made in Rice, or in Sapan-wood, or Lignum-aloes, or Saltpetre, or in Elephants, or in Beasts Skins, or in Ivory, or in other Commodities: and in fine, this Service is sometimes esteemed and paid in ready Money; and it is for the ready Money that the Rich are exempted. Anciently this Service was esteemed at a Tical a Month, because that one Tical is sufficient to maintain one Man: and this computation serves likewise as an assessment on the days Labour of the Workmen, which a particular Person employs. They amount to two Ticals a Month at least, by reason that it is reckon'd that a Workman must in 6 Months gain his Maintenance for the whole year; seeing that he can get nothing the other six Months that he serves the Prince. The Prince now extorts two Ticals a Month for the exemption from the six Months Service.

His other Revenues do arise from the Commerce, which he exercises with his Subjects and Foreigners. He has carried it to such a degree, that Merchandize is now no more the Trade of particular persons at Siam. He is not contented with selling by Whole-sale, he has some Shops in the Bazars or Markets, to sell by Re-tail.

The principal thing that he sells to his Subjects is Cotton-cloath: he sends them into his Magazines of the Provinces. Heretofore his Predecessors and he sent them thither only every Ten Years, and a moderate quantity, which being sold, particular persons had liberty to make Commerce thereof: now he continually furnishes them, he has in his Magazines more than he can possibly sell; and it sometimes happens that to vend more, that he has forced his Subjects to cloath their Children before the accustomed Age. Before the Hollanders came into the Kingdom of Laos, and into others adjacent, the

King of Siam did there make the whole Commerce of Linnen with a considerable profit.

All the Calin[1] is his, and he sells it as well to Strangers as to his own Subjects, excepting that which is dug out of the Mines of Jonsalam [Phuket] on the Gulph of Bengal: for this being a remote Frontier, he leaves the Inhabitants in their ancient Rights, so that they enjoy the Mines which they dig, paying a small profit to this Prince.

All the Ivory comes to the King, his Subjects are obliged to vend him all that they sell, and Strangers can buy only at his Magazine. The Trade of Saltpetre, Lead and Sapan, belongs also to the King: they can buy and sell them only at his Magazine, whether one be a Siamese or Stranger.

Arek, a great deal of which is exported out of the Kingdom, can be sold to Foreigners only by the King: and for this end he buys some of his Subjects, besides that which he has from his particular Revenues.

Prohibited Goods, as Powder, Sulphur and Arms, can be bought or sold at Siam, only at the King's Magazine.

As to the Skins of Beasts, this Prince is obliged, by a Treaty made with the Hollanders, to sell them all to them; and for this purpose he buys them of his Subjects: but his Subjects do convey away a great many, which the Hollanders buy of them in secret.

The rest of the Commerce at Siam is permitted to all, as that of Rice, Fish, Salt, Brown Sugar, Sugar-Candy, Ambergreese, Wax, the Gum with which Varnish is made, Mother of Pearl, those edable Birds-Nests which come from Tonquin and Cochinchina, which Navaratte reports to be made of the Sea-froth in some Rocks, by a kind of small Sea-Birds, which resemble Swallows, Gumme Gutte, Incense, Oyl, Coco, Cotton, Cinnamon, Nenuphar, which is not exactly like ours; Cassia, Dates, and several other things, as well the growth of the Kingdom, as brought from abroad.

Every one may make and sell Salt; fish and hunt, as I have declared, and without paying any thing to the King. It is true, that the necessary Policy is used in Fishing; and Oc-Pra Tainam, who receives the particular Revenues of the River, hinders those ways of Fishing, which destroy too much Fish at once. . . .

[1]See p. 72.

Commerce requires a certain liberty: no person can resolve to go to Siam, necessarily to sell unto the King what is carry'd thither, and to buy of him alone what one would carry thence, when this was not the product of the Kingdom. For though there were several foreign Ships together at Siam, the Trade was not permitted from one Ship to the other, not with the Inhabitants of the Country, Natives or Foreigners, till that the King, under the pretence of a preference due to his Royal dignity, had purchased what was best in the Ships, and at his own rate, to sell it afterwards as he pleased: because that when the season for the departure of the Ships presses on, the Merchants choose rather to sell to great loss, and dearly to buy a new Cargo, than to wait at Siam a new season to depart, without hopes of making a better Trade.

In a word, 'tis neither the natural Riches, nor the Manufactures of the Kingdom of Siam, that should tempt one to go thither. The natural Siameses, ruin'd as they are by impositions and services, cannot carry on a great Trade, though they should have all the liberty imaginable. The Trade is manag'd only with the superfluous Money, and in the places where the Impositions are very great, there is scarcely found Money necessary for life. The vast summ levied on the people returns slowly to the people, and especially in the remote Provinces; and the whole does not return, because that a great part thereof remains in the hands of those, that tend upon the receipts and expences of the Prince. And as to that part which returns to the people, it remains not in their hands for their uses; it soon goes thence to return to the Princes Coffers: so that it must needs be, that all the small Trades do cease for want of Money; which cannot be, but the general Commerce of a State does greatly suffer. But this is yet much truer at Siam, where the Prince annually accumulates his Revenues, instead of expending them....

As to the King of Siam's Chamber, the true Officers thereof are Women, 'tis they only that have a Priviledge of entering therein. They make his Bed, and dress his Meat; they cloath him, and wait on him at Table: but none but himself touches his Head when he is attir'd, nor puts any thing over his Head. The Pourveyors carry the Provisions to the Eunuchs, and they give them to the Women; and she which plays the Cook, uses Salt and Spices only by weight, thereby never to put in more nor less: A practice, which, in my opinion, is only a Rule of the Physicians, by reason of the King's unhealthy disposition, and not an ancient custom of the Palace.

The Women do never stir out but with the King, nor the Eunuchs without express Order. 'Tis reported that he has eight or ten Eunuchs only, as well white or black. The late Queen, who was both his Wife and his Sister, was called Nang Achamahisii. It is not easie to know the King's Name [Narai], they carefully and superstitiously conceal it, for fear lest any Enchantment should be made on his Name. And others report, that their Kings have no Name till after their death, and that it is their Successor which names them, and this would be more certain against the pretended Sorceries.

Of Queen Achamathisii is born, as I have related in the other Part, the Princess, the King of Siam's only Daughter [Yothathep], who now has the Rank and House of a Queen. The King's other Wives (which in general are called Tchaou Vang, because that the word Tchaou [chau], which signifies Lord, signifies likewise Lady and Mistress) do render Obedience to her, and respect her as their Soveraign. They are subject to her Justice, as well as the Women and Eunuchs which serve them; because that not being able to stir out, to go plead elsewhere, it necessarily follows that the Queen should judge them, and cause them to be chastised, to keep them in peace. This is thus practised in all the Courts of Asia; but it is not true neither at Siam, nor perhaps in any part of the East, that the Queen has any Province to govern. 'Tis easie also to comprehend, that if the King loves any of his Ladies more than the rest, he causes her to remove from the Jealousie and harsh Usage of the Queen.

At Siam they continually take Ladies for the service of the Vang, or to be Concubines to the King, if this Prince makes use thereof. But the Siamese deliver up their Daughters only by force, because it is never to see them again; and they redeem them so long as they can for Money. So that this becomes a kind of Extortion, for they designedly take a great many Virgins meerly to restore them to their Parents, who redeem them.

The King of Siam has few Mistresses, that is to say eight or ten in all, not out of Continency, but Parsimony. I have already declared, that to have a great many Wives, is in this Country rather Magnificence, than Debauchery. Wherefore they are very much surprized to hear that so great a King as ours has no more than one Wife, that he had no Elephants, and that his Lands bear no Rice; as we might be, when it was told us that the King of Siam has no Horses, nor standing Forces, and that his Country bears no Corn nor Grapes, altho' all the Relations do so highly extol the Riches and Power of the Kingdom of Siam.

The Queen hath her Elephants and her Balons [barges], and some Officers to take care of her, and accompany her when she goes abroad; but none but her Women and Eunuchs do see her. She is conceal'd from all the rest of the People; and when she goes out either on an Elephant, or in a Balon, it is in a Chair made up with Curtains, which permit her to see what she pleases, and do prevent her being seen: And Respect commands, that if they cannot avoid her, they should turn their back to her, by prostrating themselves when she passes along.

Besides this she has her Magazine, her Ships, and her Treasures. She exercises Commerce; and when we arrived in this Country, the Princess, whom I have reported to be treated like a Queen, was exceedingly embroiled with the King her Father, because that he reserved to himself alone almost all the Foreign Trade, and that thereby she found herself deprived thereof, contrary to the ancient Custom of the Kingdom.

Daughters succeed not to the Crown, they are hardly look'd upon as free. 'Tis the eldest Son of the Queen that ought always to succeed by the Law. Nevertheless because that the Siameses can hardly conceive that amongst Princes of near the same Rank, the most aged should prostrate himself before the younger; it frequently happens that amongst Brethren, tho' they be not all Sons of the Queen, and that amongst Uncles and Nephews, the most advanced in Age is preferred, or rather it is Force which always decides it. The Kings themselves contribute to render the Royal Succession uncertain, because that instead of chusing for their Successor the eldest Son of the Queen, they most frequently follow the Inclination which they have for the Son of some one of their Concubines with whom they were enamour'd.

Simon de La Loubère, *A New Historical Relation of the Kingdom of Siam*, London, 1693, pp. 94–5, 112–13, 100–1.

15
Reception in the Palace at Lopburi and Phaulkon's Chapel

GUY TACHARD

The Jesuit Guy Tachard (see Passage 12), who emerged as the éminence grise *of the French adventure in Siam in the period 1685–8, wrote, or rather assembled from a variety of sources, an official account of his second journey. The unpublished account,* Voyage du Père Tachard à Siam, *in the Archives Nationales is often more revealing, and, as Michel Jacq-Hergoualc'h (*Etude historique et critique du 'Journal du Voyage de Siam de Claude Céberet' Envoyé Extradordinaire du Roi en 1687 et 1688, *Paris, L'Harmattan, 1992) has pointed out, is often in complete contradiction with the account of one of the two envoys to King Narai. However, there are agreements at some points, including that of the reception in the palace at Lopburi at the audience in which the Dauphin's compliments and presents were presented. The hyperbole of La Loubère's speech is typical of the time.*[1]

THEIR Excellencies the Envoys were still in a courtyard outside this chamber when they saw the King of Siam, who was waiting for them seated on his throne. Immediately they gave a deep bow, to which the monarch

[1]See, for example, *The Discourses at Versailles of the First Siamese Ambassadors to France 1686–7*, edited by M. Smithies, Bangkok, Siam Society, 1986. Lanier, whose work on Franco-Siamese relations published in 1883 remains an important text, remarked that the speeches were close to idolatry.

replied by bending his body fairly low. They bowed again on entering the room reached by climbing seven or eight steps, and gave a third when they were near their seats before giving their speech, which Mr de La Loubère pronounced in these terms:

'Great King, whose friendship and alliance will always be the most esteemed by princes who would obtain thereby greater real grandeur, the Dauphin of France had charged us to demonstrate to Your Majesty the extraordinary esteem he attaches to your royal friendship and your magnificent presents. The only son and presumptive heir of Louis the Great, he places the alliance and friendship of Your Majesty at the highest level of advantages which come with the greatest birthright in the world. Your Majesty's magnaminity and wisdom demonstrate the value of Your Majesty's great and royal qualities, which like a most exquisite perfume have spread their aroma to the extremities of the earth. He hopes that Your Majesty will agree to accept the presents he is sending Your Majesty, and desires with passion that by this sign and by all the assurances which he charged us to give on his behalf to Your Majesty, that Your Majesty will be entirely persuaded of the high esteem and extreme affection he has for Your Royal Person and in which qualities he wishes to raise his august princes, his children, for the good of the two kingdoms.'

The King of Siam replied to this discourse in a most obliging manner, saying 'that he received with both great esteem and gratitude the presents of so noble a prince, that he did not doubt that he was the worthy heir of the incomparable virtues and great qualities of the king his father, and that he hoped there would always be between the French and the Siamese the link which His Majesty and he had so well established; that he had learnt with pleasure of the numerous posterity which God had granted His Royal Highness, and France and the universe itself could not have sufficient descendants of Louis the Great.' After that the monarch asked several questions of the envoys concerning the health, age and interests of the Dauphin, and his spouse the Dauphine, which they answered, and then the king withdrew.

I have spoken of the two fine mansions which Mr Constance [Phaulkon] had caused to be constructed in the city of Siam

[Ayutthaya] and Louvo [Lopburi]. We must speak here of another still finer which he built for God. This chapel, at Louvo, was almost finished when the Chevalier de Chaumont came, and mass was said here all the time he resided, but it then had no decoration. One can say now that there hardly exists a private chapel which is richer or more spacious. It does not have that regularity and symmetry which accords with the taste of architectural experts, because Mr Constance, having no architect, had it built according to his own designs; but it could hardly be bettered. Marble so precious, rare and esteemed in the Indies has not been spared. In whichever direction one casts one's eyes, from the top of the chapel to its foundation, one sees only gold and paintings. The pictures in which are shown one by one the principal mysteries of the Old and New Testaments are not exquisite but the colours are astonishing, and the painter, a Japanese, makes one realize that if the fine arts were sufficiently esteemed and as well cultivated in the Indies as they are in Europe, the Indian and Chinese painters would scarcely have to give way before the most gifted of the European masters. The tabernacle, on which work is currently being carried out, will be very big, and all of solid silver. There is no embroidery on the hangings, but the material from which they are made is extremely rich and light. The roof of this chapel is triple, in the manner of the pagodas, and is covered in *calin*, which is a kind of very white metal, between tin and lead, and much lighter than either. A breast-high balustrade surrounds the body of the building, and separates it from the two houses which Mr Constance has had built in Louvo, because the Siamese take this precaution and seek to indicate their veneration of sacred places by separating them from other buildings for the use of men. In front of the doorway which faces the street is a fairly big courtyard shaped like an amphitheatre, which one reaches by going up twelve to fifteen steps. In the middle of this is a large stone cross which will be gilded, placed on a broad pedestal, the structure and decoration of which derive from a very different architecture from ours. All around this courtyard is a kind of gallery three feet high, in which one finds small recesses placed at regular intervals for placing lamps which are lit from the first vespers of important festivals to the following day.

Guy Tachard, *Second Voyage du Père Tachard et des Jésuites envoyés par le Roi au Royaume de Siam*, Paris, Horthemels, and Amsterdam, Pierre Mortier, 1689, pp. 208–11.

16
The Death of King Narai

FATHER DE BÈZE

Father de Bèze was born in Nevers in 1657 and went with Father Leblanc to Siam in 1687, where he stayed thirteen months before going, still with Leblanc, to Pondichéry after the so-called revolution of 1688. De Bèze was held a prisoner of the Dutch in Malacca for six months, then interned in Middelburg, in Holland. He was set free in 1691 and returned to France, where he appears to have been asked by the king's confessor, the powerful Jesuit, Father de la Chaize, for an account of the events leading up to and including the revolution. He then travelled overland intending to go to China, but reached Chandernagor near Calcutta in 1693, where he died a year later after serving in the mission there.

De Bèze's account, which incorporates a text of Leblanc (who also died in 1693, in Mozambique, en route *for China), was not published in his lifetime and gives a great deal of information relating to Phaulkon, which is not relevant here. But his account of the last days of King Narai, when he was one of the very few allowed to see him, is of interest. Petracha was manoeuvring to become king; Paumart was a French missionary with some medical background who was given, on account of this, much greater freedom when his colleagues were incarcerated.*

THIS was the time when Pitracha decided upon the final act in this outrageous tragedy by putting the King's two Brothers to death. As I have related already, the younger Brother came to Louvo [Lopburi] before Pitracha's revolt took place, in response to an invitation from his sister and much more to an invitation from his niece, the Crown Princess [Yothathep]. She was ambitious and did her best to prevail upon him to come up, believing it was Pitracha's real intention to recognize the claims of this uncle whom—so it is believed—she had espoused. In the end he came up with her and Pitracha did nothing more at first than have him watched. After he had gained the upper hand Pitracha still knew that the inhabitants of the Capital were solidly in favour of the elder Prince who had kept clear of contact with him, and was deaf to his sister's messages concerning the intentions of the rebel which she believed were honest.

Pitracha now deputed several of his most trusted followers who were courtiers to go to the Prince as though to pay homage to him and then abduct him by a back door which gave on to the river.

Pitracha now found himself master of both Princes, but he dared not despatch them on his own authority lest he bring down upon his own head the hatred of all the common folk and of the majority of courtiers in his own following as well—men who had joined it under the impression they were acting thereby in the interest of the Princes. His aim therefore was to cause it to be believed that the warrant for their death came from the King himself. With this intention in his mind he resolved to go and see the King and have a discussion with him in private during which, he would make it appear, that the Princes' death-warrant had been conveyed to him.[1]

A number of courtiers were in attendance and saw him enter the King's apartment, but only one of their number, a man in closest intimacy with him, followed him inside. We had the account from a physician who chanced to be in attendance upon the King at that moment.

Catching sight of Pitracha, the King was seized with a fit of such violence that he fell to the ground as one dead. When restored, His Majesty upbraided Pitracha with the unworthy manner in which he was treating his Sovereign; with the death of his adopted son [Phra Pi] and of Constans [Phaulkon]; for the imprisonment of his Brothers. He then gave voice to his grief on our account, that we, whom he had brought out from France upon the recommendation of our King, should now be subjected to ill-treatment and reduced

[1]The incident is not related by other French writers, but a last visit is recorded in the *Annals of Ancient Ayuthia* [Translator's note].

to great want. Pitracha replied that since ill-health had prevented His Majesty from attending to Affairs of State, he, Pitracha, had been obliged to assume control upon the advice of the Court, until such time as His Majesty's health be restored; that Pra Pi and Oya Vichaiyen were found guilty of death by the Privy Council. As for the King's Brothers, Pitracha promised to send them to the King and never to do them any harm—words which the King's Sister brought up against him later on when he had the hardihood to say that the King had ordered that they be put to death, for she was present throughout the interview. Referring finally to our party of Jesuits, he protested that we had received no ill-treatment and if we needed money, His Majesty had but to give the order and he would send us money. The King signified his pleasure and Pitracha made a point of telling the courtiers that he received this order simultaneously with the order to put the King's Brothers to death. By conjoining the two orders he rendered each order more credible than it would have been alone. He sent the money to us with a deal of ceremony to prove that he carried out the King's orders punctually.

In the course of the conversation between the King and Pitracha, the King bewailed the fact that he no longer had the authority to send for Dr Paumard and myself, Pitracha again gave his word to allow us to speak to the King. This promise he intended to make good and, sending for us, he let us know that the King desired to see us, but he warned us against discussing matters of religion or recent happenings and told us he would cut off our heads if we dared do anything that contravened his orders. He knew however that we were unlikely to observe his orders and made allowance accordingly by repeating them to those who watched over the King.

So altered, so downcast did we find the poor King, it was not easy to recognize him as the King we had known. He began by bewailing the straits to which he was reduced; he then dwelt upon his grief over the death of Constans, a minister, he averred, who had ever laboured faithfully for him and rendered the State good service; the grounds upon which he was condemned to perish lacked any foundation in fact. When the guards found His Majesty launched upon that subject, they protested that long discourse was harmful to their charge in his present state of infirmity and brusquely carried him away. We were given no time even to broach the subject of Religion and were sorely vexed to have missed an opening of such promise for a final attempt to convert this Ruler—the more so as we had reason to believe that he had contemplated adopting the Christian Faith, at least on his death-bed, and had sent for us on that account. He had so often displayed a marked bias in favour of Christianity.

While still restless upon this score, we received notice of permission to see the King once more; he had displayed such grief that no time had been given him for discourse with us; he was so insistent to see us again that Pitracha had not the heart to deny him this comfort seeing he was at death's door. We went, fully determined to begin our discourse with a reference at the very outset to the King's salvation, cost us what it might. Thus, when the King confirmed his first words to us by laying bare his chest for us to see his wasted flesh, we adjured him not to hope that any human agent has the means to repair such wastage save by a miracle; rather should he strive to obtain a new and happier life which outlasts life here. The Chinese interpreter refused to translate words such as these and persisted, despite our entreaties, assuring us that for himself it was a matter of life or death. The reason for this was that Pitracha was aware that his threats would hold greater terror for this man than for us and had impressed them upon him accordingly under pain of death. The King was most anxious to know what we were saying, but I had only been six months in the country and did not know enough of the language, still less the Court language which I was only beginning to study; Mr Paumard had been ten years in Siam but did not know it either. In consequence we were unable to gather from the King whether or not he desired to be baptized. He was carried away again for, sick though he was, he had been lifted from his bed and brought into the antechamber. The King died two days later at the tenth hour that Sunday night, the tenth day of July.

E. W. Hutchinson, *1688 Revolution in Siam: The Memoir of Father de Bèze, S. J.*, Hong Kong University Press, 1968, pp. 106–9.

17
An Account of Siam Presented to Louis XIV

CHEVALIER CLAUDE DE FORBIN

The Chevalier Claude de Forbin, later Count, was a virile Provençal marine who went to Siam as lieutenant to the Chevalier de Chaumont in 1685 when he was twenty-nine. At the request of King Narai, engineered by Constance Phaulkon, the King's chief minister, he stayed on in Siam, according to him so that he would not inform the court at Versailles of the real value of the liaison with that distant country. After several almost impossible missions given him by Phaulkon, and one attempt to poison him, he decided to return as soon as he could to France, indirectly, through his favourite, Phra Pi, taking leave of King Narai, who had made him admiral of his fleet and commander of the troops in the new fort at Bangkok. He returned to France from Pondichéry in the company of Céberet (see Passage 13), returning from his mission of 1687–8, during which they were able to compare their impressions; Forbin, having lived in the country over a year, had the advantage of longer experience.

On his return to Versailles, he saw the three most powerful men concerned in the Siamese imbroglio: Louis XIV himself, the Marquis de Seignelay, Secretary of State for the Navy, and the king's confessor, the Jesuit Father de la Chaize. What he declared he told them is reproduced, in translation, below. Forbin was not absolutely neutral in his observations; he was trying to redress the imbalance created by Tachard and Choisy. He also wished to draw attention to the foolhardiness of placing reliance on a single person as mercurial as Phaulkon for the French enterprise in Siam.

Forbin was born in 1656 in Gardanne, near Aix-en-Provence, and rose to be a squadron commander in the navy. He retired at the age of fifty-nine after taking part in numerous battles in the Wars of the Spanish Succession, and then wrote his memoirs, which first appeared in 1729. He died near Marseilles in 1733. His memoirs contain an account of his stay in Siam which was nothing if not eventful. The episode of the conflict with the Makassarese in Bangkok is described in detail, and shows him to be brave and resourceful (his description of his surgery on Beauregard, whose intestines had spilled out of his split stomach, is not for the squeamish; no one was more surprised than Forbin, perhaps, that Beauregard recovered). Not all his time in Bangkok was so adventurous. He filled his idle moments in catching crocodiles.

CHARMED at the manner in which I was received [in Paris], I was present at the king's table. His Majesty honoured me with many questions about the Kingdom of Siam. He asked me first of all if the country was rich. 'Sire,' I replied, 'the Kingdom of Siam produces nothing and consumes nothing.' 'That is saying a lot, in few words,' His Majesty replied, and continuing to question me, he asked me what was the style of government, how the people lived, and from where the king obtained all the presents which he had sent.

I replied that the populace was very poor; that there was neither nobility nor rank since all were slaves of the king, for whom they had to work for part of each year, unless he chose to dispense them of this obligation by elevating them to the rank of mandarin; that this rank, which raises them from the dust, does not protect them from the wrath of the monarch, in whose bad favour they can easily fall, and this is always followed by severe punishment; that even the barkalon [Phra Klang] himself, who is the chief minister and fills the most important position in the state, is as exposed as all the others; and he holds such a perilous position only by grovelling before his master like the least of the populace; and that if he falls from grace, the mildest punishment he can receive is to be sent back to the plough after having been severely chastised; that the people feed themselves on some fruits and rice, which are very abundant in their country; that, believing in metempsychosis, no one dares eat anything that has lived for fear of eating his father or one of his relatives; that in what concerned the presents sent to His Majesty, Mr Constance [Phaulkon] had exhausted the treasury and spent so freely it would not be easy to make good the expenditure; that the Kingdom of Siam, which virtually forms a peninsula, could be a very convenient entrepôt to facilitate commerce in the Indies, facing as it does two seas, one on the east towards

China, Japan, Tonkin, Cochinchina, Laos, and Cambodia, and the other to the west facing the Kingdom of Arakan, the Ganges, the coast of Coromandel, Malabar and the town of Surat; that the merchandise of these different nations could be transported in all years to Siam which is a focal point and like a fair, where the Siamese can make profit by retailing their commodities of trade; that the principal revenue of the king consisted in trade which he virtually monopolizes in his kingdom, and that only rice, areca from which betel is made, some tin, some elephants and some skins of the wild beasts which fill the country are sold; that the Siamese went about almost naked, except for a cotton length they wore from the waist to the calf, they have no kinds of manufactures, except for some muslins which only the mandarins have the right to wear like a kind of shirt on ceremonial occasions; that when a mandarin had managed to come by a small sum of money, he had nothing better to do with it than to hide it, otherwise the king would seize it; that no one in the entire kingdom possesses any property, which all belongs by right to the king, which results in the greatest part of the land remaining uncultivated, no one wishing to take the trouble to cultivate land which would be taken from him as soon as it was in a good condition; that finally the people are very sober, an individual who can earn fifteen or twenty francs a year had more than the necessary wherewithall to maintain himself.

The king then asked me what kind of money was used in the country. 'Their money', I replied, 'is a round piece of silver, like a rifle shot, marked with two Siamese characters, which are the hallmark of the king; this ball, which is called a *tical*, is worth 40 French sous. In addition to the tical, there was a half-tical, and another silver coin called *faon* [*fuang*], with a value of five sous. For small change, they use seashells, which come from the Maldive Islands, and 120 are worth five sous.'

'Let us talk a little of their religion,' the king said to me. 'Are there many Christians in the Kingdom of Siam, and does the king really think of embracing Christianity himself?'

'Sire,' I replied, 'this monarch has never thought of such a thing, and no mortal would be so bold as to suggest it. It is true that in the discourse which Mr de Chaumont made on the day of his first audience, he mentioned religion; but

Mr Constance, who was serving as interpreter, cleverly omitted this point; the Apostolic Vicar who was present, and who understands Siamese perfectly, was fully aware of this; but he dared say nothing about it, for fear of bringing about the wrath of Mr Constance, who would not have pardoned him if he had opened his mouth on the subject.'

The king, surprised at this discourse, listened to me very attentively. I added that in the private audiences Mr de Chaumont had during his embassy, he often spoke of the Christian religion, and that Constance, who was ever the interpreter, cleverly played the role of a person with two different characters, saying to the King of Siam what flattered him, and replying to Mr de Chaumont what was appropriate, without there being, either on the king's or the ambassador's part, anything concluded but what it pleased Constance to give the other to understand; that I knew this again from the Apostolic Vicar himself, who was present at all their private meetings, and who had spoken about it to me in great secrecy. With this, the king began to smile, and said that monarchs were very unfortunate to be obliged to depend on interpreters who were often not faithful.

Finally the king asked me if the missionaries had much success in Siam, and in particular if they had converted many Siamese. 'Not one, Sire,' I replied, 'but as most of the people living in this kingdom come from different nations, and that among the Siamese there is a great number of Portuguese, Cochinchinese, and Japanese, who are Christians, the good missionaries take care of these and administer the sacraments to them. They go from one village to another and enter the houses, under pretext of practising medicine and giving away minor cures; but with all that, their industry has so far produced nothing in favour of religion. The greatest good they do is to baptise the children of Siamese they find abandoned in the countryside; for the people, who are very poor, only bring up some of their children, and abandon the rest, which is not a crime for them. It is in the baptism of these children to which is reduced the entire fruit of the missions in the country.'

On leaving the king's table, the Marquis de Seignelay asked me to pass by his chambers, where he questioned me at length on everything which might concern the king's interests, and in particular he enquired if one could establish important trade relations with Siam, and what was the purpose Mr Constance might have in showing so much concern for calling in the French. I satisfied him on the last point with many details of all that I knew of the views and designs of the Siamese minister.

'Concerning commerce,' I replied, 'as I informed the king, the country produces nothing, and can only be regarded as an entrepôt to facilitate trade with China, Japan and other kingdoms in the Indies; and, given this, the outpost which was begun by sending troops was absolutely pointless, since what the [French Indies] company already had was sufficient.

'In regard to the fort of Bangkok, it would remain in French hands for as long as the King of Siam and Mr Constance were alive; but if either passed away, the Siamese, both in their own interests, and encouraged by the enemies of France, would not hesitate to chase our troops out of a position which made them masters of the kingdom.'

Two days later, the Cardinal de Janson [a relative of Forbin] told me to go and seek out Father de la Chaize, who wanted to talk to me about the new French outpost in the Kingdom of Siam. 'My cousin,' said the Cardinal, 'take great care of what you say, for you will speak to the sharpest man in the kingdom.' 'I am not worried,' I told him, 'I have only the truth to tell.' At daybreak, I was led into a secret stairway, and presented to His Reverence by Father Vatable.

This reverend father really only spoke to me about religion and the purpose of the King of Siam in having Jesuits in his realm, building a college and an observatory for them at Louvo [Lopburi]. I told him that Mr Constance, who wanted above all the protection of the king [of France], promised more than he could deliver; that the college and the observatory would perhaps be built during the King of Siam's lifetime; that the Jesuits would be given board and keep; but that when the king died, one would need to find funds from France for maintaining the missionaries, it being most unlikely that a new king would be willing to maintain them.

When Father de la Chaize heard me speak thus, he said, 'You are not in agreement with Father Tachard.' I told him I only spoke the truth, that I was unaware of what Father Tachard had said, but his friendship with Mr Constance, who, to arrive

A Siamese Buddhist priest, from Guy Tachard, *Voyage de Siam des Pères Jésuites envoyés par le Roi aux Indies et à la Chine*, Paris, Seneuze et Horthemels, 1686.

at his designs, had omitted nothing to seduce him, could well have blinded him, and so made him suspect: that during the short time he had stayed in Siam with Mr de Chaumont, he had been able to attract the entire confidence of the minister, and that he had even served as French secretary for him on some occasions, and I myself had seen missives written in the father's hand, signed 'From His Excellency the Minister' with, underneath, 'Tachard'. On hearing this, the reverend father smiled, but soon taking up his serious and modest demeanour, which he forsook but rarely, he asked if the missionaries had much success in the kingdom.

I told him what I had told the king, adding that what held back progress in the Gospels most was the harsh and austere life of the talapoins. 'These priests or monks of the country,' I told him, 'live in continual abstinence; they only feed on daily charity offered them. They distribute to the poor what they have in addition to their necessities, and keep nothing for the following day. They never leave their monasteries except to seek alms, and that they do without speaking. They just present their bowl, which in truth is soon filled, for the Siamese are very charitable.

'When the talapoins go about the city, they carry in their hand a fan which they hold in front of their face to prevent them seeing women. They live very continently, and do not cease to follow this rule unless they wish to leave the order to marry. The Siamese have no public prayers, nor sacrifices. The talapoins gather them together sometimes in the temples and preach to them. The usual subject of their sermons is charity; this virture is a great recommendation throughout the kingdom, where one almost never sees the poor reduced to begging for their food.

'The women there are naturally very chaste; the Siamese are not malicious and the children are so submissive to their fathers that they allow themselves to be sold without objection, when their parents are forced to do so to provide their needs. This being so, you must never expect to convert any Siamese to the Christian religion, for, apart from being too uncouth for them easily to absorb the truth of our mysteries, and that they find their morality more perfect than ours, they do not esteem our missionaries sufficiently since they live in a manner less austere than their talapoins.

'When our priests want to preach the Christian truths in Siam, the people are so simple and docile, they listen as though one were telling them fables or children's stories. Their complaisance allows them to approve all kinds of religions. According to them, paradise is a great palace where the sovereign master dwells. This palace has many doorways through which all kinds of people may enter to serve the master for whatever task he designates. It is more or less, they say, like the palace of the king with several gates, where each mandarin has his particular functions. So it is in heaven, where is found the palace of the All Powerful, all religions are as many gates which lead into it, since all the beliefs of men, whatever they are, tend to honour the supreme being, and approach him, though in a manner which may be more or less direct.

'The talapoins never disagree about religion with anyone. When one speaks to them about the Christian religion or any other, they approve of all that they are told; but when one tries to condemn their religion, they reply coldly, "Since I had had the complaisance to approve your religion, why do you not approve of mine?" As for external penitence and the mortification of passion, it is not proper to speak to them about it, since they set us the example and surpass by much, at least externally, our most reformed creeds.

'Furthermore, Father,' I continued, 'the Jesuits do not lack enemies in these missions. Your missionaries, who have superior talents to others, easily manage to attract the favour of monarchs, whom they use to uphold their creed; from there it is difficult for jealousy not to lead to the formation of cabals directed against them, not only in Europe, but even in the Indies.

'During my stay in Siam, many Chinese, who have wit and understanding, confessed to me that they did not understand how people with the same belief who had left their land and crossed vast oceans, hoped to attract the unconverted to them, when they were not in agreement among themselves in their conduct; some lived with much modesty and charity, and others gave themselves over to hatred and dissention, not to say more. This is the language all the Chinese used with whom I spoke. This truth is so constant and so public in the Indies, that not only do I think I should inform you of it, but more should broadcast it at every occasion that presents itself.'

Count C. de Forbin, *Mémoires*, Amsterdam, Girardi, 1729.

Other Viewpoints, Other Times (Late Seventeenth to Late Eighteenth Century)

18
Persian Views of Siam

IBN MUHAMMAD IBRAHIM

Ibn Muhammad Ibrahim was the Secretary of the Ambassador, Haji Salim Mazandarani, sent by Shah Sulaiman the Safavid (r. 1666–94) to the King of Siam, Narai, in return for an embassy to the court at Isfahan. The Persian embassy was also enjoined to make contact with the Persian community in Siam, which had been influential until the rise in the star of Constance Phaulkon, who consequently is deemed 'the sly, ill-begotten Frank minister'. A number of influential families today (notably the Bunnags) trace their origins to the Persians who settled in Ayutthaya in the sixteenth and seventeenth centuries.

The convoluted style of The Ship of Sulaiman *does not make for easy reading, but it contains a wealth of detail about Siam and is, alas, the only non-Western source to be used in this volume. The Ambassador, who like Chaumont was also aiming to convert the king (though to a different religion), had the misfortune to die—or, in the words of Ibn Muhammad, to 'set out for the regions of the Ruler of all men'—soon after arriving in Siam and before reaching the capital. The Siamese insisted that one person in the embassy be named to replace him, and after much dithering, and to the regret of Ibn Muhammad,*

Ibrahim Beg was named Ambassador by the travelling Persians. Here are described the town of Suhan (Bangkok), with its Turkish governor, on the way to Shahr Nav (Siam, or Ayutthaya), and how Narai adopted Persian court dress and his daily routine. Ibn Muhammad, like visiting Westerners, is astonished at the religious freedom found in the country and staggered by some of its customs. He is no more an impartial observer than many of his Western counterparts, and his comments on religion and the priesthood, in particular, show a total lack of comprehension of the practices in Siam.

Suhan [Bangkok] a Flourishing Town along the River to Shahr Nav [Siam].

AGAIN we boarded boats and in one more day we came to the town of Suhan. This community is attached to Shahr Nav and is extremely fertile and beautiful. A wondrous river of fresh water flows through the town and continues down to the sea. On both sides of the river for several farsakhs are orchards which are not partitioned by walls or fences. There grows every sort of fruit tree, lemon, orange, coconut and mango, as well as the betel tree, which for beauty and grace rivals the free, swaying cypress. In fact, every fruit native to Siam was available in that village.

All around us were trees that never feel the withering touch of autumn, trees as flourishing as the youthful hopes which old men nourish in their hearts. Most countries of Below the Winds evade the grip of autumn. The meadows and the trees keep their skirts free from the chill touch of winter. But this garden spot is surely the most blessed of all these regions.

Throughout the whole year the countryside stays fresh, the meadows are full of roses and the heavy trees bend with fruit. The leafy branches swayed and whispered all around us holding their outspread arms one above the other. Juicy fruits shake and glisten in every gentle breeze....

The Embassy is Received by the Rajah, Chelebi, and Presented with Finer Boats.

When we arrived at the outskirts of the town we were met by a man called Chelebi. He was from among the people of

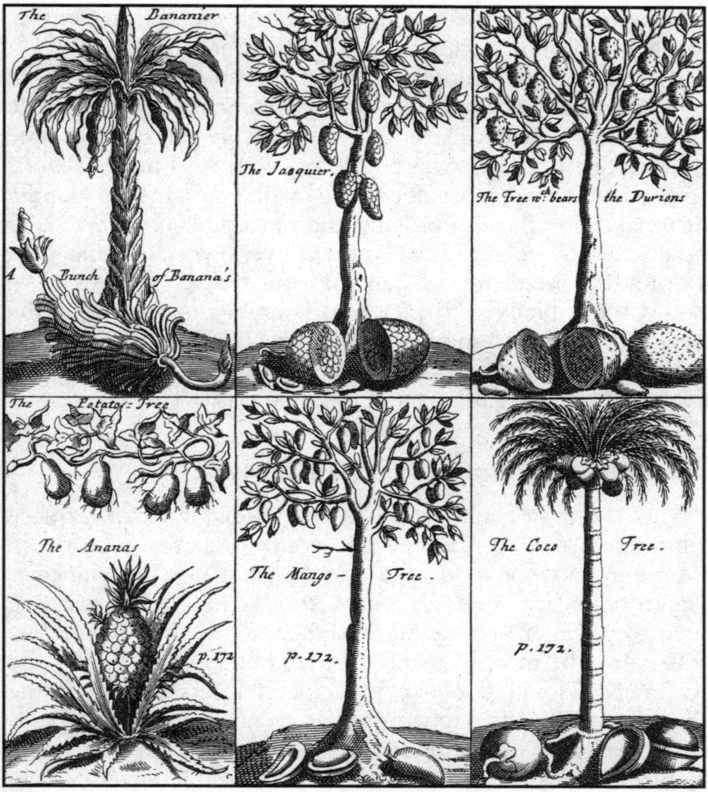

Six types of fruit tree, from Simon de La Loubère, *A New Historical Relation of the Kingdom of Siam*, London, 1693.

Rum [Turkey], had settled in this country and enjoyed the honor of lately converting to Shi'ism. Chelebi was presently the rajah of that region. He came out to meet us in a long boat which the natives call a kamucha. This kind of boat is a conveyance of honor for ministers and officials in Siam.

After bowing down before the seal of Sulaiman's signet ring, Chelebi ordered forth a gold-painted ship of great length. It was made from one huge piece of wood and contained a high throne in the middle. Fifty sailors rowed this boat with gilded oars. We were informed that this special boat was the king's 'parade horse' and that it was only fit and proper that Sulaiman's firman honor her humble throne.

Attendants also brought before us seven other boats, each of which had two house-like constructions built in the middle for seating. Ten people could easily sit in each house. The interior of the cabins was furnished with rugs and cushions and the doors were decorated with curtains of landra material. The officials cordially announced, 'Each of you is to be allotted a separate boat. Indeed, we appreciate that your journey has been full of hardship but that is all over now. Board these boats with peace in your hearts and enjoy the king of Siam's kind indulgence.' After boarding the boats the curtains were drawn open for the view and we proceeded up the river past the gardens and the orchards.

The Siamese Concern for Reporting Details.

One of the customs in Siam is that a special body of Siamese interpreters and scribes at the court prepares reports on everything anyone says or does, no matter how insignificant. The reports are then presented to the king. The Siamese seem very eager over details and there is nothing which they consider to be more low and mean than telling a lie. They are so concerned with the exact truth that if a person changes the slightest detail when giving an account of an event, he is considered an out and out liar. This preoccupation with being precise even leads them to condemn exaggeration in literature and poetry.

The Rise of the Sly, Ill-begotten Frank Minister.

There is one other cause of this deplorable situation [the recent decline in Iranian prestige]. To begin with the Siamese themselves are much like the fabled Nasnas,[1] devoid of intelligence and any practical abilities. Since they can scarcely undertake the simplest task with a hope of success, the king is cautious and never confides to any great extent in the natives. When Aqa Muhammad passed away, the king was in need of foreign support. Taking advantage of the situation, an

[1]A mythical creature.

ill-begotten Christian [Phaulkon] rose to power and filled the empty position. Formerly this Frank had been employed as a humble worker on ships. Thus he illustrated the true saying, 'Once the lion leaves the jungle the jackals venture forth.'

The Frank's Talents and Evil Influence.

In a very short time this Christian learned the language, customs and laws of Siam and day by day, in the eyes of the king, he cultivated a reputation for managing affairs. The Siamese king has made this man his chief minister and confidant, without bothering to test the coin of his character or establish to what degree his opinions or abilities are an advantage to the state. In accord with the firm rule that the low and base resent the good fortune of others, the Frank has endeavored to weaken the king's character and encourage the royal fickleness. He causes the king's sight to stray from the straight path of practising justice.

The King's Character.

Contrary to all the other kings and overlords of Below the Winds, the king of Siam sincerely was interested in raising himself, of acquiring distinction and improving his way of living, his household and his possessions. He was eager to learn about the other kings of the inhabited world, their behavior, customs and principles. He made a great effort to enlighten himself and sent everywhere for pictures depicting the mode of living and the courts of foreign kings.

When the Siamese king finally came to gaze at the illustrations on the page, which the artist Destiny painted with the pen of Fate's decrees, and there beheld the heavenly court of the Khaqan, the ruler with a lucky star and that court was depicted in accord with, 'Indeed He painted your face and great was the beauty of your portrait' and he heard of the noble life and refined manners in Iran, guided by right reason, which faculty distinguishes man from beast, the king grasped the clear fact that perfect kingship, glory and higher forms of government are the exclusive privilege of Iran.

Thus dressing himself with sincerity, he has abandoned his

former style of clothing and he has started to wear Iranian clothes, our kind of long embroidered tunic, trousers, shirts and shoes and socks. When his servants ask what kind of weapon he wishes to wear, he replies, 'What one wears must conform to one's rank and I find the Iranian style dagger alone worthy of my waist.' But he has turned his head aside from wearing the turban because of its weight. He declares, 'My head has no desire for the elaborate crown of Jamshid. This simple cap of felt is proper to my station.'

Since the king first broadened his horizons with education up until this present day, he has been secretly devoted to Iran and has cherished hopes of effecting friendly contacts with our royal court. Now these hopes have been fulfilled. According to the king's own statement, he has often sent gifts to the governor of Haidarabad and different rulers of India, as well as to kings of various other regions. He has been especially practising this sort of diplomacy since his present prime minister has facilitated contacts for him with the Christian kings.

The King's Personal Faith and Creed.

As for the faith of the Siamese king the situation is not very clear. Outwardly it would appear that he is also cursed with a weakness for idolatry. But every so often he shows interest in the faith of his particular prime minister. This is especially true at the present moment and due to the Christian prime minister many Franks of different nations have come to Siam and they have brought their priests with them.

It is a fact that the Siamese are not at all firm in their own religion but in accord with, 'the people follow the religion of their overlords' Siamese men and women will join whatever religion their employers adhere to. Thus the Iranians who have settled in Siam and begun to raise a family, brought all their household into the fold of Islam. In the same way the Christian community has managed to convert about five to six thousand natives to its faith.

When this fact is brought to the king's attention, he says that he has no interest in the matter and that the people may adhere to whatever religion they wish as long as they remain part of his peasantry. Thus every nation which comes to Siam converts some of the natives to its own religion. What faith the king really holds in his heart, 'God knows best the secrets of His servants.'

The Life and Daily Routine of the King.

As was mentioned earlier, the rulers and governors of Below the Winds have no real majesty and power and they do not maintain a grand entourage or a professional army. What they call an army is really only a mob of peasants assembled in times of danger. The population at large is divided into small groups which are represented by a minister and each minister has his own corps of officers.

The ordinary people are forced to work like slaves for the king's administration and they receive no pay for their time and labor nor are they able to raise the least complaint or refuse to serve. Only when the administration has no need of them are the natives free to pursue their livelihood, but the population is small and there is so much work to be done that the Siamese men would never be able to do everything just by themselves.

For that reason it is common for women to engage in buying and selling in the markets and even to undertake physical labor, and they do not wear veils or cover themselves with modesty. Thus you can see the women paddling to the surrounding villages where they successfully earn their daily bread with no assistance from the men.

In the past there were absolutely no craftsmen in Siam but recently a few people from outlying regions have come and established themselves in the city and they now produce some of the basic commodities. But there is a dearth of skilled workmen and for this reason it is not common to come across many fine buildings or other elaborate constructions. In fact all the houses in Siam are simple and are made of reeds and wood. Only the king's estates have been planned with any degree of care and skill.

The king's estates include temples built of wood and brick as well as private houses which were actually constructed by the Iranians. The latter buildings are not lacking in taste and beauty but the Siamese go so far as to think these works rival the palace of Khavarnaq[2] or the achievements of Chosroes.[3] The interior of the king's apartments are painted with vermilion and red clay and the roof, which is made of wood, has been plated with sheets of tin and gold. These buildings are the king's actual living quarters.

The Court Scribes.

Another Siamese practice pertaining to the king is that day or night several scribes are on hand to record every detail of the king's conversations, whom he addresses and exactly what is said in reply. It does not matter how trivial the talk may be, it is meticulously recorded. The scribes also keep record of whatever service a person renders to the king. Even if it is only a question of the king drinking water, they record who brought him his drink.

The Practice of Pawning Human Beings.

Here it may be mentioned that pawning men or women is one of the most common practices in Siam. For a certain sum the Siamese will pawn themselves or their sons and daughters. An attractive girl will go for ten to fifteen thousand dinars. Whoever is doing the pawning keeps the money as long as he wants, one day or ten years, and when he has attained his end with that capital and regained his dignity, he pays back the loan in full. No interest has been subtracted in advance. Thus he frees the pawnbroker from the binding agreement and recovers the person who was the pledge.

It is a lamentable fact that Siamese parents are like wild animals and feel no close ties with their children. Even if they have several sons, which makes their life easier, they show no signs of humanity and do not raise their children with affection.

It is also common for men to pawn themselves and while they cannot pay back the loan, they work for the pawnee as if they were his slave. Only when they have paid back the borrowed money in full are they free from their servitude. Otherwise they may remain in their master's chains until the

[2]A seven-domed palace.
[3]A title.

true Proprietor, God, claims the cash of their existence and forecloses on the loan of their life....

Ibn Muhammad Ibrahim, *The Ship of Sulaiman*, translated by John O'Kane, London, Routledge and Kegan Paul, 1972, pp. 50–1, 52, 59, 99–100, 120–1, 138–9, 148–9, 131–2.

19
Reception of the Phra Klang and Ayutthaya and Its Surroundings

ENGELBERT KAEMPFER

Engelbert Kaempfer was born in 1651 in Lemgow, Westphalia. He studied medicine in Hamelen, Hamburg, and Lubeck, languages at Cracow, and then went to study in Konigsburg in Prussia. He joined the service of Charles XI, King of Sweden, and went on an embassy to the Grand Sophy of Persia in 1683, passing through Russia. From Isfahan he decided to join the Dutch East Indies Company, as Chief Surgeon of the fleet, but did not leave Persia until 1688. He was in Batavia in 1689, and in 1690 left on a journey to Japan, passing through Siam en route. *He left Japan in 1692, was in Leiden to take his 'Doctor of Physik' degree in April 1694, and then returned to Germany, where he died in his native Lembow in 1716.*

Kaempfer is important in the records of Siam in several respects. He was the first German to record his impressions of the country. He also went at a particularly vital time, after the French adventure was over, and Petracha was installed on the throne, with Kosa Pan, former ambassador to France, as his Phra Klang (effectively Minister of Foreign Affairs and Commerce). His is one of the very few published accounts of a visit to Siam in the empty years from the end of the seventeenth to the beginning of the nineteenth century. Tachard, it is true, went back to Siam in 1699, but an account of his brief visit was never published. He found the place much changed, the merchants gone, and the capital empty.

Kaempfer's work was not published in his lifetime. After his death, his notes and papers were bought by Sir Hans Sloane, Secretary of the Royal Society in London, who engaged a Swiss scholar, John Scheuchzer, to translate Kaempfer's History of Japan ... together with a Description of the Kingdom of Siam, *which was first published in English in London in 1727.*

Kaempfer notes that the fort at Bangkok built by the French was completely razed. He gives a succinct account of the French adventure in Siam. He writes of Kosa Pan, whom he had to visit in his official capacity (Kaempfer and his party did not seek to see the king, but presented a letter to the Phra Klang), and gives his impressions of the capital 'Juthia, or Judia ... which in some descriptions of Travels is wrongly called India, perhaps by a mistake of print'. After describing the city and the palaces in some detail, he then considers the temples and the suburbs. He pays particular attention to the Phu Kao Tong, the Golden Mount, and to a double temple of the Phra Klang. He spends a great deal of time on conjectures, all wrong as it happens, of the origin of Buddhism, and then describes his departure for Japan. He concludes with remarks about the monkeys, glowworms, and mosquitoes on the banks of the Chao Phraya.

EVERY thing being ready, we went away to the audience in the following order. First, Opera Sijot the Moor, then the three other Mandarins, each in his prow. Next follow'd the prow, which carried the Letters for the King and Berklam,[1] which were writ in Malayan and Dutch, and kept each in a Purse embroider'd with gold. The purses were laid in a golden bason, which was cover'd with an embroider'd cloth, and put into a box of Pinang [betel-nut], adorn'd with pearls according to the custom of the Country. With these Ornaments they were plac'd upon a stool right under the middle of the Canopy. The Interpreter sate before them upon a Carpet. We follow'd next to the prow with the King's Letters in a particular short prow sitting under a Canopy lin'd with red. In this order we went up the River, coasting for some time the walls of the City, and then turning in towards the Berklam's House, where he gives public audience, and appears with all his pomp and splendor. We went ashore on this side of his House,

[1]The Phra Klang, Kosa Pan, formerly ambassador to Louis XIV.

and walk'd the remaining part of our way thither. The Court was dirty and nasty enough, but however in somewhat better a condition, than that of his other House, where we had had a private audience of him some Days before. Entring the Court we took notice to the left of an open House, or Room, almost square, without walls, the floor of which was cover'd with boards and full of people, some sitting, some walking and conversing together. A large Elephant compleatly harnass'd stood in the Stable to the right. Opposite to the entry was a stony staircase, leading to the Berklam's House, where we were to have our audience. We went up the same and then pull'd off our Shoes. This House hath but one single Room, or rather lofty Hall, like a Church. It is white within and full of Dust and Cobwebs. Seven square pillars on each side, supported the ceiling, which was rais'd under the third roof, and neatly enough painted with red branch'd work. About the middle of each pillar hung a large plate of chinese Copper. In the wall between the pillars were long openings with shutters instead of windows. There were two entries into the Hall, with a window between them; Poles of Bambous were fix'd to the pillars on each side of the Hall hung with white Cloth, behind which, between the pillars and the wall, were the Berklam's servants and domesticks, without any order, some sitting, some lying on the ground. Before sate the Mandarins, as Oja Tewejaata, a Mahometan, set over the Querry of the King's Elephants, next to the Berklam on his right, Oja Pipat, Deputy Berklam to his left, both with golden Boesets before them. Boesets are cubical boxes made of Pinang, and marks of the King's favour, which he presents his Mandarins with, when he gives them their names, and raises them to that dignity, which is never done without having first ask'd advice of his Astrologers. Below these two there sate several other Siamish, Chinese, and Mahometan Mandarins. I counted twenty three to the Berklam's right, and one and twenty to his left. Seven of the chief on each side sitting uppermost, had golden, and two others which sate next them silver Boesets standing before them. The Letters, with the purses, bason and other ornaments, were plac'd before the Berklam about four or five paces from him. We sate in the middle between the two rows of Mandarins, a Pinang bason with Betel and Pinang minc'd, and Jasmin and other flowers laid round the borders for ornaments sake, was set before each of us. The Berklam, as representing the person of the King sate in a particular enclos'd apartment, at the upper end of the Hall, behind an embroider'd Carpet laid over a pole of Bambous and rais'd about two or three foot above the ground, shewing only the upper part of his Body. Two gilt Umbrello's were plac'd before him, one at each side. Behind him were two golden Daggers, laid upon as many cushions, and a state Scimeter as above describ'd stood at each side. Two European pictures hung behind him on the wall encompass'd with branch'd work, instead of frames, after the Country fashion. Having all seated our selves, the Berklam ask'd Mynheer van Hoorn by the Interpreter, how the General of our East India Company did, how long he had been in the Indies, what Troops we had now at Batavia and at Bantam, which of the two was the better Country, as also who we, the Captain and I were? These and some other questions being severally answer'd, the purses containing the Letters were open'd, and the Letters having pass'd through the hands of several of the Mandarins then present, read aloud. The Interpreter not understanding some of the Malayan expressions, Mr Moses and Daniel were desir'd to help him out. The audience having lasted about three quarters of an hour, we were conducted by the Berklam's Son, who till then had been behind his Father, through his other House to our prows, and from thence to dinner, which stood prepar'd for us.

Peja prah' klam (Foreigners pronounce it Berklam) is High Chancellor, and hath the direction of foreign affairs. He is a more comely Person, and of better aspect, than I ever met with amongst this black race of mankind who are generally short siz'd and look almost like Monkeys. He is also of a quick understanding and lively action, for which reason he was a few years ago sent Ambassador to France, of which Country, its Government, Fortresses and the like, he would often entertain us in his discourses; and the hall of his House, where we had a private audience of him, was hung with the pictures of the Royal Family of France, and European Maps, the rest of his furniture being nothing but Dust and Cobwebs.

This Island, with the City upon it, is of the shape of the sole

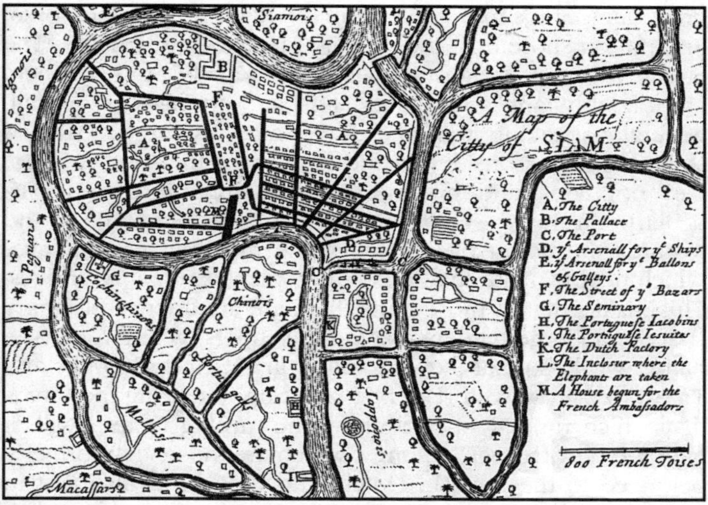

Map of Ayutthaya showing its network of canals, from Simon de La Loubère, *A New Historical Relation of the Kingdom of Siam*, London, 1693.

of a man's foot, with the heel turning westward, and hath about two German Miles in circumference. It is situate in a Country all flat, as far as the Eye can reach, on a low ground, which is cut through by many Canals coming from the River, and by them divided into so many Isles and squares, that one cannot go far without the help of Boats. It is surrounded with a Brick wall, which on the South and North is four fathoms and a half high, clean, well condition'd and adorn'd with Battlements, but the rest of it is lower, neglected and decay'd. This wall is open in many places, where there are small gates towards the River. On the inside there are ramparts rais'd against it at different distances for placing Cannons upon them. At the lower end of the City appears a large bastion advancing into the water, besides several small ones. The first is furnish'd with Cannons against the Ships coming up. To fence the City-wall against the wasteing of the current, a narrow bank, or key is left, which is built upon in many places. Divers great Canals go out of the River quite through the City some from East to West, others from North to South, and abundance of smaller Canals being derived from the great ones, Ships may come from the River up into the Town, and put on shore near the principal Houses and Palaces. The Streets run in a streight line along the Canals; Some of them are tolerably large, but the greater part very narrow, and all, generally speaking, foul and dirty: Some also are overflow'd at high water. Considering the bigness of the City, it is not very populous, and in some parts but thinly inhabited, particularly on the West side on account of its remoteness, and towards the South by reason of the morassy ground, over which people make shift to get upon planks, or paltry bridges. This makes that in those parts there are abundance of empty spaces and large gardens behind the streets, wherein they let nature work, so that they are full of grass, Herbs, Shrubs and Trees, that grow wild. The first Street upon entring the City is that which runs Westward along the turning of the Wall: it hath the best Houses, amongst which are those, that formerly belonged to the English, Dutch, and French, as also that in which Faulcon resided. The middle Street, which runs North towards the Court, is best inhabited, and full of shops of Tradesmen, Artificers, and Handicraftmen. In both these Streets are seen above one hundred Houses belonging to the Chinese, Hindostanians and Moors, as they call them. They are all built alike of Stone, very small, being but eight paces in length, four in breadth and of two Stories, yet not above two Fathoms and a half high. They are cover'd with flat tiles, and have large doors without any proportion. The rest of the Streets are less inhabited, and the Houses of ordinary Inhabitants are but mean and poor cottages, built of Bambous (which is a hollow reed, two or three Spans thick) and boards, and carelesly cover'd with Gabbé Gabbé, Branches and leaves of Palm Trees growing wild in Morassy places. The Mandarins or Ministers of State and Courtiers live in separate palaces, with Courtyards to them, which are very dirty. The Buildings in general, though rais'd with Lime and Stone are but indifferent, and the apartments neither clean, nor well furnish'd. The booth, or Shops of the town are low, and very ordinary, however they stand in good order, and in a streight line, as the Streets are. The many Canals occasion a great number of bridges. Those which are laid over the great Canal are of Stone, with Ballisters of the same, but as there are no Waggons, nor Carts in this place, they are narrow; in the middle they are high and eighty paces long; but the Bridges over the by Canals are of no Architecture, and for the greatest part of wood.

Round the City lie many Suburbs and Villages, some of which consist of inhabited Ships, or Vessels, rather than Houses, containing two, three, or more Families each; they remove them from time to time, and float them particularly when the waters are high, where Fairs are kept, to sell their Goods there and get their Livelyhood by it. The Houses in the common Villages, that stand upon firm Ground, are generally built of Bambous, reed, planks, and other ordinary stuff; some of the Houses in the Villages along the banks of the river stand on pales a fathom high, that the waters, which overflow the Country for some months, may freely pass under the Houses. Each House is furnish'd with Stairs, or a Ladder, to come down in dry weather, and with a boat, to go about it at high water. Other Villages stand on higher and dry ground, and consequently not being subject to those Inundations their Houses want neither such stairs nor boats. On those eminences also stand Temples, Convents, burying Places, where they bury their dead, and Yards where they burn their bones and ashes, and erect costly Pyramids over them. On the South-side, at a small distance down the River, the Dutch have their Factory and Magazines very splendidly and conveniently built on dry ground. Lower down on the same bank are other villages inhabited by Colonies of Japonese (the best Soldiers of former Kings), Peguans and Malaccans. On the opposite side of the River stands a village inhabited by a Portuguese race begot on black Women, and further down stands a Church, dedicated to St Domingo, to which belong the Fathers of the Dominican Order. Behind it stands another small Church, which is kept by two Fathers of the Order of St Austin, who with the foresaid three Dominicans live peaceably together in a House built of Reed. Not far from hence, on the same plain, stands a Jesuit Church nam'd St Paul, after the chief Church at Goa, belonging to the Fathers of this Order, who through all Asia are better pleas'd to be call'd Paulins from that Church than Jesuits. South West of the City, opposite to that side of the River, where it lets out the branch Klang Nam Ja the Metropolitan Bishop Mr Louis had caus'd a stone Palace to be built, together with a fine Church, which is now lock'd up since his Imprisonment.

Engelbert Kaempfer, *A History of Japan ... together with a Description of the Kingdom of Siam*, translated by John Scheuchzer, London, 1727, Vol. I, pp. 26–9, 38, 42–4, 49–52.

20
The Harbours of Phuket

ALEXANDER HAMILTON

Alexander Hamilton was one of the few persons to make contact with Siam in the eighteenth century. He was a sea captain who visited Phuket, Bangkok, and Ayutthaya between 1700 and 1719 during various journeys along the west coast of the peninsula. Gerini, a demanding scholar, considers him a 'well informed writer', and notes that he is the first person to mention Patong Bay; he would hardly recognize it if he saw it today.

When in Phuket he saw several white elephants, but this did not compensate for the overall decline in the prosperity of what was known as Junk Ceylon. This curious form was apparently a corruption of Ujong (the Malay word for 'cape') Salang (a Malay variant of the Siamese place-name Chalang or Thalang). The island had had some fame at the end of the seventeenth century, when Desfarges, the French commander, having withdrawn ignominiously from Bangkok and victualled in Pondichéry, anchored his fleet there in 1689 and in vain attempted to negotiate terms with the new king, Petracha. But Hamilton noted that the rapacious Chinese governors and tax farmers, combined with pirate raids selling captives from an already (and still) thinly populated coast, contributed against the well-being of the place, something Warington Smyth (Passage 48) was to note nearly two centuries later.

THE next place of any commerce on this coast [the West coast of the Malay Peninsula] is the island of Jonkceyloan; it lies in the dominions of the King of Siam. Between Merjee [Mergui] and Jonkceyloan there are several good harbours for shipping, but the sea coast is very thin of inhabitants, because there are great numbers of freebooters, called *salleiters*, who inhabit islands along the sea coast, and they both rob, and take people for slaves, and transport them for Atcheen [Aceh], and there make sale of them, and Jonkceyloan often feels the weight of their depredations.

The north end of Jonkceyloan lies within a mile of the continent, but the south end is above three leagues from it. Between the island and the continent is a good harbour for shipping in the south-west monsoons, and on the west side of the island Puton [Patong] bay is a safe harbour in the north-east winds. The islands afford good masts for shipping, and abundance of tin, but few people to dig for it, by reason of the afore-mentioned outlaws, and the governors being generally Chinese, who buy their places at the court of Siam, and, to reimburse themselves, oppress the people, in so much that riches would be but a plague to them, and their poverty makes them live an easy, indolent life.

Yet the villages on the continent drive a small trade with shipping that come from the Choromandel coast and Bengal, but both the buyer and seller trade by retail, so that a ship's cargo is a long time in selling, and the product of the country is as long in purchasing.

Alexander Hamilton, *A New Account of the East Indies*, Edinburgh, 1727, quoted in G. E. Gerini, 'Historical Retrospect of Junkceylon Island', *Journal of the Siam Society*, Vol. 2, Pt. 2, 1905, p. 45.

21
A Royal Reception of Spaniards from the Philippines

ANON

In the apparently anonymous Historia General de las Filipinas *(Vol. 15, Pt. ix, Ch. x, pp. 240–66) appears, according to that mine of information, Sir John Bowring (Passage 35), a little-known account of an embassy sent by the Governor of the Philippines, Don Fernando, ostensibly from Philip V, King of Spain, to the King of Siam in 1718.*

In the best nepotistic tradition of the time, the Ambassador, Don Gregorio Bustamente Bustillo, was the governor's nephew, his deputy was General Don Benito Carrasco Paniagua, and the motive was 'to establish with that King [of Siam] and this new kingdom of Castille and the Philippine Isles and their wealthy commerce, a friendly peace'.

The then ruler of Siam, Thai Sa (r. 1709–33), was a grandson of the usurper Petracha, and the dynasty appeared to be settling down. The interest of the Spanish account is that the reception of the envoys followed very closely the form established in the reign of King Narai. There was the formal audience of reception, the exchange of presents, festivities, and a farewell audience.

Unfortunately, there is little by way of description of the country as a whole in this account, but this would undoubtedly be known about by reports of Spanish missionaries, some of which were later published as Cronicas de la Apostolica Provincia de San Gregorio, *Manila, 1738 (Pt. i, Ch. xxi, pp. 667–73).*

Absolutely nothing came of the embassy, largely because the return Siamese mission was shabbily treated: 'The Governor of Manila, then busy with other concerns, paid no attention to this [Siamese] captain [bearing a letter for the proper reception of the mission], nor to those who accompanied him; their treatment was abominable. . . .' The Siamese would not allow an adjutant of the governor, sent at the behest of Carrasco, to land: 'The Spaniards had lost their credit with that nation, those who had been so ill-treated hating the nations of Europe and their mean friendships.'

ON the 23rd of May, about eight o'clock in the morning, there arrived at the ambassador's palace two mandarins of the first class on two elephants, with more than forty guards each. They were favourites of the King, and in his name bade the ambassador welcome; and they were sent to know whether, in the palace in which he was lodged, anything were wanting in the service or the adornments suitable to the rank of his person. The ambassador gave a gracious reply, and informed them that all was perfect, as arranged according to the order of so powerful a lord as the great King of Siam. They came also to know the day on which he wished to deliver the letter; and it was agreed on both sides that it should be on the 8th of June, that there might be sufficient time for preparations. On this day, a great number of mandarins assembled at this palace, to whom was delivered a special letter for the Sovereign, which they received with much pomp; and the ambassador proceeded, with a splendid train, through the streets of the city. He went to the house of the Lord Barcalan [Phra Klang], who returned to him the letter for the King, which was transcribed in the idiom of the country, in order that he might deliver it himself on the day of the embassy; and having received it with much ostentation, he returned to his palace, accompanied by mandarins and guards, where grand refreshments were served.

This affair was delayed on account of various difficulties in complying with the ceremonials of the kingdom, and they were properly overcome. On the 22nd of June, at five o'clock in the morning, the King's guards assembled in the hall of his palace, and in the adjoining street, composed of archers, fusiliers, and lancers, and that of the elephants; a suitable number of horses, adorned, especially the one prepared for the ambassador: and in the same manner came great mandarins and Portuguese. At six o'clock, the ambassador issued from his private room into the hall, and gave orders to start, the standard of our royal arms going in front. He mounted on horseback, and, with a great noise of trumpet and drums, they proceeded to one of the gates of the city, where he embarked; and going up the river, they reached the gates of the Royal Palace, in which were an innumerable company of mandarins to receive him.

He entered the first hall, in which were many elephants of war; in the second hall, many squadrons of archers and soldiers; a still greater number of arquebusiers in the third hall. He passed through a great many halls, in which there were many mandarins, who prostrated themselves in token of respect; and the ensign, elevating the royal standard, passed the rest of the train who accompanied him. The ambassador took the letter from the frame, and began to mount a carpeted staircase, where the Barcalan and the generalissimo of arms received him. He entered here, and in rather more than an hour came out with a flame-coloured field-coat with flowers of gold—a badge which confers nobility on those who receive it at the hands of the King. He immediately delivered his despatches to the King, in the same manner and place in which was delivered that of the Most Christian King of France, and in which he receives the King of Cambodia when he makes his visit in person. The ambassador saluted his Majesty in the European manner, with his hat, and his short sword placed on one side, and with shoes faced with a kind of embroidery, and with heel-pieces. His seat was at a distance of six cubits from the throne, with six carpets, the Barcalan and the generalissimo of arms being without any.

In this order the ambassador addressed the King, and discussed the affairs of his embassy, which met with success. This being ended, the King commanded his prime minister to show them the white elephant, and the one with short tusks, which those of the train saw; and the service in which they eat and drink, which are large vessels or mangers of gold, and their tusks were enclosed at intervals with this metal; and of the same were the chains which confined them in their separate apartments, and a rich and large pavilion for their accommodation. From thence they took them to see the State horses, which were adorned, some with pearls, others with diamonds, others with emeralds and rubies; and the reins were thick cords of gold of exquisite workmanship, every one admiring the wealth displayed. They saw the artillery, which was in one of the divisions of the palace, containing in it bronze cannons of forty pounds. About eleven o'clock in the day, the ambassador embarked with all his train, and returned to his palace, in which he found a splendid banquet prepared by the King's command. The covers were of silver and gold, in such abundance that the admiration was universal; the royal pages serving them with an exquisite variety of delicacies; which lasted until five in the evening. The servants departed with presents of jewels; and to a great number of Siamese who had assembled to see so solemn a ceremony, the ambassadors threw a quantity of silver money.

Quoted in Sir John Bowring, *The Kingdom and People of Siam*, London, Parker and Sons, 1857, Vol. II, pp. 124–7.

22
Phuket in 1784

THOMAS FORREST

Thomas Forrest was, like Alexander Hamilton (Passage 20), a sea captain but plying the seas of the region towards the end of the eighteenth century. He was born about 1729, but little is known about his early life, including his place of birth. He was a midshipman in the Royal Navy in 1745, and went to India as fifth mate in an East India Company ship in 1751. He went almost at once to Fort Marlborough, Benkulen, in West Sumatra, and operated out of there for several years, becoming a 'free merchant' by 1760. He travelled to Bali, and in 1774–6 went on an extensive voyage of exploration in the spice islands and New Guinea in the 10-ton ship Tartar, *which he wrote up. He seems to have had a knack of getting on well with local people, being without prejudice or pretention. He took along his German flute, and in a Papuan longhouse persuaded a girl to sing for him while he performed on his flute. In Mindanao, according to Bassett (in an introduction to a reprint of the book, in 1969), he transcribed minuets for the Raja Muda to play on the violin, and had his wife sing Malay songs inspired by Virgil's* Eclogues. *In 1784, he adapted a Malay song to part of the third sonata of Corelli and played it on his flute to the Sultan of Aceh. These activities, according to the doyen of Malay studies of the time, William Marsden, earned him the title among the Malays of 'Kapitan Gila', the mad captain.*

He went to London in 1777 when the East India Company granted him permission to publish his account of his journey to New Guinea. The first edition of A Voyage to New Guinea and the Moluccas ... *appeared in 1779, quickly followed by a second edition and a French translation in 1780. This brought him fame and contact with eminent worthies, including Sir Joseph Banks, President of the Royal Society.*

The same year he was nominated to command a ship in the Bengal Marine at Calcutta, which led to his subsequent book, A Voyage from Calcutta to the Mergui Archipelago *(1792). His patron, the Governor-General of India, Warren Hastings, was replaced in 1785, and thereafter Forrest sold pepper as an independent sea captain, commanding a ship for a syndicate of Calcutta merchants. He is known to have had three sons, one of whom worked for Scott and Light, traders in Phuket and Penang, whom he met in 1784. It is thought Forrest died in Calcutta in 1802, but like his birth, this is obscure.*

Forrest visited Phuket just before the Burmese raids which were to lay waste the island. His description of it follows.

THE Island Jan Sylan (called Junk Ceylon in our maps) is situated on the east side of the Bay of Bengal, and is divided from the continent by a narrow isthmus of sand about a mile in length, and half a mile in breadth, which isthmus is covered only at high water (the tide rising on the springs about 10 feet), and shuts up on the north part, an excellent harbour, called Popra [Pak P'hrah].

The name Jan Sylan is a corruption from Oojong Sylan (point or promontory of Sylan), the south point projecting a little way into the sea, and probably the name was given to it before it became an island at high water, and before it was disjoined from the continent, as it is at present: the word *oojong* being a Malay word signifying point, and the inhabitants in general speaking Malay, from their intercourse with that people, had it been considered as an island, the word *pulo*, signifying island in the same tongue, a word of easy pronunciation, if once affixed to it, would most probably never have left it.

There are several small islands adjacent to it, from one to six miles in circumference; and one beautiful island lies about sixteen miles east of it, called Pulo Panjang (Long Island): it is about 23 miles long, and 8 broad, of moderate height, gently sloping from the middle to the sea on each side. Pulo Panjang is divided from the main by a strait called Callat Leheere (Throat Strait), with 2 fathoms water in the shallowest part.

Jan Sylan has no high hill upon it, but several of moderate height; and, as may be expected from its size, no considerable river; but several creeks that run to the sea, generally through flat marshes of mangrove trees, from pleasant brooks in the interior parts; they keeping purposely the skirts of the island in a state of nature, I suppose, to prevent invasion; and their vessels consist only of few prows [prau, prahu] about the size of Indiamen's long-boats, and small canoes, that find their way up these creeks, to the well-cultivated plains abounding with rice fields in the middle of the island.

Besides the harbour of Popra above-mentioned, there is another capacious harbour [Patong] on the south-west part of the island, as the natives informed me; but I never was in it. The place where ships generally anchor is in a good road, well sheltered behind a small island now joined to the main island at low water, lying in 8° 10′N. lat.

On the main opposite to this island is a creek that leads to the village of Terowa [Tha Rua], consisting of about 80 houses, on a plain, through which runs a pleasant brook, with many windings, over a gravelly bottom.

After having with much difficulty got up this narrow creek, where oars cannot be used, on the upper part, paddles only, and perhaps against a strong current, one is much pleased to reach the pleasant rivulet above-mentioned; and here resides Pee-peemont [P'hya P'himon], the governor, or viceroy, from the court of Siam. This governor, when I was there in 1784, had three assistants, or perhaps rather colleagues, as they partook of his power: their names were Pee-Tukerat [P'hya Dukkharas], Pee-Siring [P'hya Surindr-raja], and Pee-Lancrac [P'hya Lankaraks]. Each of these officers had about sixty followers, a kind of retainers, who in a great measure live on the community; for, receiving little pay, they oppress the inhabitants: their arms are a musquet and bayonet, sword and dagger. I have often seen them attending their masters at Pee-peemont's house, where they all met frequently upon business. . . .

I travelled thither with Capt. James Scot [Scott], who resided then at Terowa, on some commercial business, his vessel lying in Popra harbour, a very sensible and intelligent gentleman, to whom I was much obliged for his civilities and services on many occasions. We travelled on an elephant, through a path worn like a gutter, in some few places, where it was over a flat rock, the path being worn by the elephant's feet, and so narrow as not to be above an inch or two wider than his hoofs: I wondered how the huge animal got along. This bad road was for a very little way through the skirt of a wood; and about two miles from Terowa we got into the open country again, full of rice fields and well watered, yet not swampy. In about three hours we reached the governor's house, which is larger and more commodious than the one at Terowa, and seven miles distant from it. In his garden we found limes, oranges and pummel noses [pomelos]. Chysong, the son of a Chinese with whom I lived, told me the island produced most tropical roots and fruits; and I am persuaded many of our vegetables might be raised, the climate is so cool; very like what it is at Pulo Pinang.

The governor gave us a very good dinner, but did not eat with us. He did not speak Malay, but had a linguist who spoke Portuguese. Our drink was the water of young coconuts and sherbet. After dinner we were entertained with three musicians, who played on such like string instruments as the Chinese play on at Canton. Having drank tea we took leave.

They have a good many elephants, which they get from Mergui; none wild, no horses; they have bullocks and buffalos for labour; wild hogs and deer, a few tame goats, no sheep, domestic dogs and cats. They have the common poultry, but not in abundance. The climate is very agreeable; no violent heats; the rains come on gently in July, and continue until November, with frequent intermissions: fine weather then succeeds, with very cool north-east winds at night, which must be favourable to the cultivation of vegetables, as it is at Calcutta....

The people of Jan Sylan, though they generally understand the Malay tongue, from their intercourse with that people (greater formerly than now), speak the Siamese language, and write as we do from left to right. They write remarkably straight, though without lines.

They resemble in feature the Malays, with a good deal of the Chinese look; are well made, rather slender. They are allowed to marry as many women as they can maintain; but the first wife rules the household, as in China: and, as in China and Pegu, no woman can leave the country. Chysong had but one wife.

Thomas Forrest, *A Voyage from Calcutta to the Mergui Archipelago*, London 1792, pp. 29–36, quoted in G. E. Gerini, 'Historical Retrospect of Junkceylon Island', *Journal of the Siam Society*, Vol. 2, Pt. 2, 1905, pp. 61–71.

23
The Fall of Ayutthaya to the Burmese

FRANÇOIS-HENRI TURPIN

François-Henri Turpin (1709–99) did not *come to Siam; indeed, he only seems to have gravitated between Caen, where he was born and where he taught history in the university, and Paris, where he tried unsuccessfully to live by his pen and where he died in penury. But he obtained his information about Siam from the missionary, Bishop Brigot, who was in the country from 1741 until the fall of Ayutthaya in 1767, when he went via Burma to Pondichéry.*

The details of how Turpin obtained his facts from the Bishop of Tabraca (Mgr. Brigot) are interesting, and recounted by Adrien Launay in his Histoire de la Mission de Siam 1662–1811 *(Paris, P. Téqui, 1920):*

'In 1769 the bishop left Pondichéry to return to France. On his arrival in Paris, he paid calls on several ministries, particularly on the Duke of Praslin, the Minister for the Navy, Mr Bertin, Secretary of State, and Mr Boutin, Financial Administrator, who received him pleasantly, appeared to be interested in his fate, and asked him to write and even publish "accounts of China and India concerning natural history, government and commerce". The bishop began this work, wrote some notes to which he added details given by Mr Davoust [another missionary]; then, after contacting a hack writer,

Turpin, he gave him his manuscript as well as the memoirs about Siam of Mr Aumont [a missionary in Ayutthaya since about 1700, and in the 1730s working in the Siamese city of Mergui]. Turpin was inspired by these works while allowing his imagination to guide him, without bothering too much about exactitude, which in truth was rather difficult for a man who had never travelled. He published a work entitled Histoire Civile et Naturelle du Royaume de Siam, et des Révolutions qui ont boulversé cet Empire jusqu'en 1770. *The surprise and dissatisfaction of Mgr. Brigot and the directors of the Seminary of Foreign Missions was great when this work appeared, for "they found reprehensible things" in it. The bishop complained bitterly. Turpin took note of his objections; he corrected the pages which were found particularly objectionable, and which we are unable to indicate, and replaced them by others closer to the truth. The work was translated into English by Cartwrigt [*sic*] and later inserted in the collection of voyages by Pinberton [*sic*]. With useful information, it contains other details in which exactitude is not the dominant note, but at the time it appeared, it was still the best of anything that had appeared on Siam.'*

It was virtually the only new book to appear in the West in the eighteenth century dealing exclusively with Siam, and the account of the fall of Ayutthaya is undoubtedly close to the truth; this was something Brigot had personally witnessed. No other Western accounts are known to survive, for the Dutch abandoned their post in Ayutthaya a little before its inevitable fall to the Burmese. The Brigot–Turpin version is therefore given here in full. The importance accorded to the Christians in the defence of the city should doubtless be taken with a generous pinch of salt.

WHILE storms shook the whole empire, the King of Siam,[1] shut up in his seraglio, consoled himself with his concubines for the miseries of his subjects. The news that the enemy had evacuated Tennasserim and Mergui had given room to believe that the danger was over, and that the state had no farther occasion for protectors. In short, the Bramas [Burmese] were at the gates of the city, and they had

[1]Suriyamarin, r. 1758–67.

not the shadow of an army to oppose them. The King awoke from his profound sleep at the noise of the inhabitants of the country, who rushed in crowds to take refuge in the royal city. They employed them to repair the fortifications: they raised columns forty feet high to mount cannon on. The Christians refused to assist at this labour, convinced of its inutility, and that they would crumble under their own weight.

The enemy, before they began the attack on the royal city, laid waste all the territory. They were certain of finding subsistence in the back country, of which they were masters, and their destructive policy was to oblige the Siamese to surrender by famine. One of their detachments extended its ravages to the very gates of the city. Bancok, a fortress which defended the approaches to it, was destroyed; the gardens, stripped of their ornaments, were covered with ruins. A college the missioners had established in the environs was reduced to ashes. After this excursion the incendiaries retired with precipitation to the main body of their army, and their retreat for a moment allayed the alarm.

At this period two English vessels arrived. The captain brought the King an Arabian horse, a lion, and several valuable articles. This captain, whose name was Powny, had on some occasions proved his courage. The King, who had more confidence in his valour and talents than in his cowardly and effeminate courtiers, begged him to undertake the defence of the city; but the Englishman, convinced that he should be badly seconded by a people void of courage, refused the honour of the command: the example of the Dutch, who had withdrawn, confirmed him in his repugnance to accept it. They would not have abandoned their factory, which contained such valuable effects, if they had thought the Siamese capable of seconding of them in the common defence. He was irresolute on the part he should take, when he suddenly found himself attacked by the Bramas, who, masters of Bancok, took their dispositions to batter him with cannon.

The brave Englishman, too weak to defend himself, and too brave to submit, took the wise resolution to tow his vessel up to the narrows, where the barbarians were endeavouring to fortify themselves; but the fire from the artillery of the ships destroyed their works, and carried death among their ranks. Protected by their cannon, the English could defy the fury of the Bramas with impunity. The inaction they experienced on board their ships wounded their pride, and, impatient to punish their aggressors, they made several descents, and throwing themselves in order on their undisciplined enemies, they made a dreadful carnage of them.

Powny, forced by necessity, consented to undertake the defence of the city, on condition that they would furnish him with cannon, and whatever was necessary for attack and defence. His demand was complied with, and, as a pledge for his fidelity, the Siamese required him to deposit his merchandise in the public magazine. This condition wounded his pride, but he was obliged to submit to it. He delivered thirty-eight bales of valuable effects, and embarked the rest in different ships, and after having settled every thing with the ministers, he went on board his own ship, where he prepared to justify the opinion they entertained of his courage. He ordered descents, which were all murderous to the enemy: their forts, scarcely erected, were destroyed: every day was marked with their defeat or flight. In order to profit by these advantages, he wrote to the court of Siam for cannon and ammunition, but he experienced a refusal. The Siamese, suspicious, were fearful of his becoming too powerful, and of their being dependant on a foreigner. Their distrust fettered their protector: it was to forge those very chains they feared to wear. The ministers replied, that as the enemy was preparing to make an attack on the other side of the city, they wanted all the cannon they had to repulse them.

The Englishman, irritated at this infraction of their promises, resolved to abandon a people who could neither fight themselves, nor supply their friends with the means of defending them: but before he sailed, he published a kind of manifesto against the Siamese Monarch to justify his desertion. He seized six Chinese vessels, one of which was loaded on the King's account; the other five came to trade at Siam, and were stopped in the gulph, where they were much surprised to find themselves stripped of their effects. The Englishman, to indemnify them for what he had taken, gave the captains letters of exchange drawn on the King of Siam, to the amount of the thirty-eight bales he had deposited with him. After having thus secured himself, he boldly passed before his enemies, who, instead of troubling his retreat, congratulated themselves on being freed from a rival who alone could hinder their success.

His departure raised the courage of the Bramas, who now only having to fight against effeminate men, every where carried desolation. The pagodas became a prey to the flames, and the lead they stripped from them served them to make balls. The enemy, for a long time master of the country, had not allowed the lands to be sown; and, uselessly cruel, they even envied the Siamese the bounties of nature. But the fruitfulness of the soil produced an abundant harvest, neither the reward of the labourer, nor the produce of sowing. The grains of rice which the year before had fallen from the hands of the reapers, took root, and came to maturity. This unexpected bounty was a great consolation to people threatened with famine. But what should have been a resource to them, was the cause of their misfortune: the inhabitants being spread over the fields to gather in the rice, were surprised by the Bramas, who led them captive to their camp.

While the Bramas, spread through all the provinces, warred against man and nature by their devastations, the King and his superstitious ministers put all their trust in their magicians. The officers and soldiers, led away by this example, consulted them on the means to render themselves invisible, that they might attack the enemy without being seen; and the hopes of learning a secret which favoured their cowardice, prevented them from exposing themselves to sight till it had been revealed to them. The illusion was so strong, that experience was unable to convince them of the vanity of that lying art. The chiefs, as cowardly as the subalterns, seemed only to have taken arms to turn them against their fellow citizens. They dispossessed them of their money and corn, under pretence of providing for the wants of the soldier, to whom they distributed but the most worthless portion of their plunder, and that trifling bounty served them as a veil to cover their extortions.

A Siamese Prince, who had been exiled to Ceylon, was touched with the miseries of his country. He forgot that he had been ill treated; he was still powerful enough to raise an army, which he had the generosity to offer to his persecutors. The court of Siam, too proud to accept the assistance of a banished man, whose zeal censured his injuries, rejected his offers with contempt, and instead of seeking him as a protector, sent several detachments against him, which were sometimes victorious, sometimes defeated. This conduct was the more imprudent, as it divided their forces at a time when the army of the Bramas became every day stronger by the junction of discontented Siamese.

It was in the month of March that the enemy's army advanced to within two leagues of the city. It was arrested on its march by the death of the general, who was carried off by a quincey. It was judged expedient to hide his death from the soldiers, and the secret was only disclosed by the dissentions which broke out among the chiefs, who all wished to assume the command; but soon united by their thirst for plunder, they put themselves in motion, to proceed to the pillage of the most celebrated and richest temple in the environs of the capital. They flattered themselves with finding the foot of an idol which was of massive gold; but the King of Siam had the precaution to remove into his palace this monument of public worship, which the barbarians, though superstitious, would but have little respected.

The Bramas, irritated at being deprived of this prey, revenged themselves on the walls of the temple, which they demolished, and on its ruins erected an edifice consecrated to profane uses. The other pagodas built round the city were not spared. They were built with brick and surrounded with ditches, which appeared to defend them from fire or the assaults of an enemy. The Christian churches, on the contrary, were only constructed of stakes and boards, less fit to protect them than to facilitate the progress of the flames. But, in spite of their weak state, they were maintained by the vigilance and courage of those who had the charge of defending them; and the enemy did not set a foot in them till after the Siamese and Chinese had experienced frequent defeats.

The 7th of September, 1766, they got possession of a very high tower,[2] about three furlongs distant from the royal city. They planted a battery of cannon on it, to bear on the strand, which made them absolute masters of the river. The danger becoming more pressing, the Siamese had no hope but in the Christians, whose heroic valour had been proved in the last

[2]The Phu Kao Thong.

The ruins of a pagoda at Ayutthaya, from Henri Mouhot, *Travels in the Central Parts of Indo-China (Siam), Cambodia, and Laos ...,* London, John Murray, 1864.

revolution. They gave them the defence of the bastions; they granted them thirty pieces of cannon, balls, and powder. Six thousand Chinese were ordered to defend the Dutch factory, and a large pagoda contiguous to it; and, by a particular favour, they made them a present of rather better than four hundred pounds sterling.

The Christians were but eighty-four in number to defend different posts, exposed to the surprisals of a numerous army. This brave militia were not trained to military discipline, nor to the use of arms; a sword and musket in their hands would have been a subject of derision in the eyes of an European soldier. But notwithstanding their awkwardness, they were the flower of the Siamese army, and there was only the abuse of their courage to be apprehended from them. The first days passed in skirmishes, but at length the enemy, having united his forces, got possession of five large temples, which were converted into so many fortresses, from whence they battered the advanced works, and especially the church of St Joseph, the roof of which was shot through, without the least injury to the multitude assembled in it.

On the 8th of December they were informed that the besiegers were preparing a fresh assault. The Christians immediately marched out of the church with drums and trumpets; they engaged, and made a great slaughter of the enemy, who were rather vanquished by their fears than the arms of the Christians. This first success inspired them with courage to become the aggressors in their turn: they attacked the Bramas, who were entrenched in a pagoda; nothing could withstand them: they returned with an elephant, a brilliant pledge of their victory. Their name became formidable to the enemy and the boast of their fellow citizens.

The Portuguese, who dwelt about two short leagues from the bishop of Tabraca, also gave striking proofs of their bravery: they cut to pieces a number of Bramas who had attempted to storm their college. Confounded and disheartened at the uselessness of their attacks, they retired filled with admiration for this handful of Christians, whom they feared much more than fifty thousand Siamese, who had neither the courage to wait for them, nor to pursue them in their retreat. It is true that these Christians, though more courageous, were not better disciplined, and it was that fault which caused the loss of the French quarter. The guard was buried in a profound sleep, when the Bramas, recovered from their first terror, set fire to the upper part of the bishop's quarter. The Christians took refuge in crowds in the church, where the cries of the women and children announced a peril, the horrors of which were redoubled by the darkness of the night. One Christian, who had strayed, was unmercifully massacred; the others made an obstinate defence; and though surprised, they appeared invincible. The enemy, every where repulsed, attempted an attack on the Dutch quarter.

The reputation of their courage drew many Siamese and Chinese to their quarter, who, under their shade, thought themselves sheltered from the tempest. All contributed to the general defence: they raised walls on the ruins of destroyed pyramids: the Chinese found among them a great deal of silver: the Christians had the leaden gutters for their share, of which they made balls.

The city, ready to fall into the power of the Bramas, would have been buried in its ruins, if they had not had recourse to negociation to soften the besiegers, already armed with torches to reduce it to ashes.[3] The Bramas, proud of their superiority, replied that they had no other conditions to prescribe than for them to surrender at discretion, and that they were determined to use all the rights that victory gave them. Such hard laws were rejected, and hostilities recommenced. On the 28th of April, 1767,[4] the city was taken by assault. The riches of the palace and pagodas became a heap of ashes and ruins: the golden images of the false gods were melted, and the blind rage of these barbarians deprived them of the rewards which had awakened their cupidity. Their own fury robbed them of their prey; and to revenge their loss, they made their resentment fall on the inhabitants, whom they burnt on the soles of their feet, to make them discover the places where their treasure was hid. They violated their weeping daughters before their eyes.

The priests, suspected of concealing riches, were run through with darts or lances, and many were knocked on the head with clubs: the fields, as well as the pagodas, were

[3]Suriyamarin, seeing defeat inevitable, offered to become a vassal of Burma.
[4]The date is usually given as 7 April 1767.

strewed with the dead: nothing was to be seen but carcases floating down the rivers, and the stench attracted swarms of flies, who revenged the country by the ravages they caused in the army during its retreat. The great officers of the kingdom, and the Monarch's favourites, were loaded with irons and condemned to row in the galleys. The King, witness of the miseries of his courtiers, endeavoured to escape the horrors of their fate; but he was discovered, and massacred at the gate of his palace.[5]

The King, priest-torn from the silence of his retreat,[6] was led captive with the Princes and Princesses of his blood; and all, through fear of death, owned they had concealed treasures. When the avarice of the enemy found nothing further to glut itself with, and the country only presented the spectacle of the dead and the dying, the victorious army began its march towards Pegu. It led in its train the King of Siam, who, instead of courtiers, had only the companions of his captivity, less wretched than himself, as they had not fallen from such a height.

F-H. Turpin, *Histoire Civile et Naturelle du Royaume de Siam, et des Révolutions qui ont boulversé cet Empire jusqu'en 1770,* 2 vols., Paris, 1771, translated as *History of Siam,* in John Pinkerton, *A General Collection of the Best and Most Interesting Voyages and Travels in all Parts of the World,* London, 1814, Vol. 9, pp. 647–52.

[5]Suriyamarin is said to have fled and starved to death ten days later.

[6]This refers to the previous king, Uthumphan, who reigned for ten days in 1757 before abdicating in favour of his elder brother and becoming a monk.

24
The Missionaries and King Taksin

FATHER CONDÉ

After Mgr. Brigot's departure from Siam at the fall of Ayutthaya (see Passage 23), Mgr. Le Bon was named Bishop of Metellopolis to succeed him, and eventually reached Siam in 1771. He was well received by King Taksin, who enlarged the land accorded to the Church of the Holy Cross in Dhonburi, and gave two barges to the mission.

A Breton born at Auray in 1750, Father Condé became vicar of the Siamo-Portuguese parish in Thonburi in 1773, in which year Mgr. Le Bon requested the king to allow Christians to take the oath of allegiance without swearing it before the image of the Buddha. This received no reply. But then all people were ordered by the king to follow Buddhist law and not to kill animals, to which the Muslim and Christian communities objected. In 1774, Taksin forbade Siamese and Mons to convert to Christianity or Islam under pain of death, a fate which would befall anyone seeking their conversion (this was a rather more severe interdiction than that already given to the mission in 1731).

Things went from bad to worse for the mission. The bishop, Condé, and another priest, Garnault, were put in prison in 1775. Apart from the question of the oath of allegiance, they refused to admit that King Taksin, who was already the subject of hallucinations, could fly in the air. They were freed after a year of incarceration, and received by the king as though nothing had happened; he even offered them tea in the palace. They were then forbidden to leave the country, and, with another change of mind, ordered to remove from the kingdom in 1779 when in December they left for Malacca. Condé was named Bishop of Rhésie and Apostolic Vicar in succession to Le Bon in 1782, and arrived in Bangkok in 1784 after the death of Taksin. He died the following year on his way to Kedah, where he hoped to be enthroned.

Here are extracts of Condé's very long account of the tribulations of the missionaries, which originally appeared in the Lettres Edifiantes *(Vol. XXV, pp. 390–401), and here come in a translation by Sir John Bowring.*

IT is a very old custom in the Kingdom of Siam, and may be considered a fundamental law of the country, to take an oath of fidelity to the King. This custom is not in any way contrary to our holy religion, but among the heathen it is taken in the following manner:—On the appointed day, all the mandarins and officials have orders from the King to repair to a pagoda, filled with idols, where are assembled the talapoins, priests of their false gods. The latter take pure water, over which they make prayers and perform sacrilegious ceremonies, afterwards plunging into it the sabre and arms of the King. This done, the mandarins call upon the idol and their other gods to witness, while they drink a little of the water, which, through the prayers of the talapoins, has the power of destroying all who become traitors to their sovereign.

Among the Christians are several [three, in fact] mandarins who, like the rest, receive the King's order to repair to this pagoda, and take the oath of fidelity in the heathen fashion. Fear of the King, who is terrible when his will is opposed, had induced them to join the rest; but although not actually drinking of the water, they pretended to do so. Their names were written down, and the ceremony was complete; but our religion admits of no dissimulation, and we constantly repeated to them that the pretence alone made them guilty in the sight of God. In September, 1775, our Christian mandarins resolved to do as we recommended, and sacrifice life rather than fail in Christian duty. On the appointed day, which this year was the 21st September, they absented themselves from the water of sacrifice; and on the 22nd, they were accused at the tribunal as having refused to take the oath of fidelity. They persisted in saying that they would not do so after the heathen manner, as it would be contrary to our religion, and that they had taken it as Christians do, which was indeed the case. The affair was reported to the King, with malicious exaggerations, while he was celebrating a religious festival, which was to last three days. He gave orders to have the affair examined into, and if the Christian mandarins were traitors, they should be put to death. They were therefore immediately all three thrown into prison, with chains on their feet and necks, a cangue (an instrument of torture) on the throat, their feet and hands thrust into stocks....

On the 25th September, the day on which the affair was brought before the King, the chief of the tribunal sent for the bishop, my fellow-pastor, and myself.... We were conducted before him as criminals, and not as we were accustomed to be received on other occasions. The King was very wrathful; and immediately our mandarins were brought forward, with chains on their feet and necks, an honour which we had not yet received. The King put several questions to us, but his irritation prevented him from understanding our replies. We assured him that we did not hinder Christians from tendering him the oath of fidelity; that they had indeed taken it in our presence, but that our holy religion forbade its followers to participate in pagan superstitions.... We would have spoken at greater length, but the King would not listen. He gave orders to have us seized, stripped, bound, and beaten with rods. The order being given, we were dragged away, and stripped of our cassocks and shirts. I cannot express the feelings of that moment. We both received the benediction of the bishop; and hardly had the venerable prelate bestowed it, when he was thrown upon his back, to be dragged from the presence of the King. I saw no more. Each was bound to a pillar, on the bank of the river, in presence of the people and of the whole Court.... We were seated on the ground; a cangue ten or twelve feet long on our necks, the two ends of which were fastened to a wooden pillar; our feet tied by a cord, by which we were bound to the pillar at the foot of which we sat: another cord, tied round the body, bound us closely to a pillar behind us; our hands being tied to the cangue, which was on our necks, so that we could not stir. The other three Christians were in the same condition, as the King directed that each should receive fifty blows, which were immediately inflicted. We heard their cries, but no blows were given to ourselves, though the reason for this forbearance was not known...; a moment later we saw fetters and chains brought for ourselves....

After having loaded us with irons, we were taken to the dwelling of the Barcalan, close to the river (the Barcalan is the mandarin charged with the foreign affairs; everything relating to foreigners being taken before his tribunal); there the cangue was put on our necks, and our hands and feet were placed in the stocks. In this state we passed the night of the 25th and 26th, accompanied by guards. They questioned us all night, yet without listening to us....

About seven o'clock in the morning, we were dragged to the palace, and immediately after, the King ordered us to be brought before him. He put the same questions to us that he had done the evening before, and we gave the same answers. He grew angry, and declared we should be put to death: he gave orders that we should be seized; we were stripped and bound, as on the preceding evening, and each received on his bare shoulders one hundred blows. They were counted aloud, the King remaining present. At the very first stroke, I felt the blood flow, and expected every moment to breathe my last.... At length the scene was over, and we retired wounded and bleeding....

We were taken to prison, where were many Christians, who showed us every kindness. Four or five days after, we were conducted to the palace, where those are imprisoned who have taken part against the King....

We were left in chains nearly a year, till the 2nd September, 1776. Every day we were assured that the King was about to pardon us, but still he delayed....

Some time after our imprisonment, the Birmans came with a powerful army, sacked two or three of the provinces of Siam, and besieged one of the strongest towns in the kingdom. The King sent troops, who were unable to resist them. He set out himself, with a troop of Christian soldiers; but his presence, which had once been so powerful to animate the soldiery, had no effect.... The town was taken and sacked; the King himself appeared to lose courage. Up to that time he had always been victorious; he was heard to complain of his misfortune, declaring that he had injured no one.... During this time we were treated with some consideration; but our irons were not removed, neither was the chain which bound us each to a pillar. We could sit or stand, but were unable to walk....

On his return from the army, the King appeared sad and confused: it was feared that the enemy would come to the capital, and, in that case, Siam itself was lost....

At length, on the 14th of August, the eve of the Assumption, the King, who caused all the other prisoners to be brought before him, to pardon or to punish them, directed the high mandarins to examine us, and send us back to our people.

They came to set us free, and every one testified pleasure. Nevertheless, we were taken in our shirts, with irons on our feet and a chain round our necks, into the hall, beyond the palace, before the mandarins. They told us that the King pardoned us, but that we must give in writing an acknowledgment of our fault, and a promise that we would not again commit it. We had always dreaded this demand; which we refused....

The mandarin directed his guards to take us back to prison, but not to that in the precincts of the palace. We entered our new prison, not knowing how things would turn out.... Every one assured us that on the next day (16th August) we should be permitted to return to our church, and so we expected; but, on the contrary, the morning of the 16th saw us again fettered and taken back to the prison of the palace. Nevertheless, we were told that we should soon be restored to freedom....

On the 1st September, the King himself began to inquire into the affair: he was told that it was being examined into. The next day they notified to his Majesty that all thought we ought to be released. The King gave orders that it should be done, and immediately retired, without speaking of any other affair....

Three months after our release, the King sent for us to an audience. The bishop was ill and could not go, but my fellow-pastor and myself attended. The King showed us every mark of attention and friendship, placing himself below us, offering us tea (which he does not do to the very highest mandarins), and repeatedly inviting us to drink it. He appeared as if he wished to atone this day for all he had caused us to suffer during the past year.

Since that time, he has frequently given us audience, and received us graciously; but our holy religion differing from his, we are often forced to contradict him. He persists in declaring that he can fly; and being annoyed at our saying it was impossible, he did not send for us for more than a year. No longer being admitted at Court, we have gone much among the people....

Quoted in Sir John Bowring, *The Kingdom and People of Siam*, London, Parker and Sons, 1857, Vol. I, pp. 359–69.

Early Contacts with the Bangkok Dynasty (1824–1851)

25
Siamese Amusements

JAMES LOW

James Low (1791–1852) was a controversial servant of the Honourable East India Company with, at the time, the rare distinction, shared by only one other person—his rival, the better connected Captain Burney—of being fluent in Malay and Siamese.

Born in Scotland, he entered the East India Company as a cadet in 1811, rising to lieutenant in 1817 and captain of the 46th Madras Native Infantry in 1826. He was transferred to the Penang presidency in 1818 where he studied Malay and Siamese, and in 1824 was sent on a mission to Chao Noi, Chao Phraya Srithammaraj, generally known to Westerners as the Raja of Ligor (Nakorn Srithammaraj). This formidable person was a legitimate son of King Taksin and the adopted son of a previous viceroy of Nakorn Srithammaraj, who in 1821 had led the Siamese invasion of Kedah to bring its sultan to heel. Low was to seek the so-called raja's assistance or, at least, benevolent neutrality in the first Anglo-Burmese War of 1824. When at 'Ligor' he learned that the raja was not a semi-independent ruler, as was thought in Penang, but a Siamese official subject to the court in Bangkok.

After conducting surveys in the newly acquired territories of

Lower Burma, Low was sent on another mission, this time to Perak, in 1826, where he exceeded his instructions, promising aid in a treaty with the ruler if Siam interfered. He led a raid into Perak the following year, capturing a pirate stronghold and arresting its leader, Nakhoda Udin, a Siamese subject. Chao Phraya Srithammaraj objected that this was in contravention of a recently signed treaty. Low was duly reprimanded, but finally exonerated and reinstated in 1827.

Low was never again used on diplomatic missions or military expeditions. He was made Superintendent of the newly acquired Province Wellesley, opposite Penang, where he stayed for twelve years, profitably developing a number of spice plantations of his own. He also acquired a native wife. His wealth and lifestyle made him several enemies. He was transferred to Singapore as Assistant Resident from 1840 to 1844 and promoted to lieutenant-colonel. He was retired from the Madras army service in 1845 and spent the next five years looking after his plantations. He left Penang in 1850 after more than thirty years in the Malay peninsula, to settle in Scotland, where he died two years later near Edinburgh.

Low wrote prolifically; Cordier's Bibliotheca Indosinica *has some thirty references to articles in numerous scholarly publications. He wrote the first book in a Western language on Thai,* A Grammar of the T'hai or Siamese Language, *published in 1828 in Calcutta (he took leave to oversee its publication), using movable type in Siamese. He wrote on white elephants, coal deposits along the Siamese coast, Siamese government, and Buddhism. He translated the Kedah annals from Malay, and left a valuable account (published in 1838) of his political mission to 'the Raja of Ligor in Siam'. Below are extracts from the second part of an article 'On Siamese Literature' dealing with entertainments, games, and amusements, subjects frequently commented upon by visitors to Siam, but only systematically dealt with by La Loubère and Gervaise before.*

THE Siamese, from being of a lively temperament, and of strong but versatile passions, like other semi-barbarous tribes, are much addicted to gaming, and also to many other less pernicious amusements. The Government checks the unbounded licentiousness to which gaming would lead by licensing gaming houses, where only games of chance may be played. At the great festival called *Wantroot* or *Songkhraan* (*Sankrânti* of Hindoos) a general licence is sometimes given to the people to gamble free of duty. The women are said to indulge in the pernicious delusion with equal eagerness as the men. The same passion for playing is found among the Burmese.

The universality of the game of Chess need not here be insisted on. The Siamese are alike remarkable with other Asiatics for their clear-headedness at this game; and, were all other proofs of their possessing a considerable share of mental perspicacity removed, this one would redeem them from the charge of being deficient in it....

The *Len rua* are boat races. The distance to be rowed over is about two miles. It is chiefly the officers of Government who indulge in this amusement. They use paddles; the rowers sing *he he rua*, a boat-song.

Len khwai are buffalo races. The course is about two hundred yards long, and a straight line at each end is a starting post, and in the centre a house where the judges of the race sit; two buffaloes start at a time at the sound of gongs, one from each post, and to the right hand severally. The aim is for either buffalo to overtake the other before he has gone twenty times over the course. Two only start at once.

The course is very broad and is separated in the middle by a row of people. So that it in fact becomes a sort of narrow oblong figure, the compassing of which forms one round.

There are no riders, but each owner seizes the rope which, as usual, is passed through the cartilege of the animal's nose, and goads him on, being relieved at short intervals in this operation by persons stationed betwixt and at the posts. The person whose buffalo overtakes that of the opposite party must seize the rope it is held by, or he does not win.

The Siamese of Bangkok have no buffalo fights like those exhibited in the Burman Provinces, in which the owners ride their buffaloes and urge them on, and where lives are occasionally lost. Large bets are made at Siamese races....

Len Plaa Kat is a very fanciful kind of amusement—being neither more nor less than a fish fight. The *plaa kat* is a fish which grows to two or three inches in length at the utmost. It is found in shallow rivulets and is sought after with great avidity. The males are selected and kept separately in bottles.

Bets are laid and two of these bitter enemies are slipped into a large bottle where they generally fight until one is killed or disabled.

This game is discountenanced by the king as contrary to the principles of the Buddhist religion, which enjoins humanity. But the customs of barbarous nations are often at variance with the creed they most vehemently contend for. The Chinese also keep a species of fish called by them *Sampan or ho Sampan* for the purpose of fighting them. This fish (the *Ikan puyu* of Malays) is about a span in length and it fights with much vigor and bitterness. The Chinese lay large bets on the issue of a battle of this kind. The *Puyu* seems a diminutive species of perch.

Chon nok nok are fights of various kinds of birds.

Cock-fighting, or *Len chon kai*, is generally prohibited but is nevertheless practised secretly. They do not arm the bird like the Malays.

The Siamese have borrowed many juggling feats from the Hindoos and Chinese, but they have a great aversion to snakes. So much so that at the sight of one some Siamese will appear affected, as if by hysterics, and consequently they do not introduce them into their exhibitions. The Mons or Peguers, teach snakes to move to the sound of a flute in the manner of the tame snakes of Indian jugglers.

Len chok moei, or boxing matches, are common at all great festivals and entertainments. They are often very bloody, and would frequently end in the death of one or both of the parties, did not the king, or other great man present, stop the battle before it becomes dangerous. They arm their hands with hard cord, which is warped round them. The Hindoos use the same, and also arm their fingers and knuckles with horn or silver knobs. They strike straight forward or in any manner most likely to tell according to their unscientific practice. They are allowed to use their knees, feet, and heads in combat.

There are no set number of rounds. The king if present, or if he is not, some one of his courtiers regulates the barbarous sport, and rewards the victors. It is not favorable to the formation of a good opinion of Siamese advancement in civilization, to find at such exhibitions the king, his family and his household of both sexes, with the courtiers, and the populace, women and children including. They excuse the inconsistency of prohibiting fights amongst the brute creation, and exhibiting combats of men, by the remark that the latter have reason to guide their choice of actions. Women have been known on occasions of the kind alluded to, to enter the ring and obtain by a stout battle the applause of the Siamese fancy. The spectators follow the example of the king in throwing pieces of money to the successful combatants, i.e. those who have much punished their opponents....

Waau are paper kites, ranked as male and female. The Siamese are extremely fond of this amusement. The kite is about five or six feet high, and with the cord may, in some instances, cost seventy [Straits] dollars....

People of all ranks and ages in Siam smoke tabacco: it is made into segars [cigars]. Even amongst the great, the Indian hookah has not been yet introduced, although pipes are frequent.

The segar is presented along with the betul mixture to a stranger on his entering a house. Tea accompanies it in some houses; if the visitor has come from a distance he is presented with food immediately, or is invited to stay to dinner....

The Siamese challenge each other to trials of improvisitorial skill—such are questions and replies in verse—and discussions on Bali [Pali] learning. Some one also of a party repeats the name of an animal, tree, or any substance, and the person who accepts the challenge must give the name of one of the same genus, having a like termination—and the trial is kept up until one of the competitors fails to produce a name which shall chime with his adversary's.

Riddles are also proposed and a failure to expound them incurs forfeits of a fanciful kind. Both men and women engage in this amusement and the forfeits are adapted to each sex, much in the manner that we find them in the British game of a similar nature.

James Low, 'On Siamese Literature', *Asiatic Researches*, Calcutta, Vol. XX, Pt. II, 1836, pp. 374, 386–92.

26
White Elephants and Wat Phra Keo

GEORGE FINLAYSON

George Finlayson accompanied his fellow Scot, John Crawfurd (Passage 27), on the 1821–2 mission to Siam and Cochin-China. Like him, he was a medical doctor who had seen service in India. Unlike him, he had no experience of South-East Asia, though he had Crawfurd's impatience and occasional intolerance. Finlayson's account of the mission was published in 1826, two years before Crawfurd's, but had neither its authority nor its perspicacity. It appeared, however, with an extensive introduction by no less a person than Sir Thomas Stamford Raffles. Finlayson was in failing health even in 1823, and by the time his book was published, he was already dead.

Finlayson was chiefly interested in natural history, but complained he had little opportunity to study this during his stay in Siam. After the first interview with Rama II, Crawfurd and his party were given the ritual conducted tour of the royal palace. Finlayson here describes extensively the white elephants, and gives a summary account of Wat Phra Keo, though without naming it; this is, in fact, the first published description of it.

THE streets [inside the palace] were remarkably dirty, so that for the greater part of the way we had to walk up to the ancle in mud and water. However, no offer was made to procure us our shoes until we had gone through the whole ceremony of seeing the strange sights of this palace, a tedious and not very gratifying ceremony, which occupied us nearly two hours. The sun had, after the shower, shone out with intense power; the stones over which we passed had in consequence been rendered very hot, and the alternate passing from these stones into the wet and puddles rendered the promenade not altogether agreeable to persons unaccustomed to walk bare-footed.

We were first conducted to the stables of the white elephants, which, being held in great veneration by the Siamese, are kept within the inner enclosure of the palace, and have habitations allotted to them quite close to those of the King himself.

Of white elephants there are at the present time no fewer than five in the possession of the King, whence we may infer that this variety is far less rare than we are accustomed to believe, at least, that is so in the further peninsula of India. It has, however, seldom happened that so many have been collected at one period, and the present is regarded as auspicious in consequence of an event so unexpected, and so much desired. A white elephant is still reckoned as beyond all value, every effort is made to take them when they are by chance discovered, and the subjects of the King can perform no more gratifying service than that of securing them. They, and indeed all elephants, are the property of the King only.

The appellation white, as applied to the elephants, must be received with some degree of limitation....

We next proceeded to visit a temple situated at a short distance beyond the hall of audience. The court is spacious and neat, containing, besides the temple, a handsome small building, in which their sacred books are deposited. At each of the principal gates are placed gigantic earthen images, of grotesque form, with clubs in their hands, and at each angle of the temple brass figures of a fanciful animal, somewhat resembling a lion. Besides, there were other figures made of clay, paltry in appearance and absurd in design. The temple is of a pyramidal form, highly wrought with minute figures, somewhat in the Chinese style. The character of the ornaments, like that of the paintings on the stern of a Chinese junk, is operose, unmeaning, and grotesque; yet the general effect was in the present instance not unpleasing to the spectator, who regarding it at some distance, overlooked the minuteness alluded to....

But to return to the temple. I have observed that it was of a pyramidal form, the point terminating in a slender spire, about 200 feet high. Within, the building constituted a single lofty chamber, about 50 feet long, and nearly as much in breadth, paved with stones. In the centre were placed, on irregular stages, a countless number of small figures of Buddha, intermixed with bits of looking-glass, scraps of gilded paper, and Chinese paintings. Surmounting the rest was a figure of Buddha, about a foot and a half high, in a sitting posture, made, as our guides would have us to believe, of emerald.

Wat Phra Keo, or the Temple of the Emerald Buddha, from Frank Vincent, *The Land of the White Elephant . . .*, New York, Harper and Brothers, 1874.

The stone was either the Chinese figure-stone, or Heliotrope, but it was placed at too great a distance for us to be able to say exactly which. There was here nothing in the shape of an altar, nor any convenience save the floor on which to place fruit and flowers, the usual offerings made to Buddha. A number of vagrant, idle people, had followed us. They entered the temple, and behaved with a degree of noisy indecorum, which could not fail to surprise us.

Surrounding the temple, and forming its enclosure, there is a paved passage, covered in above, and supported by pillars. The walls of this passage are covered with rude paintings of allegorical subjects, chiefly taken from the story of the Ramayana, a celebrated epic poem of the Hindus. It would appear, indeed, that many of the absurdities of the Hindu religion are intermingled with that of Buddha. There are in Bankok a few Brahmans, who are entertained by the king, and have built a small temple. The Siamese cultivate a lock of hair on the forehead, which lock they preserve from birth to the age of twelve, fourteen, or sixteen, untouched. At the expiration of this period, they institute a great feast; presents are made by all the relations and friends of the family, and the occasion is rendered one of great joy. The Brahman then, sprinkling a little water on the head, and repeating certain prayers, cuts the lock. When the children of the king undergo this ceremony, an artificial hill is constructed, on which the Brahman performs the ceremony.

Close to the temple stands the pyramidal building, in which the sacred books are kept. You ascend to it by a flight of steps, covered with plates of tin, as is also the floor of the room. The books cannot be very numerous. They are contained in a pyramidal upright cupboard, richly ornamented with small pieces of mother-of-pearl.

Returning by the road we had entered, we repassed the inner and second gates of the palace, when we found ourselves in the enclosure where we had halted for some time before entering the audience-hall. The only objects worthy of remark in this place were several ridiculously and uselessly large brass guns. They must, from their size, be equally unserviceable and unmanageable. They seemed, however, to pride themselves not a little in possessing guns of such a calibre. They appeared to have been uncommonly well cast.

Having now been shewn all that was thought worthy of notice, we were reconducted to the room in which we had first halted. It was again soon filled with the rabble. A plentiful dessert of sweet-meats was introduced, and the Moorman [escort] was particularly desirous that we should partake of it. But it was impossible to overlook the mean condition of those left to entertain us, the disreputable appearance of the building, or the jeering and disrespectful conduct of the herd of spectators that crowded round us. It seemed as if the court had said, *See them feed.*

George Finlayson, *The Mission to Siam and Hué, the Capital of Cochin China, in the Years 1821–2*, London, John Murray, 1826, pp. 150–1, 155–6, 158–61.

27
Visiting Bangkok

JOHN CRAWFURD

John Crawfurd was a remarkable, if self-opiniated, Scotsman who passes in and out of the pages of South-East Asian history in the early years of the nineteenth century. Born in 1783, he studied medicine at Edinburgh, and in 1803 went to India as an assistant surgeon in the Third Regiment of Native Cavalry. He was transferred to Penang in 1808 where he spent three years, learning fluent Malay in the time, and during the British occupation of Java from 1811 to 1816, held a number of posts there, the most important being British Resident at the Court of the Sultan of Yogyakarta. From 1817 to 1821 he was in Britain, where he published, in 1820, a three-volume History of the Indian Archipelago *which was seen to be his attempt to equal Raffles's* History of Java. *The Marquis of Hastings, Governor-General of India, appointed Crawfurd, in 1821, to head a mission to Siam and Vietnam. His record of this was published in 1828. Rama II, whom he met, was advancing in years, and many of his negotiations were conducted with the future Rama III, Prince Chetsadabodin.*

The mission accomplished little; the court was divided on the merits of trade with outsiders.

Crawfurd went on to become Resident (Governor) of Singapore from 1823 to 1826, in succession to Raffles, its founder. He was made Civil Commissioner in Rangoon on leaving Singapore, and then Ambassador to Ava in 1827, an account of which mission was also published in 1828. Crawfurd, at the age of forty-five, returned to Britain for good in this year, a Fellow of the Royal Society, the Literary Society, and of the Geographical Society. He gave all his manuscripts to the British Museum in 1842, but continued to publish extensively, producing a Grammar and Dictionary of the Malay Language *in 1852 and a* Descriptive Dictionary of the Indian Islands *in 1865, before dying in 1868.*

Essentially, he was an eighteenth-century gentleman rather lost in the nineteenth century world of commerce, notwithstanding his years of service in the East India Company. But he acquired a nineteenth-century arrogance with regard to native peoples. He was not the perfect diplomat and did not inspire, unlike Raffles, great affection. Abdullah bin Abdul Kadir, in the Hikayat Abdullah, *wrote of him: 'Colonel Crawfurd was by nature inclined to impatience and outbursts of temper. He did all his work slowly, without hurrying. He was conscientious as well as capable, and he was also a man of education. Yet in spite of this he was fond of material wealth. He was tight-fisted and gave himself airs. His temperament made him intolerant of listening to long-winded complaints. Neither had he the ability to enquire fully into people's affairs.'*

For all his faults, his account of Siam as he found it in 1822 is detailed and valuable, and the first comprehensive description of the country since the end of the seventeenth century. Here he describes Wat Suthat and nearby buildings, and gives some insights into more mundane matters; Westerners were extremely rare in Bangkok in his day, and the visit of his party clearly created a great stir and curiosity.

DURING the visit ... all the temples, but particularly the larger one, were, on account of the holidays, crowded with visitors, and this incident afforded us a striking picture of the manners and habits of the people. The votaries were of all ages and sexes, and the women were not less numerous than the men. The bulk were Siamese, but there were also Cochin Chinese, Cambojans, people of Loo [Laos] and Pegue, and a great number of Chinese. Instead of the gravity and decorum which might have been looked for in a temple, the demeanour of the visitors was noisy, clamorous, and playful. They were at one moment prostrate before the idols, and at another engaged in some frolic, or singing an idle song. One man, for example, coolly lighted his segar [cigar] at an incense-rod which a devotee had just placed as an offering before one of the idols, and another deliberately sat down before an image and played a merry air on a flageolet, while many were engaged at the same shrine in performing their devotions.

The women mixed in the crowd, unveiled, as indeed they always are, and were neither shy nor timid; on the contrary, there was considerable familiarity between the sexes; and our conductors, Mohammedans, hinted to us, although I cannot pretend to say with how much truth, that the temples were frequent places of assignation. All this levity certainly formed a very striking contrast to the decent and reverencial devotion of a Christian, or even of a Mohammedan people, and struck us with surprise.

The women were the most decorous in the performance of their religious duties, and also the most assiduous. They went about sprinkling the images with perfumes, and making offerings to them. The oblations were of various descriptions—such as lighted incense-rods; fresh lotus, and other flowers; chaplets of artificial flowers, and cloths of various descriptions. There were, indeed, few of the many idols which I have mentioned, that were not decked with a scarf of silk or cotton cloth, commonly of a yellow colour, the offering of some votary. The Chinese, on their part, burned sacrificial paper, and hung up, as votive offerings, from the roofs of the temples, banners of cloth or paper with Chinese inscriptions upon them.

No officiating priests were to be seen; and, in truth ... there was not a Talapoin within the precincts of the temple, except the few whom we met in the library, and these were distant from the crowd, and appeared to take no share whatever in what was passing.

I should mention, that those who frequented the temple

were not confined to the lower classes. One group of well-dressed females was pointed out to us, consisting of above thirty persons. These were one of the concubines, and an infant-child of the Prince Krom-chiat, with their attendants. The infant, apparently not above three years of age, appeared to have been well-tutored, for he went through his prostrations with great composure before the principal image in the central temple. Several of the followers were young and handsome; and we were somewhat surprised, at hearing our conductors request us to point out any amongst them that we might desire to form a matrimonial connexion with during our stay in Siam.

Our appearance in the crowd excited a degree of curiosity, which stopped short only of rudeness.—We were followed wherever we went. Our presence was sometimes announced by shouts, and a hundred idle questions were put to us, which either our interpreters would not explain to us, or we had no time or inclination to answer. A strong inclination was also felt to ascertain, by personal examination, the quality and texture of our dress, and the nature and use of the trinkets which we had about our persons. In all this, the ludicrous importance and vanity of the Siamese character was conspicuous, even among the lowest persons whom we encountered.

April 13.—We made an excursion this morning through the town of Bang-kok. The ground on which it is built is a rich tract of alluvial land, low, but not marshy, and intersected by numerous winding creeks and canals. We crossed the river, from our dwelling, towards the palace, which lies along the western bank of the river. A kind of canal surrounds it, and this, which was navigable, and communicated with the river, we entered in our boats at the southern angle of the fortification, passing under the walls, which had some mean bastions, with small embrasures, but no cannon. The canal was crowded with merchant-boats, loaded with rice, salt, cotton, dried fish, oil, dye-woods, &c. As we passed along, there was pointed out to us, on our right-hand, the residence of the fugitive prince [Snguon] who, under countenance of the Siamese Government, lays claim to the throne of Kamboja: it was a very poor dwelling, indeed.

In our progress, we had to pass under a bridge, which,

after the profusion of expense which we had lately witnessed in the temples, afforded a surprising example of the stupid inattention of a despotic Government and a superstitious people to all objects of public convenience and utility. The value of a very few of the brass images which we saw yesterday, would have been sufficient to build a noble bridge at this place, where it was so much required; but the one which we now saw, consisted of a single plank, and was elevated to the giddy height of at least thirty feet. The passengers, for safety, took hold of each others' hand as they passed along it. Out of politeness to us, and in deference to the prejudice which I have already alluded to, that makes it a dishonour to have others pass over our heads, those who intended to go over, halted until our boat had gone through.

After passing on between two and three miles behind the palace, we came to a spacious temple [Wat Suthat], which was commenced by the present King about two years before, and was not yet finished. This was of the same general form as those I have already described, but in costliness and magnificence far excelled them. The doors and window-shutters, and the capitals and pedestals of the wooden columns, were curiously and laboriously carved almost throughout, exhibiting figures of flowers, trees, and animals: this carved work was again richly gilt. The central temple, which, in this case, was raised on a very elevated terrace, consisted but of one chamber, or fane, measuring fifty-eight and a half English feet in height, seventy-one and a half in length, with a breadth equal to the height. A single brass [bronze] statue of Gautama occupies this noble chamber, for such it unquestionably is. The image, exclusive of the pedestal, measures, in its sitting posture, twenty-nine and a quarter feet: from the point of one knee to that of the other is twenty-two feet nine inches. This was an ancient statue [Phra Buddha Chakyamuni], lately brought down the river, from the town of Sokotai, by order of the King. The minor images in the gallery of the quadrangular inclosure of this temple were one hundred and sixty in number, all of plaster, and most of them in an unfinished state.

At the temple we found that the festivities of the season were celebrating with deafening tumult and discord. The principal chamber was crowded with people, and a noisy band of music was playing before the idol. In the same situation there was a set of comedians, who excited the mirth of the crowd by their extravagant and ludicrous buffoonery.

The Prah-cha-di, or 'tall thin spire', with a broad base, appears to be a favourite emblem of the Buddhist religion. Accordingly we noticed that the whole loose earth of the area of the temple now visited, was here and there raised into little temporary conical mounds, on the top of each of which a rod was fixed, containing a slip of paper, on which was written the name of the votary who had taken the trouble of erecting it. In the course of the day we frequently observed floating along the river and canals, on the stems of banana-trees, numerous little mimic temples, which contained similar mounds of sand or earth with those I have just described.

Close to this temple of Gautama our conductors showed us a Hindoo place of worship [Wat Prarn]—a novelty in this part of the world, and therefore calculated to excite our curiosity. There were three temples within one inclosure, each consisting of a long brick building, with an ordinary tiled roof. Access to them was from one end, while the altar and images were at the opposite one. They were dreary and comfortless-looking places, destitute of all ornament, and their poverty and simplicity afforded a remarkable contrast to the wealth and magnificence of the Buddhist establishment in their neighbourhood. There was no mistaking the religion which had the countenance and protection of the State. One of the three buildings contained fifteen large handsome images, all in a standing posture, of brass, with their crowns, amulets, and drapery gilded. The most distinguished was a figure of Mahadewa, nine feet high. There were several smaller ones of the same deity, with figures of Prawati, Padmi, and Vishnu, and one statue of Brahma. A second building appeared to be dedicated to Ganesa, whose statue was the most conspicuous. Here were also four statues of Mahadewa. The third building appeared to be dedicated to the worship of the Linga, of which there was a large gilded figure in the centre of the altar, surrounded by forty or fifty small brass images—such as those of Siwa, Ganesa, Naraina, Hanuman, the Bull Nandi, &c. &c. We were told that all these images had been brought, at different times, from Western India.[1]

There was no one in attendance at the temples, but the priests attached to it lived at no great distance, and one of them came at our request. He was an elderly person, of slender form, and still retained much of the peculiar features of the Hindoo. He had a white scarf over his shoulders, and, in opposition to the cropped heads of the Siamese, he wore his long hair tied in a knot behind. He informed us, through our interpreter, that he was a Brahmin, and the fifth in descent from his ancestor who had first settled in Siam, and who, according to his statement, came from the sacred Island of Ramiseram, between Ceylon and the Main. He was gratified at the slender acquaintance which we displayed respecting the Hindoo religion, and took a pleasure in continuing the conversation with us on this subject.

Not far from this temple were erected two enormous wooden-posts, or pillars, joined at the top by a cross-beam. Each of these pillars was certainly not less than seventy feet high, and in size equal to the main-mast of a ship of four or five hundred tons. Certain ceremonies of the Buddhist worship, the nature of which I could not ascertain, are annually performed at this spot.[2]

The tide having retired and left the creek, by which we had reached the temples which we now visited, dry, our boats were previously sent round to a convenient wharf, higher up the main river, and we walked to where they were. This led us to a very extensive bazaar, paved throughout with brick, and with a row of very good shops on each side, chiefly in the occupation of the Chinese. Among the articles exposed for sale, were large quantities of Chinese crapes, which are much worn by the Siamese women, principally in the form of scarfs. These shops also contained considerable quantities of Indian printed goods, and English chintz and broadcloths.

Quitting the bazaar, we passed under the walls of the Fort or Palace. This has no ditch, the curtain no embrasures; and the bastions, although having embrasures, are without cannon.

[1]Many are now in the National Museum in Bangkok.

[2]The ceremonies at the Giant Swing, or Sao Ching Cha, were in fact Brahmin. See Young (Passage 49).

As a place of strength it is too contemptible to deserve any notice. . . .

May 21.—The re-appearance of the epidemic *cholera* spread great alarm amongst the people, a matter which was apparent enough from the precautions which they took against its attacks. The King, under some superstitious imagination, which I am unable to explain, directed the people to keep at home, and abstain from all work for seven days. The temples at this time were more frequented than usual, and numbers of persons were to be seen wearing shreds of white cotton yarn round the neck as amulets, whilst others endeavoured to recommend themselves to the good will of the gods by purchasing fowls and other animals from strangers, with a view of giving them their liberty and saving them from slaughter. The secular superintendant of the great temple, which was the first we visited, called upon us in the course of the day, and said that he had no fear of the *cholera morbus*, as he made frequent prostrations before the idols, and wore a skein of cotton thread round his neck as a charm. As he spoke, he pointed to this potent amulet!

John Crawfurd, *Journal of an Embassy from the Governor-General of India to the Courts of Siam and Cochin China*, London, Henry Colburn, 1828, pp. 115–20, 158.

28
An Audience with Rama III

HENRY BURNEY

Henry Burney was to follow in John Crawfurd's ambassadorial footsteps (Passage 27), both in Siam and Ava, and with rather more success. Times had changed, there was a new king, Rama III, on the throne in Bangkok, and British successes over Burma had caused the Siamese to be rather more circumspect of the power which had laid low their traditional enemy.

Burney was born in Calcutta in 1792, and joined the East India Company as a cadet in 1807. He was well connected, being the nephew of Madame d'Arblay (Fanny Burney). He took part in the conquest of Java in 1811, from which date he was stationed at Penang, rising to become Military Secretary to the Governor from 1818 to 1824. Like James Low (Passage 25), he learned during his time in Penang fluent Malay and Siamese, and was also sent on a mission to Nakorn Srithammaraj, to the 'Raja of Ligor', shortly after Low, in 1825. Captain Burney was selected to go as Envoy to Siam late in 1825, and managed to obtain a political and commercial treaty with the Siamese in June 1826. He was greatly helped in his negotiations by the arrival of news, in February, that the British had successfully concluded the war with the Burmese.

Burney's account of his mission was published in Bangkok in 1910 in the unwieldy Burney Papers. *Here is his account of his first audience with the king, Rama III, in 1826, who had been less than two years on the throne. Mr Hunter, alluded to here, was a resident British merchant whose name will occur several times in these pages. The audience is remarkably similar in form, not only to Crawfurd's four years earlier, but also to those of Chaumont (Passage 10) and La Loubère (Passage 14) in the seventeenth century; Burney, however, took along his son, and the Siamese love of children is evident in the consideration shown to him by the king.*

EARLY on the morning of the 16 Instant the day fixed for our introduction to the King, the Governor General's letter was brought to me, and at 10 a.m. we left the house in four boats. The first conveyed the Sepoys and their drum and fife. The second Captain Macfarquhar, my Interpreter, and myself, with the Public Letter. The third our chairs of ceremony, and the fourth Captain Sutherland, Mr Hunter and a band of Siamese Music. We were followed by two or three hundred small boats with Siamese Officers, and those whom curiosity had brought to witness the Scene, which we attempted to make as imposing as possible. On our arrival at the opposite side of the river, Captain Macfarquhar and myself got into our chairs and the rest of the Gentlemen mounted the small horses which were in waiting with tolerably decent appointments. We proceeded thus, accompanied by Jose Pediada and Beneditto,[1] as far as the gateway of the second Court, where the Native Christians only pulled off their Shoes and Stockings whilst we were requested to dismount, to leave our Sepoys and walk a short distance into a Hall in which we found Pya Phiphut, Pya Chula and his son and other Siamese Officers in waiting, with several state Elephants standing outside. We were detained in this Hall for about half an hour, and then summoned into the presence of the King, who we were informed had taken his seat on the throne. We passed through a body of Siamese Troops seated on their Hams within a railing each side of the road, which was lined by 2 or 300 Drums and other instruments that played a grave tune. At the door of the Hall of Audience, Pediada, Beneditto and all our Siamese attendants fell on their Knees and fore-arms, in which posture they moved before and on each side of us. The moment we entered and saw the King, which we could not immediately do, as he was seated on a throne 10 or 12 feet high at the farther end of the Hall, which appeared to have been purposely darkened, we made three profound bows, whilst the Siamese struck their heads on the ground, and raised their hands joined to their foreheads the same number of times. We then moved on, preceded by Pya Phiphut and Pya Chula about twenty paces where we again bowed, and the Siamese made their obeisances three times. We then set down on the Carpet which covered the floor. Pya Phiphut was lying about 8 paces before me, and between us Pya Chula, Pediada was on my left—my own Interpreter immediately behind me—Captain Macfarquhar on my right, and next to them were Beneditto and Radsitha. The rest of the Gentlemen sat behind us, whilst a little before and on the left of us, the Public presents which we had brought were all arranged. At a signal from Pya Phiphut, I rose, holding the Governor General's letter over my head, and advancing 6 or 8 paces beyond that Pya, where a Gold Vase had been placed, I deposited the letter upon it, and then taking out the English address, which I had prepared, read it out with a loud voice and placing it by the side of the Governor General's letter, retired to my seat, keeping my face towards the King. The whole of the English

[1]Portuguese interpreters.

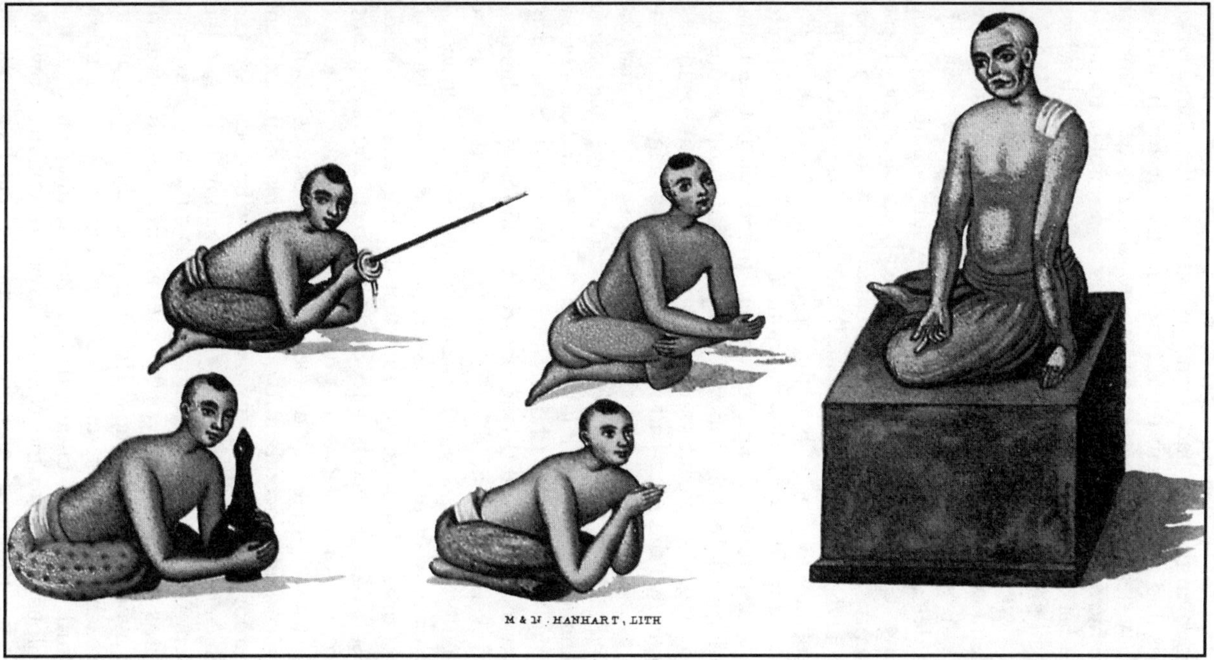

The mode of approaching superiors, from Sir John Bowring, *The Kingdom and People of Siam*, London, Parker and Sons, 1857.

Gentlemen then, as had been previously settled, joined their hands and raised them three times against the forehead. His Majesty desired that we should approach him nearer, and we were moved 8 or 10 paces in advance. Pya Phiphut then read out a list of the presents, and a complimentary speech which he had prepared in my name. The first questions His Majesty asked were, whether I had come from the same Governor General who had deputed Mr Crawfurd to Siam, and how long the present Governor General had been in India. He next demanded 'what is the object of your coming here and of the Governor General of Bengal sending me these presents'. I replied that the presents were tokens of friendship and good will, and that I had been deputed to His Majesty to tender to him the congratulations of the Right Honble the Governor General of India, upon his accession to the great throne of Siam, to cement friendship between the Siamese and English Nations, and to submit propositions for improving the wealth and commerce of both countries. Fearing that the King had not noticed that a Siamese translation was annexed to my English address and desirous of having it then read if possible, I added that that paper explained the objects of my Mission and I rose and delivered it into the hands of Pya Chula. The King directing the paper to be given to the Prah Klang observed 'I am much obliged to the Governor General.' The King then demanded, what is the cause of the present War between the English and Burmese. I took care to shape my reply so as to bear on the subject of the Burmese Captives, and said that the Burmese had made unjustifiable incursions into our territories, had burnt and destroyed some places on our Chittagong frontier, and had carried away some of our subjects. His Majesty asked if the war had commenced before or since the arrival of the present Governor General and observed that the Burmese are old enemies of the Siamese, and that he is happy to hear of the present War. He next asked, if the War is difficult. I answered that it is difficult wherever the enemy can take advantage of their woods and swamps. His Majesty desired us again to approach him closer, and we were moved 6 to 8 paces forward. He then enquired if I had learnt whether the populous nation to the North of Ava are coming down to assist the Burmese—and on my replying that I had not, he observed that there are now at Bangkok several Laos Chiefs whom I may see and interrogate on the subject. The King then asked if I proposed to wait here until the arrival of the Governor of Ligor, and I replied that I did, as I had some affairs to submit to the consideration of His Majesty in conjunction with that Chief. He next enquired after the health of the Governor General, and of the King of England, and in replying to the latter question I took occasion to state that Great Britain was never in a more flourishing condition than at present. He then asked how many years I had been in India, and when it was my intention to return to England and enquired of the Prah Klang, whether Mr Crawfurd or I am the higher Officer. The Prah Klang answered, that Mr Crawfurd is a Captain of Merchants, and I a Captain of Soldiers. The King demanded, whether every English Minister and Officer is not obliged to go to war in the same manner as those of the Siamese and Burmese Nations. I replied that our Officers are divided in some respects in the same manner as the Chinese, into Mandarins of Letters and Military Mandarins, and that war is the business of our Military Officers. The King then directed, that whatever I had to say respecting trade or any other matter I should communicate to the Prah Klang, to whose best attention he was further pleased to recommend us in very strong terms. He took particular notice of my Son—asked his age and where he was born, and at the close of the Audience, the Prah Klang presented to the Boy a number of Toys and other Articles, which the King had ordered to be prepared for him. A Siamese Officer bearing an instrument in the shape of a sceptre, and seated on the floor a little in advance of Pya Phiphut, then rose upon his Knees and made three obeisances to the King, who took up his *Kris*, and a noise like the stroke of a wand was heard, at which Curtains of Gold Cloth were quickly drawn before the King's throne. The whole of the Siamese then made the usual obeisances towards the Curtains.

Immediately below the King's throne were seated the Princes of the blood. On each side were the principal Ministers according to their relative ranks. The first two persons on the King's right were the Yomarat and Kalahom, and on the left the Chakri and Prah Klang. There were several Chinese and Cochin Chinese, and we noticed particularly some Laos

Officers who were richly dressed and much resembled, in the opinion of Captain Macfarquhar the Goorkha Chiefs. After the Audience we were taken to see the white Elephant, and one or two of the Temples, and returned home with the same state as we had set out.

The King appeared to us to bear a strong resemblance to the King of Ligor—he had no crown, which I am assured he never wears excepting on the day of his Coronation. He wore no [*sic*] loose transparent muslin dress over his rich Cloths of Gold in the same manner as the Courtiers covered their surat Kim Khaul vests, and his fingers displayed a profusion of diamond rings. The Hall of Audience appeared 120 feet long by 60 broad and about 40 feet high. Even after we had the last time been desired to approach, we were perhaps 40 feet distant from the throne. I must own that although the dresses of the King and his Ministers were rich, the *tout ensemble* much disappointed me. There was a kind of second hand finery in the hall of Audience, which displayed not one handsome lustre, whilst to each pillar was fixed a large Chinese painting on glass of a European Officer or Lady. The throne is in shape like a boat placed upon a platform with a small Canopy the whole covered with gold. The Concourse of Spectators which flocked around us, joined to the Soldiers and other attendants about the Palace, was very great. At our entrance into the Hall of Audience we could scarcely move from the number of Courtiers and other Officers who were lying prostrate on the ground. The King's questions were repeated by Pya Phiphut to Pya Chula, who repeated them to Jose Pediada, who interpreted them to me in English. Having my own interpreter immediately behind me, I often understood the King's question long before it reached me through the Official Channels. My replies were taken in the same manner to Pya Phiphut, who made them much longer by first repeating all the Kings titles stating that his great Excellent and infallible Majesty had been pleased to ask such a question, to which I begged with all humiliation, to submit such an answer. Nothing however can be more contemptible than the appearance of the Soldiers, and I cannot credit what however the Native Christians assured me was the case, that the Soldiers we saw on this day were the King's body guard, and some of his best description of Troops. They were a poor, thin ill-set race, many of them with old Sepoys coats. Their Muskets were old, rusty Arms held in every possible way, and as to accoutrements they had scarcely any. The most formidable body of Troops consisted of a party of stout able bodied men each armed with a thick stick. The Siamese Soldier when detached against the Burmese frontiers is supplied, I am informed, with a Musket, a Bamboo full of rice and a hoe, with which last instrument he digs a hole for himself, in which he sits concealed until some of the enemy come near enough to be surprised.

Henry Burney, *The Burney Papers*, Vajranana National Library, Bangkok, 1910, Vol. I, pp. 42–8.

29
The Top-knot Cutting Ceremony

FATHER BRUGUIÈRE

Father Bruguière is quoted no less than ten times in Sir John Bowring's massive work on Siam (Passage 35); less, it is true, than Pallegoix, and less extensively, but nevertheless his writings clearly impressed the British envoy. All these citations were taken from the Annales de l'Association de la Propagation de la Foi. *An annotated, translated, and abridged version of his letter to Monsieur Bousquet, Vicar-General of Aire, appeared as 'Notices of the Religion, Manners, and Customs of the Siamese' in* The Chinese Repository, *Vol. 13, No. 4, April 1844, pp. 169–217. The original appeared in the* Annales de l'Association de la Propagation de la Foi, *Vol. XXV, 1831, pp. 63–215. Pallegoix too quotes Bruguière, notably over the story made famous by Anna Leonowens whereby city gates required human sacrifices. She deceitfully made it appear as though this was still being done in King Mongkut's reign. Bowring writes: 'Of an ancient ceremony frequently referred to by travellers, which requires the immolation of three human beings when any new gate was constructed in a Siamese city, I could find no vestige in Siam. Though many details are given of the proceedings in a letter from Bishop Bruguière, Pallegoix doubts the existence of such a usage. It has probably fallen into desuetude.'*

Barthélemy Bruguière was born at Raissac-d'Aude in 1792, ordained priest in Carcassonne in December 1815, and taught philosophy and theology in a seminary. He joined the Foreign Missions in 1825, and left for Siam the following year with the title of Bishop of Capse (Capsu, or Capu, according to Bowring). Like many of his fellows, he became entangled in disputes with Portuguese missionaries, and in 1831 was named Apostolic Vicar in Korea. He died suddenly in October 1835 when travelling to Manchuria.

The top-knot cutting ceremony (to which Finlayson in Passage 26 alluded) is another rite which has largely fallen into disuse, and which is extracted (in Bowring's translation) here. It should be noted that Bruguière only talks of the ceremony in relation to a prince, but in fact all classes used to observe the rite to a greater or lesser degree, according to situation. A very few families still observe the tradition.

WHEN a prince of the Royal family attains to the age of thirteen or fourteen years, he is removed from the palace, puts on a new dress, and a talapoin [priest] cuts his hair. On this occasion, men of the highest rank and intelligence among the four nations in Siam come to the Court in the costume of their respective countries. A kind of mountain, with a pathway to the top, is made, where a tent is erected, and a little below it the figure of one or two elephants, which furnish water that falls into a basin at the base of this artificial mountain. When all is ready, the civil and military officers place themselves in two files, and the procession in this order leaves the palace. The prince who is the object of the ceremony is seated on a chair, which is borne upon the shoulders of the officers. He has on his head a high bonnet, not peaked, and slippers on his feet, and gold bracelets on his arm; a kind of rattle is shaken before him, to signify that he is yet in his infancy;—they also play on the flute, tambourine, and trumpet. The princess who is to be his future wife goes before with her hands joined, holding a plume of peacock's feathers. When the *cortège* returns to the

An artificial mountain, known as Mount Khrai-lat, erected for the tonsure ceremony, photograph by John Thomson, 1865.

palace, the prince prostrates himself before his father, and the King takes him by the hand and leads him into the temple, where the ashes of their ancestors are deposited, when he adores them.

This ceremony is repeated for three consecutive days. On the fourth day the talapoins cut his hair in the ancestral temple, and he receives a white dress, instead of the red one he wore during the ceremony. The same day, he goes to the artificial mountain, accompanied by a great retinue, where he washes his hands in the basin, and then ascends with three or four lords to the top of the mountain, into the pavilion, where he is supposed to go through with some superstitious ceremony. There is some resemblance between this Siamese ceremony and that of the ancient Romans, when their young men took the *toga virilis*.

Quoted in Sir John Bowring, *The Kingdom and People of Siam*, London, Parker and Sons, 1857, Vol. I, pp. 32–3.

30
Personages at Court

CHARLES GUTZLAFF

Missionaries, mostly Protestant and often American, came aplenty to Bangkok in the reign of Rama III (r. 1824–51), somewhat giving the lie to the impression that the kingdom was closed to outsiders during this period. F. A. Neale (see Passage 32) shows us this was not true in so far as the military was concerned. Charles Gutzlaff was one of the earliest of such missionaries, much more at home in dealing with Chinese (whose habits he deplored), and showing an intolerance of other people's religious viewpoints equalled to the earliest Catholic missionaries in the seventeenth century. Sir John Bowring wrote of Gutzlaff's account of his stay that it was 'characterized by that extraordinary and sanguine credulity, which no amount of disappointment, no experience of facts, no opportunities of knowledge, seemed in the slightest degree to influence or control'.

Gutzlaff is not a likeable character. He survived (he wrote in May 1831) three years in Siam, in the company of his wife, living in a 'cottage' on the banks of the Chao Phraya, having 'the high gratification of seeing the prejudices of the natives vanish; and perceived with delight, that a large field amongst the different people who inhabit Siam, was opening'. He deceived himself, but did his best, by his own lights. He gives a general account of the different races in the country, notably the Chinese, the Mons, the Malays, the 'Moors', and the Lao or Shans. Needless to say, he thought little of Catholic missionary efforts.

In spite of berating the Siamese for what he calls 'self-sufficiency' (presumably meaning their disinterest in his calls for apostasy), and saying 'I regret I have not found one honest man.... Sordid oppression, priestcraft, allied to wretchedness and filth, are every where to be met', he finds solace in comparison: 'Notwithstanding, the Siamese are superior in morality to the Malays. They are neither sanguinary nor bigoted, and are not entirely shut against persuasion.'

In the extract which follows, he tries to show that he made some impression on important persons at court (no attempt is made here at a complete elucidation of all the names he drops), whereas in truth he made little or none, and he gained access to the court because of his medical knowledge, not his religious fervour. It is significant that he only mentions the example of three ordinary persons who showed some interest in his teachings. But, like the earlier missionaries, he fails to distinguish between polite interest and a desire to convert.

FAVOURED by an over-ruling Providence, I had equal access to the palace and to the cottage; and was frequently, against my inclination, called to the former. Chow-fa-nooi,[1] the younger brother of the late king, and the rightful heir of the crown, is a youth of about twenty-three, possessing some abilities, which are however swallowed up in childishness. He speaks English; can write a little; can imitate works of European artisans; and is a decided friend of European sciences, and of Christianity. He courts the friendship of every European; holds free conversation with him, and is anxious to learn whatever he can. He is beloved by the whole nation, which is wearied out by heavy taxes; but his elder brother, Chow-fa-yay,[2] who is just now a priest, is still more beloved. If they ascend the throne, the changes in all the institutions of the country will be great, but perhaps too sudden. The son of the Phra Klang, or minister of foreign affairs, is of superior intelligence, but has a spirit for intrigue, which renders him formidable at court, and dangerous to foreigners. He looks with contempt upon his whole nation; but crouches before every individual, by means of whom he may gain any influence. Chow-nin, the step-brother of the king, is a young man of good talents, which are however spoiled by his habit

[1] Prince Chudamani.
[2] Prince, later King Mongkut.

of smoking opium. Kroma-sun-ton, late brother of the king, and chief justice of the kingdom, was the person by whom I could communicate my sentiments to the king. Officially invited, I spent hours with him in conversation, principally upon Christianity, and often upon the character of the British nation. Though himself a most dissolute person, he requested me to educate his son (a stupid boy), and seemed the best medium for communicating Christian truth to the highest personages of the kingdom. At his request, I wrote a work upon Christianity, but he did not live to read it; for he was burnt in his palace in the beginning of 1831. Kroma-khun, brother-in-law to the former king, a stern old man, called in my medical help, and I took occasion to converse with him on religious subjects. He greatly approved of Christian principles, but did not apply to the fountain of all virtue, Jesus Christ. In consequence of an ulcer in his left side, he again called in my aid; yet his proud son despised the assistance of a barbarian; neither would the royal physicians accept of my advice; and the man soon died. Even a disaster of this description served to recommend me to his majesty the present king, who is naturally fond of Europeans; and he entreated me not to leave the kingdom on any account; but rather to become an officer, in the capacity of a physician. Paya-meh-tap, the commander in chief of the Siamese army in the war against the Laos or Chans, otherwise written Shans, returning from his victorious exploits, was honoured with royal favour, and loaded with the spoils of an oppressed nation, near the brink of destruction. A severe disease prompted him to call me near his person. He promised gold, which he never intended to pay, as a reward for my services. And when restored, he condescended so far as to make me sit down by his side, and converse with him upon various important subjects....

In relating these facts, I would only remark, that I maintained intercourse with the individuals here mentioned, against my inclination; for it is burdensome and disgusting to cultivate friendship with the Siamese nobles. They used to call at midnight at our cottage, and would frequently send for me at whatever time it might suit their foolish fancies. At the same time, it must be acknowledged that, in this manner Providence opened a way to speak to their hearts, and also to vindicate the character of Europeans, which is so insidiously misrepresented to the king.

I will mention also a few individuals in the humbler spheres of life; but who profited more by our instructions than any of the nobles. Two priests—one of them the favourite chaplain of his majesty, the other a young man of good parts, but without experience—were anxious to be fully instructed in the doctrines of the Gospel. They came during the night, and persevered in their application, even to the neglect of the study of Bali, the sacred language, and of their usual services in Budhism. The elder, a most intelligent man, about twenty years of age, continued for months to repair with the Bible to a forest, boldly incurring the displeasure of the king. He also urged his younger brother to leave his native country, in order to acquire a full knowledge of Christianity and European sciences, so as afterwards to become the instructor of his benighted fellow-citizens; a Cambojan priest was willing to embark for the same purpose. Finally, a company of friends invited me to preach to them that they might know what was the religion of the Pharangs, or Europeans.

Charles Gutzlaff, *Journal of Three Voyages along the Coast of China in 1831, 1832, and 1833, with Notices of Siam, Corea, and the Loo-Choo Islands*, London, Westley and Davis, 1834, pp. 26–31.

31
The Funeral Pyre of the Late Second King

EDMUND ROBERTS

Edmund Roberts came as envoy of the United States in March 1833, following in the steps of Henry Burney (Passage 28). His visit occurred like so many visitors at a time of a royal funeral which prevented much serious discussion of business, even supposing the Siamese desired such, and Roberts himself was quick to see perceived offences to his dignity and person. Like Burney, his treaty (in duplicate in Siamese and English, with Portuguese and Chinese translations annexed), dated

20 March 1833, ratified by the King of Siam and Roberts on 14 April 1836, did not amount to much. The court was unwilling to consider seriously opening the country to outside trade.

Roberts seems to have spent far more time with the resident British trader, Hunter (see Passage 28), who liked the good life, than with his fellow nationals, who were all missionaries. The Dictionary of American Biography *claims that Roberts's mission 'was to be secret, and he was given as "ostensible employment" the position of clerk to the commander of the United States sloop* Peacock *at $1,500 a year'. His mission could hardly be disguised in Bangkok (a city, some maintain, without secrets), and he had ample opportunities to investigate, as instructed, the operations of the East India Company.*

*Roberts's observations are not as detailed as those of John Crawfurd (Passage 27), and his mission much less well prepared. They had only a Chinese interpreter, and, according to Moor (*Notices of the Indian Archipelago, *Singapore, 1837, p. 203), quoted by Sir John Bowring, the presents offered did not impress: 'The presents to the King consisted of a pair or two of beautiful watches set with pearls of some value, some silver baskets, and abundance of Chinese silks. To the Pra-Klang, also, Mr Roberts gave presents to a good amount, but he did not visit any of the inferior princes. The amount of the presents might be about two thousand to two thousand five hundred [Straits] dollars; while the returns consisted of a little sugar, sticklac, pepper, tin, gamboge benjamin, anguella-wood [eaglewood], sapan-wood and inferior cardamums; the whole of which might be worth one thousand or one thousand five hundred dollars. The Siamese knew the presents were bought in China, which did not please them much; and it is said that at one time they were not disposed to accept them. The original presents for the Cochin Chinese and Siamese Courts were sent out from America in a separate vessel, but she had not arrived in China ere the* Peacock *left. But this the Siamese would not credit.'*

Edmund Roberts was born in 1784 in Portsmouth, New Hampshire. His parents died young, and he was put in the care of an uncle, a merchant in Buenos Aires, who introduced him to the world of commerce and from whom he inherited a fortune. He chartered a brig to trade with

Zanzibar, got to know the Sultan of Muscat, and through relatives of his wife was sent on a mission to the Far East to negotiate commercial treaties. He returned to Portsmouth in 1834 and was ordered to ratify the treaties with Muscat and Siam, and negotiate treaties with Cochin-China and Japan. He fell ill after leaving Siam and died in Macao in 1836.

The record of his travels in 1833–4 'suffered from official censorship', according to The Dictionary of American Biography, *and the record of his last voyage appears in W. S. W. Ruschenberger's* A Voyage around the World: Including an Embassy to Muscat and Siam *(1838). Roberts's papers were deposited in the Library of Congress.*

Here is an extract dealing with the funeral pyre of the second king, the upparat, *an uncle of the king and a son of Phra Phuttayotfa (Rama I), who died in 1832; Phra Nangklao, later known as Rama III, was to leave the position unfilled.*

OUR object in visiting the left bank of the river, was to see an immense edifice, in the form of a temple, which was erecting for the purpose of burning the wang-na, generally called the second king, who died about six months since; and whose body has been embalmed, according to the imperfect knowledge of the Siamese in this art. The body is first washed, and then a large quantity of crude mercury or honey is poured into the mouth; it is then placed in a kneeling posture, and the hands are brought together before the face in the attitude of devotion; strips of cloth are then bound tightly round the extremities, and the body is compressed in a similar manner, for the purpose of squeezing out the moisture. It is then put into an air-tight vessel, more or less expensive, according to the rank of the deceased (some of the vessels are even made of gold); a hollow tube is inserted into the mouth, passes through the upper part of the box and the roof of the house, to convey away the effluvia; a similar tube is placed in the bottom, which communicates with a vessel, placed there to receive the draining from the body. The sordes thus collected, if they belong to a prince, are conveyed, with many ceremonies, below the city, and there emptied into the river. Should they belong to the king, they are boiled until an oil separates, and this is used on certain occasions (as when his family or his

A cremation pyre, from Henri Mouhot, *Travels in the Central Parts of Indo-China (Siam), Cambodia, and Laos* . . ., London, John Murray, 1864.

descendants pay their devotions to his departed spirit), to anoint the singular image, called Seina, which is generally placed in a temple, after his death. By the process, named above, the body, in a few weeks, becomes quite dry and shrivelled.

I am fully sensible that any description I can give of the building to which I have alluded, will fall far short of the reality; in fact no language can convey an adequate description of it. The *'tout ensemble'*, when viewed at a distance, glittering in gold and flowers, recalls to our recollection the brilliant and splendid castles of fairy-land, so bewitchingly set forth in many an idle work of former days. Many hundreds of people have been employed in its erection ever since his death; the centre building is a large open dome, and probably reaches to the height of eighty or ninety feet; it is supported by immense wooden pillars of teak all in one piece—the roof is of various indescribable forms, and differs from any I have ever seen—the parts rise one above another till it comes to a point; from the centre rises a high slender spire, and from the base to its apex cannot be less than one hundred and fifty feet; the roof is covered with brass leaf, which gives it a splendid appearance at a distance: it has a great number of projections with various singular ornaments on their edges and the inside of the roof is dome-shaped: beneath it was erected a small temple, in the same form, having in the centre a high platform, to which we ascended by a flight of steps, over which was a small spire: it is supported upon four pillars and cannot be less than thirty-five feet high—the roof is ornamented with neat carved work and richly gilt—on the platform the body is to be burnt. The whole inside of the building was painted to resemble flowers, profusely gilded, and otherwise richly decorated with gold and silver leaf—the walls were made of matting covered with paper and secured to bamboo-frames, as well as the outer covering, which was painted brown, decorated with large flowers made of brass or copper leaf and pasted on, which gave it a brilliant appearance. Eight temples, one fourth of the size of the great temple, stand about one hundred feet from it, so that the whole forms a complete square, of rather less than five hundred feet on each side; these are similarly gilt and painted, and are connected with each other by a corridor inside; the covering outside is similar to the great centre temple, being painted brown and overlaid with flowers. Around the base of all these buildings are projections of about three feet, like the base of a column, having imitation mouldings: these are overlaid again with sheets of brass leaf, as well as the cornices and architraves. The entrances to all the doors have a profusion of gilt and painted ornaments as well as the base, shaft, capital, and architrave of all the columns. The great building was surrounded at proper intervals (so as not to appear crowded) with small temples or sheds standing on four columns, and neatly gilt and ornamented. A wide space on the east side was left open, on which were erected very high narrow stages, neatly built, for the use of musicians, for the exhibition of rope dancers, tumblers, and gladiators, or sword fighters, pugilists, &c. At regular intervals were raised conical umbrellas or a series of canopies, the lower one being about six feet in diameter and each covering gradually lessening to the top, which terminated in a point—they were about thirty feet in height and alternately were of silver-leaf and brass-leaf, gilt, and ornamented with flowers. The whole ground and passages were covered in with bamboo framework, as well as the passage leading to the king's palace; the latter had a covered walk or roof of the same material extending the whole distance to the entrance within the enclosure. There were four entrances through long passages to the temple-altar or place of burning, and the whole building was surrounded with hideous images of men about a foot high, low dwarf-trees being interspersed between them, protected again by a low neat network railing of iron.

Edmund Roberts, *Embassy to the Eastern Courts of Cochin-China, Siam, and Muscat: in the US Sloop-of-War Peacock, David Geisinger, Commander, During the Years 1832–3–4*, New York, Harper and Brothers, 1837, pp. 242–4.

32
Chantaburi and a Fire in the Capital

FREDERICK ARTHUR NEALE

Frederick Arthur Neale was a gung-ho military person who spent his youth in Penang, served in India, found himself 'in the spring of 1840, a dilettante at Singapore, a waster of time and dollars', when he was invited to sail on a ship leaving for Bangkok. There, he seems to have spent much time in the 'factory' of the ever hospitable Mr Hunter, the British trader long established in Siam (one of whose claims to fame was bringing the original Siamese twins to the West), and he soon obtained a 'commission in the Siamese service as a naval and military officer at the same time'. The Siamese Navy in 1840 apparently comprised fourteen vessels, chiefly commanded and officered by Englishmen, who received, as Neale admits, 'handsome salaries'. As a first lieutenant, with a hundred Straits dollars a month, 'one day I was busy on board; another I was with the cavalry four or five miles in the interior; a third, occupied in drilling the Prince's own private bodyguard; a fourth, doing a little pioneering work; and so we rang the changes on the army and navy each week-day.'

The prince in question, whom he refers to as Prince Chou-Faa (Chudamani), was the younger brother of the future King Mongkut (Rama IV), who was to be appointed Second King in 1851 when the latter ascended to the throne. Neale paints an engaging picture of the prince (whose eldest son was called George Washington) as a slightly eccentric, charming, gifted, and extremely hospitable person, with an excellent command of English. Neale ended up as his aide-de-camp before returning to England in 1842.

By his own admission, Neale never travelled inland in Siam, apart from a trip to Ayutthaya and around the shores of the gulf. He has a marked attitude of Victorian superiority which is not always attractive, but a certain freshness and vigour which can be entertaining. He describes the Siamese as good-looking, apart from their brush-like hair-styles, he praises the gardens and fruits, he found Rama III corpulent and short of breath in the one audience he was granted, and cruel in his punishments.

After returning to London, Neale seems to have moved on to the Middle East, and published his 'first-born literary production', Eight Years in Syria, Palestine and Asia Minor, *as a consequence. He followed this with his work on Siam, having made notes while in the country and claiming 'a pretty retentive memory'. The publisher's selling-point that 'The engravings have all been prepared from drawings made in the country, and their accuracy may be relied on' has to be overlooked; not one looks like anything in Siam.*

Neale describes here the south-eastern settlement of Chantaburi (Chantiboon), which was later in the century to pass to the French for a time, and a fire in Bangkok.

AT length we came in sight of the tall elegant spire of the distant watt at Chanti Boon, which was glistening like a diadem of precious stones in the sunlight; five minutes more sailing brought us to a fine open part of the country where the embankments of the river were higher than heretofore, and where lofty tamarind trees grew in abundance. Selecting the most shady of these, we landed, and having dispatched the old man in his diminutive canoe to announce our advent, we bethought ourselves of breakfast, and had it forthwith. The neighbouring country was richly cultivated and strictly guarded, for several of the plants and trees in the neighbourhood were of that class that yield costly gums, amongst others the gamboge, benzoin, or frankincense; owing to this, not a cow or any kind of cattle was seen grazing on the rich pasturage, which was profuse indeed, lest they might injure the valuable trees, some of which were saplings that had not long since been planted. The guards, however, were permitted to allow their ponies to graze on these plots, securing them by a chain fastened round the right forefoot and riveted to a peg driven firmly into the ground.

I never saw a country in every respect more fitted for the rearing of the silk-worm than the district of Chanti Boon. The fine alluvial soil was just what would nurture the white mulberry, and cause it to attain to great perfection of growth; and the climate in the spring (the period when we visited it), was just of that temperature that would best suit the delicate and cautiously reared silk-worm....

The governor's house was pleasantly situated on the banks of the river, and commanded a fine view of the surrounding country. Unlike the other houses of officials that we had visited in Siam, this one was remarkable for its cleanliness; and the few nights that we slept on shore we revelled in the rare luxury of unexceptionable clean bed linen. Of all Oriental cookery, however, the Siamese is the most execrable and unwholesome; not from the want of the wherewithal to cook (for most certainly the pork and poultry were remarkably fine), but from want of *savoir faire*, and from the abominable practice they have of eating pickled garlic, and flavouring all their dishes strongly with this unsavoury condiment.

Now-a-days, it [Chantiboon] has become a quiet, thriving, populous mercantile town, every one in and about it wearing the look of affluence and contentment; and such soldiers as reside in the district, or are in cantonment in town, make oftener use of their arms in making those stabs from which the gum called gamboge exudes than in injuring either friend or foe. The natural barrier formed by the lofty range of mountains in the immediate vicinity of Chanti Boon, is a safeguard against the pillaging attacks of the Cochin Chinese, for which the Siamese ought to be very thankful; for without this nothing but a remnant of the large revenue annually yielded would ever enter the Government treasury.

The neighbourhood of Chanti Boon abounds with wild elephants, tigers, chetahs, and a vast variety of wild beasts, reptiles, and insects; of the two latter the most destructive being the cobra de capella and the Indian white ant, the former fatal to the life of man, the latter to his household goods and chattels.

Once during my prolonged sojourn at Bangkok I witnessed a fire on the river which threatened destruction to the whole city, and all the ships and other craft in harbour. A great deal of cocoa-nut oil is consumed by the Siamese for cooking and other purposes, and generally speaking each house is provided with one or more large-mouthed jars full of this ingredient for home consumption, consisting of inflammable matter. As the houses are constructed, it cannot be a matter of surprise that fire as easily catches as it is difficult to be extinguished. A careless party of boys who were fishing in the river by

The port of Chantaburi, from Henri Mouhot, *Travels in the Central Parts of Indo-China (Siam), Cambodia, and Laos* . . ., London, John Murray, 1864.

torchlight suffered the canoe to approach so near to some of the floating houses in one of those narrow little passages (which I have before alluded to as detrimental to the salubrity of the city, from the vast amount of filth there accumulated), that the torch ignited the thatched roof of one of the houses, which was instantly all in a blaze. Snatching away the torch from the delinquent's hand, who was wholly unaware of the mischief he had committed, another of the boys made an effort to fling it into the water, hoping that it would be instantly extinguished, and thus leave no clue to the discovery of the perpetrators of the deed; but in the struggle that ensued between the first boy, who imagined himself insulted, and the one who had snatched the torch away, the latter, in flinging it from his hand, missed his footing, and falling back into the water, sent the torch in an exactly opposite direction to what he had intended, and it, all blazing as it was, alighted on the roof of another house in the back row, and in less than two minutes a double row of streets was all in flames. The alarm of fire was instantly given by the Chinese junks in the harbour, who created a frightful din with their gongs, assisted in the noise by the bells of the European vessels. The watts [temples] in the neighbourhood caught up the strain, and eventually the great watt of the white elephant sounded its huge booming gong, which is somewhere about the size of a large round table. The city, which a few minutes before had been hushed in peaceful tranquillity, was now the scene of the greatest confusion and noise imaginable. There was the murmuring of thousands of voices, that came stealing upon the ear like the roar of distant water; lights were instantly seen moving in every direction; vessels were weighing their anchors or slipping their cables, and sailing up the river in the Yuthia direction, so as to be out of reach of the fast-approaching flames. The fire was on the opposite side of the water to our house, and appeared to us at that time to be not far from the Portuguese consulate; but distant as it was, so bright were the flames, that the whole place was perfectly illuminated, and we could plainly distinguish the smallest boat moving on the river. All the Europeans on our side of the river were assembled at Mr Hunter's wharf to witness this sad but grand spectacle, as also the American missionaries. One of these gentlemen, who was certainly never born to be a soldier, evinced the greatest symptoms of alarm and terror, though the fire was fully two miles away from us, and on the other side of the river; but he had fifty horrid conjectures to make—that some canoe, or boat, or vessel would come over all in flames, and ignite our side, and then his comfortable house and nice furniture would be all burnt. In the midst of these and many other lamentations of a very melancholy character, somebody chanced to ask him where Mrs R. (his wife) and his children were. 'Oh!' replied he, struck as it were all of a heap! 'well, I guess I quite *forgat* them; I calculate they are asleep;' and with this exclamation he bolted into his house, and opening the bed-room door, roared out '*fire!*' with all his might, and then bolted back to the jetty (wharf) again, looking as pale as though he had expected to find the wharf burnt down, and all means of escape cut off. His poor wife and children, who had been frightened nearly out of their wits, came tearing down to the jetty in the utmost alarm, and when the lady found the real state of affairs, she rated poor R. most soundly for his cowardliness, and for putting her into such an awkward predicament as to compel her to run out in what she called her *she maizey* (chemise). The ladies of the party and the greater number of Yankees, finding there was no immediate danger to be apprehended to their lives and properties, *calculated* that they would go to bed again, and accordingly went; but as for brother R., no earthly inducement could prevail on him to return to his house. It was a grand sight indeed to see the swarms of people that lined the floating houses on either side of the banks of the river for miles and miles; and when the King in his state barge came rowing down the river, as is his custom on any similar calamity, then in truth it was wonderful to see the prostrate thousands in attitudes similar to that of prayer, calling to the King to save them and their property from destruction,—as though his supposed celestial influence could arrest the fiery element in its direful progress. . . .

Thus did this simple and foolish people firmly believe that the interposition of their King was all-sufficient to keep them from harm, and to make the effect more impressive, the fire was almost instantly quelled by some of the court agents having resorted to the simple plan of cutting away the moorings of that row of houses that lay nearest to the flames, and these floating down the river, and kept off by men in boats with long poles, gradually gained the centre of the stream, when, being caught by the strong current setting in that direction, they were rapidly swept round a corner, and so disappeared. As for the flames, they burnt on till the last bit of timber of the last house was fairly consumed; and then the gap occasioned by the water fairly quenched their mischievous ire, and all was dark night again.

F. A. Neale, *Narrative of a Residence at the Capital of the Kingdom of Siam ...*, London, Office of the National Illustrated Library, 1852, pp. 111–14, 199–201.

33
Smallpox and Lying by the Fire

DR DAN BEACH BRADLEY

The name of the formidable Dr Dan Beach Bradley occurs at regular intervals in the mid-nineteenth century in writings about Siam. The American missionary who served many years in Siam published tracts and his own newspaper, the Bangkok Recorder, *on a printing press he imported, and frequently fulminated against the practices he deemed wicked in the country, notably concubinage and slavery. Several of his broadsides were personally answered (usually without revealing the source) by King Mongkut himself, who displayed unusual patience in dealing with what he must have considered a thorn in his side. Even Anna Leonowens (Passage 37) recognized that the 'newspaper strictures (not always just) and suggestions (not always pertinent) aimed at his administration of public affairs, or the constitution and discipline of his household' were an intrusion. She claimed, 'He snubbed them with sententious arrogance, leavened with sarcasm.' One wonders what else she expected him to do in the circumstances; he recognized the value of the medical and education services of Bradley and could hardly throw him in jail or out of the country.*

Bradley travelled extensively in Siam between 1835 (when he first came to the country) and 1846, and kept diaries of his stay in the country until his death in 1873 (the originals in twenty-five volumes are held in the Oberlin College Library in the United States). In this passage, he describes his attempt to introduce the practice of vaccination against smallpox, which, like cholera, ravaged the population in the first half of the nineteenth century.

ONE of the first questions asked me by the Phraklang when I came to Siam was whether I could always cure the smallpox. He was disappointed when I replied that I could not but hoped to be able to introduce the practice of vaccination to prevent the annual outbreak of the dreadful scourge.

There is no disease half so destructive of life among the Siamese as the smallpox, which rages among them three or four months every year without an exception. The season of its reign is November through February, which embraces the closing of the wet season and three months of the cool and dry season. It is almost impossible to find a family of some years standing here that has not been severely visited with the smallpox at a cost of two or three or more lives. A very large majority of the inhabitants are very thickly pitted by its ravages.

Almost from the beginning of my residence in Bangkok I had been receiving vaccine material from medical colleagues in Boston and Singapore, and for years my experiments with these specimens had led to naught. By 1838 I had almost given up the hope of introducing vaccination to Siam.

The year 1838 was a particularly severe one for smallpox in Bangkok. One night during that dread season, in the midst of my wakeful dreams the thought occurred to me that inoculation might be made an incalculable blessing to this people in the absence of vaccination. In the case of inoculation, a portion of diseased matter is introduced into a healthy individual in order to induce a mild form of the disease. In the case of vaccination, cowpox virus is employed for the purpose of producing immunity from the smallpox.

Inoculation had been practiced by the families of the Baptist Mission from the first, while the other families resorted to it as a partial substitute for vaccination. The perfect success with which it had recently pleased the Lord to follow the inoculation of the missionary children and several of the native children who were living in their families, seemed an encouraging earnest of the success of general inoculation in Siam, provided the native physicians and people could be properly instructed on the subject and would use the same precautions that we took in the case of our children. Hence it occurred to me that it might be a good plan to write a treatise on the art of inoculation, inasmuch as the King [Phra Nangklao, Rama III] and several noblemen had manifested a desire to be instructed on the subject. When I mentioned this to the Phraklang, he informed me of the King's support. I decided, therefore, to prepare such a treatise and publish a few hundred copies for the Siamese physicians. The thought that this plan might be the means of saving several hundred, perhaps thousands, of lives annually from a premature grave in Siam made me impatient to be about the task.

When His Majesty was informed of the successful inoculation of our children, he straightaway sent several of the Royal Physicians to receive instructions from me. The King sent several slaves with his physicians to provide ocular proof of the benefit of the plan. I gladly treated them as well as a number of the children of the nobles, and in every case I met with success.

My treatise was soon printed, and I found it a very great aid to me in giving instructions to those whom I inoculated. With each inoculation I left a book, and strictly enjoined that the directions must be obeyed. The tract was in very great demand, and all understood it with perfect ease.

Inoculation became the all-engrossing topic of conversation in Bangkok that season. Several thousands were inoculated with perfect success. Not one death occurred, even though smallpox contracted in the natural way is quite mortal. I could but regard this as a very remarkable fact. When was it ever heard that inoculation was attended with perfect success? The very best that had ever been hoped for in inoculation was that there should be only one or two deaths among five hundred persons inoculated, and that many of these would but only barely escape death.

In order to encourage the work of inoculation, the King offered a bounty of twenty ticals (that is, about twelve dollars) for a small quill of smallpox virus sufficient to inoculate twenty or thirty persons, and to the poor who were not able to procure medicines he gave money to help them through.

At the end of the season the Phraklang sent me word that His Majesty had sent to his care three changs of silver (one-hundred-and-forty-five dollars) for me. I was not at home when the message was left. I was very pleasantly surprised at it. Although I had often heard of the King's gratitude for my public services, I little thought that I would ever see it take any other form than mere words. The Second Phraklang sent his servant to conduct me to his house to receive the royal bounty. I went and was received with particular respect. A dish of fine coffee, which was then a rare beverage in Siam, was prepared expressly for me. Some of the nobles and rulers were beginning to use it in imitation of foreigners. The Phraklang knew that I was accustomed to its daily use and had it provided for me.

He then sent for the bag of ticals just as it had come from the King's hands, counted them before my eyes, and presented them in the name of His Majesty, saying, 'His Magnificent Majesty presents this sum of money to thee, the American Doctor, as a testimony of his gratitude for thy most benevolent services in teaching the Royal Physicians the art of inoculation and thy success in bringing into Siam this great boon which has already saved many lives.'

In response I said to him, 'I, the American Doctor Bradley, beg to write a letter and bring it to the Royal Feet, to inform his Magnificent Majesty that I, having written a treatise on inoculation for smallpox and having with profound reverence presented it to thee, have now received thy royal present. Thy power and thy favor protect my head and person perfectly. Thy servant has received the favor, most highly respecting it. Now thy servant designs to keep the royal present for the purpose of defraying the expenses of writing a book on midwifery and various other medical and surgical works, with a view to distributing it among the royal and people's physicians that it may be for the advantage of the people of Siam universally; that they may increase in prosperity, health, and happiness.'

The Phraklang read it and replied, 'It is good. His Majesty much desires a work from you on midwifery. It will be a great favor, for the poor Siamese mothers suffer exceedingly by lying by the fire.'

I told him that there was every reason to believe that Siamese women in childbed could be treated after the American and English customs as successfully as the Americans and English themselves. He replied that he believed this to be the case, because it had been clearly proven that inoculation is as good for the Siamese as for the English.

The thought that Asian people are somehow radically different in internal structure from Englishmen and Americans had operated as an almost insuperable obstacle to innovations by the missionaries in obstetrical practice. The women were exceedingly tenacious of their cruel old way, and in fact outside the upper class they remain so today. They judged that the miseries of lying by the fire a month for every birth of a child were incomparably better than to suffer for all their lives with desires, as they fully believed they must, if they did not follow this custom. They were all ready to acknowledge that missionary wives were infinitely more happy than were those who had to endure the fire; but they believed that this was because such women were not born in Siam and hence were exempted from this curse.

I continued to regard inoculation as a poor substitute for vaccination, and believed that I must persist in my attempts to produce a vaccine. Success came providentially in 1840. On January 22, 1840, I began experimenting with a specimen of vaccine virus sent out by Dr S. V. C. Smith of Boston. He was ardently desirous that vaccination might become successful in Siam. I had so many times vainly tried to introduce it that I had absolutely no hope for its success; but I could not refuse to comply with the benevolent request of Dr Smith to do my best in trying with this virus. Accordingly, I called on the Phraklang and prevailed upon him to allow me to vaccinate some of his children. I vaccinated ten of his little ones and sixty-five Malay captives whom he gave me as subjects.

Nine days later I discovered to my great joy that five persons had apparently taken the disease. Every one of the five had been vaccinated from a scab that I had moistened with rain water and introduced with the point of a lancet. Those whom I vaccinated from the quill had all failed, as did most of those I vaccinated from the scab. From the five that took it, I vaccinated some fifteen or twenty Malays. From the child of Brother Robinson, whom I had also vaccinated, I vaccinated my infant child, a little Siamese school girl, and our colleague Miss Pierce.

A week later I visited the Phraklang with Miss Pierce, the Hemenways, and my wife. My chief object was to show a beautiful specimen of kinepox [cowpox] on the arm of Miss Pierce, and to induce the Phraklang to lend his special influence to propagate the kinepox among the Siamese generally. He was a good deal pleased with the sight, and he presented Miss Pierce with a bunch of flowers. I requested him to let me vaccinate those of his children who had not taken it. He immediately called them. Just at that moment the man who had charge of the Malays brought in a report that some of the slaves had contracted smallpox after I had vaccinated them, that one had died, and that others were very sick. This story frightened the Phraklang so much that he dared not let me vaccinate again in his family.

I assured him that there was some mistake in the story, and I went myself to investigate the matter. I saw nearly all those whom I had vaccinated, but found not one who had taken the smallpox. I returned and reported the same to the Phraklang, who therewith ordered his physicians to collect a number of his children and have them vaccinated. Accordingly, in the evening, the physician came to my compound with five children to be vaccinated. Prince Mongkut sent five persons also, and by the permission of Prince Chutamani I vaccinated one of his little daughters.

These experiments were so successful that His Majesty requested me to vaccinate in the palace of his brother and to instruct the physicians in the method. The series continued successfully into the month of May.

The following January, I determined that it was my duty to memorialize the King on the subject of vaccination so that he might have the whole of the coming dry season to reap the benefit of it. Having consulted with my brethren I engaged in the work with much ardor and nearly completed a long communication, showing first what was accomplished by vaccination the previous spring in order that His Majesty might refer to these successful cases for proof of the efficacy of the cowpox; and second, giving him the sum of two letters I had recently received from Drs Reynolds and Hale of Boston, giving full proof that the true vaccine virus could be procured by inoculating a cow with smallpox virus; and third, urging that some immediate and efficient measures be taken by the Royal Physicians to procure the matter and vaccinate through the Kingdom during the next dry season.

The Phraklang soon informed me that the King had perused my memorial on vaccination with much pleasure and was desirous to have me experiment on some cows and would provide me with the subjects. The Phraklang sent the owner of a flock of cows to me for the experiment and said that the cows, although on the other side of the river, should be brought across in boats if I so desired. My efforts to produce the kinepox locally proved unsuccessful on that and subsequent occasions, however, and we had to depend upon external sources of vaccine matter. A description of my futile attempts may be of some interest nonetheless.

Following my unsuccessful experiments in 1841 I returned the next season to the keeper of the King's cows, and was happy to find that he was ready for me to inoculate as many calves as I pleased, that he would do precisely as I might wish during the time of experimentation. I was surprised to find that it was the King's order to the Phraklang and the Phraklang's to him two years earlier that made him ready for me now. He was still feeling the force of that order. He regarded it as burdensome, but said that it was His Majesty's command and he could not but grant all my wishes. I went early in the morning taking with me some very finely pulverized scabs of smallpox. The subject of my experiments were two calves less than a year old. By means of a quill I blew some of the powder into the nostril of each after the manner of the Chinese inoculation for smallpox. I then shaved and scarified a place as large as a twenty-five cent piece and rubbed in a paste of the powder and put on a plaster of the same. I also scarified several places at the side of the *labia pudenda* of each and rubbed in a paste of the same there.

This experiment failed, and so when I was able to acquire another suitable specimen I took a capillary syringe and sucked a goose quill nearly half full and re-inoculated one of the calves and one cow three or four years of age. I made about seven free punctures in the side of the *labia* and then deluged each puncture by forcing the virus in by my small syringe. I then introduced a small seton of silk thoroughly wet with the virus into two of the udders of each.

Once again my hopes were dashed, but fortunately we were able frequently thereafter to vaccinate successfully with matter sent into Bangkok from Singapore.

I printed my treatise on midwifery in 1843, with excellent illustrations by a Siamese artist, and my tract on vaccination in 1844. These books I consider among the most useful we have ever published.

Because we were unable to obtain smallpox vaccine through my efforts in 1842, or through importation from outside Siam, we determined to resort to the method of inoculation among the missionary families. I procured the necessary matter in time to treat all the children except my daughter, Harriet, an infant eight months of age. We discovered too late that she had already contracted the disease, and after two weeks of increasing agony she breathed her last on December 30th. Despite my success in saving hundreds and perhaps thousands of lives throughout Siam, I was unable to protect my own beloved child from the dread disease.

William L. Bradley, *Siam Then: The Foreign Colony in Bangkok Before and After Anna*, Pasadena, California, William Carey Library, 1981, pp. 57–62.

34
Ayutthaya, Lopburi, and Phra Phutthabat

JEAN-BAPTISTE PALLEGOIX

Jean-Baptiste Pallegoix's two-volume Description du Royaume Thai ou Siam *was published in Paris in 1854. It was not translated into English, perhaps because Sir John Bowring's classic work,* The Kingdom and People of Siam, *appeared so soon after, in 1857, quoting extensively from it.*

Bowring himself writes that 'in 1830 a great impulse was given to Catholic missionary exertions by the nomination of

Monsieur Pallegoix, Bishop of Mallos, as Apostolic of Siam'. Pallegoix travelled widely in the country, and knew it well. He became a good friend of Prince Mongkut when the future king was still a monk, and Pallegoix's death in 1862 was greatly mourned by the king. The last years of Monseigneur Pallegoix's life were spent working on a Siamese–Latin–French–English dictionary. Bowring speaks of the 'touching report, made by Bishop Pallegoix, of the destruction and desolation which he found to have visited the former seat of Catholicism when he reached Ayuthia, in 1831'.

Pallegoix was by all accounts a saintly man, though his unremitting labours were scarcely rewarded by converts; the total number of Catholics in Siam in the mid-1850s was estimated to be 7,050 (including descendants of Portuguese and Vietnamese, and 600 'dispersed and in slavery')—not that the Protestant missions could claim greater success.

The first two extracts relate journeys to Ayutthaya and Lopburi made by Pallegoix as part of his mission, both places sadly fallen since their days of glory. The last extract is in Sir John Bowring's translation, and describes the journey to the pilgrimage site of Phra Phutthabat to see the Buddha's footprint there.

IN the environs of Juthia [Ayutthaya] the river divides into a number of canals, so many that it is easy to get lost. That which was properly the city is an island three leagues around, with the shape of a Chinese purse. I have covered in all directions the vast ruins which cover the surface of this island; the most remarkable are those of the palace and the royal pagodas, where there are still some colossal statues 50 or 60 feet high; the inside of the statues is made of brick and the outside of bronze, about two inches thick. According to the annals of Siam, one of these statues was made with 25,000 pounds of copper, 2,000 pounds of silver and 400 pounds of gold. The walls are all overturned, and this immense pile of ruins is covered with impenetrable bushes and shaded by ancient Indian poplars, the abode of brown owls and vultures. These ruins hide the huge treasures buried at the time of the taking of Juthia; people dig there all the time and are nearly always successful.

The new town is around the ancient city; it comprises two rows of floating shops and a population of 40,000 souls composed of Siamese, Chinese, Lao and Malays. The province of Juthia is extremely fertile in rice and abounds in excellent fish. A league to the north of the town, in the middle of the plain, is a majestic edifice called the Golden Mountain, built in 1387[1] in our era. It is an immense square pyramid about 400 feet high; each side has a fine stairway by which one reaches the broad galleries which look out all around. When you are at the third level, you have one of the finest views imaginable. At this height, there are four corridors which lead to the inside of the dome, where a large gilded Buddha statue raised on an altar has for its protection and adoration millions of bats, which continually cover it with their fetid excrement, and, flying both day and night, make a great twittering, or rather an infernal din. The dome, which is admirably built, rises 150 feet further above the galleries, and ends in a handsome and well-gilded spire....

The following day, we arrived at the foot of the mountains, and I went to install myself in the house of the chief of a Lao village, who readily received me. Seeing that there were neither pagodas nor talapoins [priests] in this village, and moreover that the inhabitants seem well disposed towards the Christian religion, I resolved to stay there. All the children and young people having offered me their services, in four days my small bamboo chapel was complete. There, every evening, instruction was given followed by prayer; in the daytime, I went into the forest to visit the neighbouring villages.

Three leagues from the place where I was, on an arm of the river and at the base of very picturesque mountains, is the celebrated town called Nophaburi [Lopburi], founded in the year 600 of our era,[2] and which was for a long time the capital of a small kingdom. If one were to judge by the ruins of its walls, its palaces and other buildings, and by the great number of pagodas still standing, one is convinced that it was a populous, rich and powerful town. I went to visit the

[1]The temple attached to the spire dated from 1387, but the spire itself in its present restored form dates from the eighteenth century.

[2]The date of the foundation of the earliest town of Lawu is not known.

palace of the famous Constance [Phaulkon] who reached the rank of chief minister in 1658;[3] a pretty little Christian church can be seen there;[4] the altar had gilded fluted columns and is surmounted by a baldachino on which is written in letters of gold *Jesus hominum salvator.* The talapoins have placed a Buddha statue on this altar and came to install themselves in the apartments of Constance; but according to the pagans themselves, as many came, died, so that today they have definitely abandoned the place. Before the ruin of Juthia, the kings of Siam took up residence in Nophaburi during the flood period and amused themselves above all in hunting elephants. The hills in the neighbourhood are planted with *ates* (or sweet-sop fruits) and excellent bananas; in the mountains there is game of all kinds; the river and the canals are full of fish which attract flocks of pelicans, wild ducks, storks, herons and other aquatic birds. The fertile plain produces good crops of rice, so that one can call this province an enchanted land, where abundance and happiness reside.

I engaged a guide, mounted an elephant, and took the route of Phra-bat [Phra Phutthabat], followed by my people. I was surprised to find a wide and excellent road, paved with bricks, and opened in a straight line across the forests. On both sides of the road, at a league's distance, were halls or stations, with wells dug for the use of the pilgrims. Soon the road became crooked, and we stopped to bathe in a large pond. At four o'clock, we reached the magnificent monastery of Phra-bat, built on the declivity, but nearly at the foot of a tall mountain, formed by fantastic rocks of a bluish colour. The monastery has several walls surrounding it; and having entered the second enclosure, we found the *abbé-prince*, seated on a raised floor, and directing the labours of a body of workmen. His attendants called on us to prostrate ourselves, but we did not obey them. 'Silence!' he said; 'you know not that the *farang* honour their grandees by standing erect.' I approached, and presented him with a bottle of sal-volatile, which he smelt with delight. I requested he would appoint some one to conduct us to see the vestige of

[3]Phaulkon came to Siam in 1678, and rose to power shortly after 1680.
[4]See Passage 15 by Tachard.

Buddha; and he called his principal assistant (the *balat*), and directed him to accompany us. The *balat* took us round a great court surrounded with handsome edifices; showed us two large temples; and we reached a broad marble staircase with balustrades of gilded copper, and made the round of the terrace which is the base of the monument. All the exterior of this splendid edifice is gilt; its pavement is square, but it takes the form of a dome, and is terminated in a pyramid a hundred and twenty feet high. The gates and windows, which are double, are exquisitely wrought. The outer gates are inlaid with handsome devices in mother-of-pearl, and the inner gates are adorned with gilt pictures representing the events in the history of Buddha.

The interior is yet more brilliant; the pavement is covered with silver mats. At the end, on a throne ornamented with precious stones, is a statue of Buddha in massive silver, of the height of a man; in the middle is a silver grating which surrounds the vestige, whose length is about eighteen inches. It is not distinctly visible, being covered with rings, ear ornaments, bracelets, and gold necklaces, the offerings of devotees when they come to worship. The history of the relic is this:—In the year 1602, notice was sent to the King at Ayuthia, that a discovery had been made at the foot of a mountain, of what appeared to be a footmark of Buddha. The King sent his learned men, and the most intelligent priests, to report if the lineaments of the imprint resembled the description of the foot of Buddha, as given in the sacred Pali writings. The examination having taken place, and the report being in the affirmative, the King caused the monastery of Phra-bat to be built, which has been enlarged and enriched by his successors.

After visiting the monument, the *balat* escorted us to a deep well cut out of the solid stone: the water is good, and sufficient to provide for crowds of pilgrims. The abbé-prince is the sovereign lord of the mountain and its environs within a circuit of eight leagues; he has from four to five thousand men under his orders, to be employed as he directs in the service of the monastery. On the day of my visit, a magnificent palanquin, such as is used by great princes, was brought to him as a present from the King. He had the civility to entertain us as well as he could. I remarked that the kitchen was under the care of a score of young girls, and they gave the name of pages to the youths who attended us. In no other monastery is this usage to be found.

His highness caused us to be lodged in a handsome wooden house, and gave me two guards of honour to serve and watch over me, forbidding my going out at night on account of tigers. The following morning I took leave of the good abbé-prince, mounted my elephant, and taking another road, we skirted the foot of the mountain till we reached a spring of spouting waters. We found there a curious plant, whose leaves were altogether like the shape and the colours of butterflies. We took a simple breakfast in the first house we met with; and at four o'clock in the afternoon we reached our boat, and after a comfortable night's rest, we left Tha Rua to return to our church at Ayuthia.

Mgr. J.-B. Pallegoix, *Description du Royaume Thai ou Siam*, Paris, Mission de Siam, 1854, pp. 84–7, 94–6; Sir John Bowring, *The Kingdom and People of Siam*, London, Parker and Sons, 1857, Vol. I, pp. 161–4.

King Mongkut and His Land (1851–1868)

35
Private Audiences with the King

SIR JOHN BOWRING

Sir John Bowring was a remarkable person. Born in 1792 and educated privately, he became fluent in most Western and Eastern European languages (as well as Arabic and Chinese), and as early as 1820 produced a volume of translations of Russian poetry. He became co-editor of the influential Westminster Review, *advocating Benthamite radical views, including the abolition of slavery, prison reform, and free trade (he produced a biography and definitive edition of Bentham's works in eleven volumes in 1843). He was a Member of Parliament from 1835 to 1837 and again from 1841 to 1847. He was also a successful hymn writer, and introduced the first decimal coin (the two shilling piece) in Britain. He was appointed Consul in Canton in 1847 and in 1854 became Minister Plenipotentiary to China, accredited to Japan, Siam, Cochin-China, and Korea, and at the same time served as Governor and Commander-in-Chief of Hong Kong, posts which he held for nine years. Near the end of his time there, Bowring and his wife were nearly poisoned by bread laced with arsenic, part of an attempt to kill Hong Kong residents in the prelude to the 1857–8 hostilities against the Government of China. He returned to England early in 1859 to remain active in public affairs, dying in 1872 at the age of eighty.*

In his posthumous Autobiographical Recollections *(1877), he considered his mission to Siam in 1855 as one of the most interesting parts of his life. The result of his mission was the famous 'Bowring Treaty', to serve as a model for most other powers, replacing the old system of export and import monopolies with virtually free trade. He was not above hinting at the use of force to obtain his ends, but in spite of that managed to establish a warm relationship with King Mongkut, then in the fourth year of his reign and anxious to prepare his country for inevitable reform.*

Bowring read carefully before his mission, and assembled the results of his reading and his own observations in Siam in a two-volume work (published in 1857), as important in its way as La Loubère's account of the country in the seventeenth century. As David Wyatt has correctly pointed out in his introduction to a reprint of Bowring's book, in 1969, 'for a man who spent scarcely a month in Bangkok, The Kingdom and People of Siam *is an unexpectedly lengthy and comprehensive work'. It drew heavily on the recently published text of Bishop Pallegoix, and on textual material supplied by King Mongkut himself (for the history of the country). It also includes the little-known account of a Spanish mission to Siam in 1717 (see Passage 21) (which Bowring translated himself). Given here is Sir John's account of his first and second private audiences with the king.*

I am located in the building called the English Factory; but the building has been reconstructed, and put in good order for my reception. I occupy two apartments above—a sitting-room, large and airy, and a bed-room, which has been newly papered, in which I sleep in a bed which is ornamented with drapery of cloth of scarlet and gold, and from which garlands of flowers are suspended. Jars of fresh water are placed on my table, with bouquets of roses; and a Siamese servant speaking English has me in special charge.

The *Rattler* arrived at one o'clock, and fired a salute of twenty-one guns. The King had requested that some of his officers might be present to witness the salute, and they are afterwards to go on board the *Rattler*. As far as I can learn, the arrangements for my entertainment have been confided to the care of Mr Hunter.

In the afternoon, wandered through the streets and into some of the temples of Bangkok. Many of the women were employed in yellowing their children with turmeric. Does the appropriation of this colour for the garments of the talapoins [monks] give it a peculiar value in the eyes of the people? The walls of the temples are covered with paintings, religious and historical. The priests were never uncivil, but often looked at us with a vacant, uninterested stare. It is their profession to be indifferent to worldly things, and the *show* of contemplation is, to a great extent, the *substance* of religious character. When that character resolves into self-abstracted musings, what is its real value to mankind? It is but gross egotism, evidencing the religious sentiments in no benevolent or beneficent shape; for who is the better for the unrevealed thoughts or undivulged meditations even of the profoundest philosophers?

The King's boat arrived at a quarter before eight p.m. to convey me to the palace; and on landing at the wooden pier on the other side of the river, I was conveyed by eight bearers in an ornamented chair to the first station. It was a semi-official reception. The troops were drawn out in several parts of the palace. We were escorted by hundreds of torch-bearers through a considerable extent of passages and open grounds, passing through gates, at each of which was a body of guards, who 'presented arms' in European fashion. When we reached one of the outer buildings near the palace walls, a brother of the Phra Kalahom [Minister of the South and military affairs] met us, and we were desired to wait the pleasure of the King. Two golden ewers containing pure water were brought in, and a note from his Majesty desiring I would leave my companions, H. S. P. and J. C. B., until they were sent for: I was to come on alone. The major-general marched before me, and told me that within the palace about a thousand persons resided, but that in the ladies' part there were no less than three thousand women. The abject state of every individual exceeds belief. While before the nobles, all subordinates are in a state of reverent prostration: the nobles themselves, in the presence of the Sovereign, exhibit the same crawling obeisance. After waiting about a quarter of an hour, a messenger came, bearing a letter for me, and a pass, in the King's hand, allowing me to pass the guards; and I was informed that without such credentials no individual could approach. It was a beautiful moonlight, and in an open space, on a highly-ornamented throne, sat his Majesty, clad in a crimson dress, and wearing a head-dress resplendent with diamonds and other precious stones, a gold-girdle, and a short dagger splendidly embossed and enriched with jewels. His reception of me was very gracious, and I sat opposite his Majesty, only a table being between us. The King said ours was an ancient friendship, and I was most welcome. His Majesty offered me cigars with his own hand, and liqueurs, tea, and sweetmeats were brought in. An amicable conversation took place, which lasted some time....

On reaching the reception place, the King came forward. Two little children of the King were playing on a crimson and gold carpet, who screamed at my approach, and were taken away. They seemed to wear nothing except wide-brimmed hats, which covered their heads. He took me to his private apartments, ornamented with beautiful pendules and watches, statues of Queen Victoria and Prince Albert, handsome barometers, thermometers, &c. He then led me through two or three small chambers, where were fine specimens of Chinese porcelain services, and other costly decorations. Almost everything seemed English. There were many new books on the shelves. The King spoke of the history of Siam, and said it was rather obscure and fabulous, but that the more veracious portion went back about five hundred years; that the Siamese alphabet had been introduced about that time. Inscribed on the apartments to which his Majesty had conducted me, were the words 'Royal Pleasure' in English, and in Sanscrit characters with the same meaning. He asked if I should like to hear Siamese music. On my answering yes, a number of young people (I could not distinguish the boys from the girls) played some rather pretty and plaintive airs, and interluded them with songs, which were less wild and monotonous than I should have expected. His Majesty then conducted me to the hall of audience, leading me by the hand wherever we went, amidst the prostrate nobles, crawling about, or bending their heads in the dust in his presence. A good deal of the conversation was repetition of the assurances of his personal esteem for me; but I fear in all a system of do-little, or as little as possible, policy, which I must meet either by obtaining what I can without delay; or, if what I can obtain be not worth the visit, I shall put off the treaty altogether, and consider this visit as one of courtesy, preliminary to a more important one hereafter....

The King inquired about the discovery of the planet Neptune: said, 'You have two terms,—one, the vulgar—leap-year, and another, the classical—bis-sextile,—when February has twenty-nine days.' He mentioned both the Latin and English names for the signs of the Zodiac—explained to me that the sacred days of the Siamese were those of the four quarters of the moon. He said he had a small magic lantern, but not a good one. He inquired if it were true that the Cochin Chinese having received the thanks of Queen Victoria for kindness to wrecked seamen, had sent a golden lion in return for those thanks. He said he should write a history of his times in English; and I offered him the aid of Mr Bell, but he did not welcome the suggestion. He gave as a reason for having fixed Monday for the audience, that the astrologers had declared it would be an auspicious day. The King closed the conversation rather abruptly, as I am told is his habit, saying it was late—half-past ten p.m.

Sir John Bowring, *The Kingdom and People of Siam*, London, Parker and Sons, 1857, Vol. II, pp. 268–71, 279–81.

36
In Procession with a White Elephant and Travelling through the North-East

HENRI MOUHOT

The explorer and naturalist Henri Mouhot is chiefly famous for being credited with the discovery of the ruins of Angkor, something he never claimed, for he was well aware that he was not their discoverer. The ruins had been known about in the West from the sixteenth century, and at least four persons had visited them in the nineteenth century before Mouhot, three leaving accounts of what they had seen. But Mouhot undoubtedly was the person who, with his detailed descriptions and illustrations, which became instantly famous (Anna Leonowens was to plagiarize them in 1870), marked the Western consciousness of the importance of the site.

Mouhot was born in Montbéliard, France, in 1826, and at the age of eighteen went to Russia and Poland for ten years, teaching French in the military academy at St Petersburg. He became interested in the new science of photography, and travelled through Europe with his brother, selling daguerrotypes with some success. Both brothers came to England, married relatives of the explorer Mungo Park, and settled in Jersey in 1856. Mouhot seems to have come across a copy of Bowring's book on Siam, published in 1857, which sufficiently fired his imagination to sail from London, in April 1858, for Singapore and thence Bangkok.

Mouhot travelled widely in Siam, Cambodia, and Laos. He spent as little time as possible in the capital, preferring to add to his collection of fauna in the wilds. He wandered in the hills around Saraburi, took in Chantaburi, spending some time in the hills there, before going through Cambodia, and, after a side trip to Petchburi, then embarked on a final journey through Korat (which province covered a vast area of what is now the north-east) and Loei to Luang Prabang, near where he died at the age of thirty-five of a fever, attended only by his two faithful servants, in November 1861.

Mouhot's discoveries in the natural sciences were important; he had a squirrel, a tortoise, a spider, and a beetle named after him. His first collection of specimens was unfortunately lost at sea, but undeterred he at once started another. His sketches and photographs of his travels greatly helped the fame of his posthumous account of his travels, which were first published serially in French in the Tour du Monde *in 1863 before a definitive edition in English appeared the following year.*

Since Angkor is now part of Cambodia, given here are extracts of his writings on the north-east, which is another of his claims to fame, as the first explorer to move through and write about those parts. It was not an easy journey, and eventually cost him his life. A reserved and solitary person, though nevertheless quick to inspire confidence in others, his letters show him devoted to his family. Also quoted here are passages from letters to his wife and brother describing the capture and treatment of a white elephant, whose procession from Korat (officially known as Nakorn Rajasima) towards the capital he fell in with. This last is given first.

[*To his wife Annette, at Saraburi, 24 February 1861*]

I arrived at Korat after a tedious and troublesome journey, for I had only a few oxen for my baggage, and was forced to walk myself. From there I went to Chaiapume [Chaiyaphum], and here an animal of the mandarin species made himself great, and under the pretext of having no elephants refused me the means of going further, and was so rude and impolite to me that I determined at once to return and protest against the very insufficient protection which had been granted to me. Indeed, I could do nothing else, not being able to go on. The elephant which had brought me to Chaiapume took me back to Korat, and there I found a mandarin from Bangkok, who had been sent to fetch a white elephant which had been taken in Laos. I begged him to let me join his party, and he lent me two elephants, one for my servant and luggage, and one for myself. I left Phrai at Korat, with the greater part of my possessions, having hired a room for him in the house of a Chinese, and a week afterwards found myself back at Saraburi, in company with this strange divinity (who, by the way, had more black then white about him), and of the grand personage who had been sent to escort him, and who had showered on him every kind of attention during the journey. He had an escort of fifty foot soldiers and several on horseback. As for me, I wanted for nothing; at every halt the mandarin sent me ducks, fish, fruit, sweet-meats, &c., and he was also kind enough to allow me eight men as night-guards to watch round my fire. In return, I discovered for him in the mountains large quantities of copper, and even gold, which delighted him.

The whole province of Saraburi was in motion to do honour to the white elephant; the King and all his court are coming here; the ministers are here already to watch over him. I decided, therefore, to apply to the Siamese, hoping to obtain more from them than from the Europeans; and

View of the mountains of Korat, from Henri Mouhot, *Travels in the Central Parts of Indo-China (Siam), Cambodia, and Laos* ..., London, John Murray, 1864.

yesterday, hearing of the arrival of Khrom Luang, the King's brother, I hastened to address myself to him. He, however, had only passed through, and was gone to Prabat, to join the King. However, I found here the man I wanted, the mandarin who has most interest in Laos, and without a letter from whom it would have been difficult to proceed. I did not know him, but I went to him to ask about the Prince, and told him what I wanted. 'I am your man,' said he; 'the Prince can only give an order for me to write a letter, such as I will give you, if you like.' I accepted gladly, and promised him in return my double-barrelled gun, which I could easily replace, 'if he would only furnish me with the means of travelling through Laos without expense, and would bring the Chaiapume mandarin to reason'. The poor governor of Saraburi was with us, and had to remain more than an hour amidst a number of others kneeling on the bare ground, while I was seated on the mat of the mandarin, by his side, eating sweetmeats and drinking tea, while he dictated a letter in which he called the governor of Chaiapume a fool, and threatened to deprive him of his office, and of this letter I was to be the bearer; and he promised me another general one on the morrow, in which he stated that if I did not receive efficient aid it might bring on a war; and this he also repeated to all the chiefs present. My cause was gained. . . .

[*To his brother*]

From Korat to Bangkok you know that I travelled in company with an animal who has a title equal to that of the greatest Siamese mandarin, and who was served by two inferior mandarins, who gave him his meals composed of cakes, biscuits, and sweetmeats out of golden dishes; and who had slaves sent before him to clear the way and cut down the brushwood and branches, for this elephant, according to the Siamese superstition and ignorance, possesses the soul of some deceased prince or king. They called him a white elephant, but in reality he had only a few spots of that colour on his body. Alas! The king and all his mandarins are now in mourning, for the object of their worship died of indigestion. Poor beast and poor king!

The entire province of Korat comprises a number of villages, and more than eleven towns, some containing as many as fifty or sixty thousand inhabitants. This little state is simply tributary, but on condition of furnishing the first and most considerable levy of men in case of war.

The tribute consists of gold or silver, and in several districts, amongst others those of Chaiapume and Poukiéan [Phu Khieo], amounts to eight ticals a head. Some pay in silk, which is weighed by the mandarins, who, as with the cardamom at Pursat, and the *langoutis* at Battambong, buy a further quantity on their own account, and at their own price....

I was again delayed a few days at Korat before I could obtain elephants, in consequence of the absence of the viceroy; but on his return he received me in a friendly manner, and gave me a letter of introduction to the governors of the provinces under his jurisdiction. He likewise furnished me with two elephants for myself and servants, and two others for my baggage; so at last I was able to set out for Chaiapume....

I was, however, much better received on my second visit to Chaiapume.... The sight of the elephants and the order from the viceroy of Korat made the mandarin as supple as a glove, and he provided me with other elephants for a visit to some ruins existing about 3 leagues north of the town, at the foot of a mountain. The superstitious Laotians say that these ruins contain gold, but that every one who has sought for it has been struck with madness.

Two roads lead from Chaiapume to Poukiéan, the first, across the mountains, is so excessively difficult, that I decided on taking the other, which, however, is much longer. The first day we started at 1 o'clock, and reached a village named Non Jasiea [?], where we were overtaken by a fearful storm. We sheltered ourselves as well as we could, and arrived before night at the entrance of a forest where we slept.

For five days we were compelled to remain in the forest on account of the weather; it rained great part of the day, and throughout the night; the torrents overflowed, and the earth was nothing but a sea of mud. I never in my life passed such wretched nights, as all the time we had to remain with our wet clothes on our backs, and I cannot describe what we suffered. The snow hurricanes, so frequent in Russia, and which nearly killed me when in that country, seemed trifling miseries in comparison. My poor Phrai was seized with a dreadful fever two days before reaching Poukiéan, and I myself felt very ill.

The passage of the mountains was easy, and the ascent very gradual; blocks of stone obstruct the road in various parts, but our oxen and elephants made their way without much difficulty. I had bought a horse for myself at Korat.

The vegetation, though not thick, is beautiful: the trees, many of which are resinous, are slender; the stems being seldom more than a foot or two in diameter, and often 25, 30, and even 40 metres in height. Under their shade are to be seen great numbers of deer, and tigers are not uncommonly met with. In the mountains are many elephants and rhinoceros. We found immense beds of stone, and in some places saw small brick buildings containing idols. During the journey one of my chests was thrown to the ground by the movements of the elephant, and broken to pieces, as, unfortunately, were all the contents, consisting of instruments, and bottles of spirit of wine containing serpents and fishes.

Poukiéan is a smaller village than Chaiapume. I met with a friendly reception from the governor, who had just returned from Korat, and had heard of my intended journey. Poverty and misery reign here; we cannot find even a fish to purchase; nothing but rice; and as soon as my faithful Phrai is on his legs again we shall leave the place.

Tine-Tine attracts the most attention. The people do not, as we pass, cry out first, 'Look at the white stranger,' but 'A little dog!' and every one runs to see this curiosity. My turn comes afterwards.

In these mountains the Laotians make offerings to the local genii of sticks and stones....

In all this mountainous region elephants are the only means of transport. Every village possesses some, several as many as fifty or a hundred. Without this intelligent animal no communication would be possible during seven months of the year, while, with his assistance, there is scarcely a place to which you cannot penetrate....

All this eastern portion, with the exception of a few villages filled with 'black-bellied savages'—so called from the manner in which they tattoo themselves—is inhabited by the same race, the 'white-bellied Laotians', who call themselves Laos, and are known by this name to all the Siamese, Chinese, and surrounding nations.

The black-bellied or western Laotians … tattoo the under part of the body, principally the thighs, and frequently wear the hair long and knotted on the top of their heads. Their language is nearly the same, and differs little from the Siamese and Eastern Laos, except in the pronunciation, and in certain expressions no longer in use among the former. …

Most of the villages are situated about a day's journey from one another, but frequently you have to travel for three or four days without seeing a single habitation, and then you have no alternative but to sleep in the jungle. This might be pleasant in the dry season, but, during the rains, nothing can give an idea of the sufferings of travellers at night, under a miserable shelter of leaves hastily spread over a rough framework of branches, assaulted by myriads of mosquitoes attracted by the light of the fires and torches, by legions of ox-flies, which, after sunset, attack human beings as well as elephants, and by fleas so minute as to be almost invisible, which assemble about you in swarms, and whose bites are excessively painful, and raise enormous blisters.

To these enemies add the leeches, which, after the least rain, come out of the ground, scent a man twenty feet off, and hasten to suck his blood with wonderful avidity. To coat your legs with a layer of lime when travelling is the only way to prevent them covering your whole body.

Henri Mouhot, *Travels in the Central Parts of Indo-China (Siam), Cambodia and Laos during the Years 1858, 1859, and 1860*, London, John Murray, 1864, Vol. II, pp. 258–9, 270, 115, 120–2, 125–6, 129–30.

37
Meeting King Mongkut and the First Day of Teaching

ANNA LEONOWENS

Anna Leonowens led two lives, a fact only recently discovered; three lives, if one includes the grossly erroneous version shown in the film 'The King and I'. Once in Bangkok, she gave out she was born in Wales in 1834, the daughter of an Indian army captain and the recent widow of another military officer, and ruined by bank failures resulting from the Indian Mutiny. In distress, then, and needing to support her two young children, she took the post of schoolmistress (which she always termed governess) to the children of King Mongkut.

Her real background was less romantic. She was born three years earlier than she held, in 1831, in a barracks in Ahmadnagor, India, of a cabinetmaker turned enlisted man married to Ann Glasscock, who was possibly Eurasian. Her father died before she was born, and her mother quickly remarried. Anna (christened Ann Harriett Edwards) seems to have received her education in a barracks school in India, and, at fourteen, managed to attract the attention of an assistant chaplain, the Revd Badger, who took her with him on a tour of the Middle East. She married a clerk in the Military Pay Office in Bombay, Thomas Leon Owens, in 1849 who sired three children (one died young), and travelled with him to Australia, England, and Malaya, where he died of apoplexy, in Penang.

In Bangkok, Anna was undoubtedly snubbed by the British consulate staff and their wives. She, in turn, snubbed the sea captains (one of whom was still asking for her hand when she left Bangkok), and her only friends seem to have been the wives of the American missionaries, whose views she espoused, probably genuinely, on polygamy, slavery, and other evils (as they saw them) then common in Siam. She by no means saw eye to eye with her employer, King Mongkut, who had been enlightened enough to employ, for the first time, a foreign lady teacher full-time in the palace, and who came to regard her as 'one great difficulty'. When her health broke down (she says), she decided to leave. Another reason was that she had received no increase in salary, and had her daughter Avis to support at school in London. She left in November 1867, went to England, put her son Louis in boarding-school, and sailed with her daughter for New York, where she taught for a time. In need of money, she put together her Siamese experiences, with as much imagination and plagiarism as truth, and published them in 1870.

Her book brought her instant success, and she tried to follow it in 1872 with a sequel, The Romance of the Harem, *which had even less regard for verisimilitude than its predecessor. Anna met the leading American literary personalities, including Harriet Beecher Stowe, whom she greatly admired, and was much in demand as a lecturer in the New World, where her less than glorious family background would have been, had it not been carefully concealed, of little or no account. She followed her daughter on her marriage to a Scottish banker to Halifax, Nova Scotia, and settled down to small town life in Canada. She found time to write two more books, neither a great success, and went to Russia in 1881 commissioned to write a series of articles on the country. She accompanied her granddaughter to Germany where she went to study music, while Anna studied Sanskrit in Leipzing. On her return, to Montreal this time, still following the steps of her daughter and son-in-law, in 1897, she managed to get an appointment as lecturer in Sanskrit in McGill University, giving her last lecture when she was seventy-eight. She died in Montreal in 1915.*

Given that so much of what she wrote in her recollections of Bangkok cannot be relied upon, and her travels outside the capital non-existent (her supposed journey to Angkor is a fabrication), selections from her most famous work have to be handled gingerly. She is unlikely to have invented much, though, about her first meeting with King Mongkut (there was a witness, Captain Bush), and about the early days of teaching in the palace, which extracts follow.

CAPTAIN B—(who, by the by, is a titled nobleman of Siam) introduced me as the English governess, engaged for the royal family. The king shook hands with us, and immediately proceeded to march up and down in quick step, putting one foot before the other with mathematical precision, as if under drill. 'Forewarned, forearmed!' my friend whispered that I should prepare myself for a sharp cross-questioning as to my age, my husband, children, and other strictly personal concerns. Suddenly his Majesty, having cogitated sufficiently in his peculiar manner, with one long final stride halted in front of us, and, pointing straight at me with his forefinger, asked, 'How old shall you be?'

Scarcely able to repress a smile at a proceeding so absurd, and with my sex's distaste for so serious a question, I demurely replied, 'One hundred and fifty years old.'

Had I made myself much younger, he might have ridiculed or assailed me; but now he stood surprised and embarrassed for a few moments, then resumed his queer march; and at last, beginning to perceive the jest, coughed, laughed, coughed again, and in a high, sharp key asked, 'In what year were you borned?'

Instantly I struck a mental balance, and answered, as gravely as I could, 'In 1788.'

At this point the expression of his Majesty's face was indescribably comical. Captain B—slipped behind a pillar to laugh; but the king only coughed, with a significant emphasis that startled me, and addressed a few words to his prostrate courtiers, who smiled at the carpet,—all except the prime minister, who turned to look at me. But his Majesty was not to be baffled so: again he marched with vigor, and then returned to the attack with *élan*.

'How many years shall you be married?'

'For several years, your Majesty.'

He fell into a brown study; then, laughing, rushed at me, and demanded triumphantly:—

'Ha! How many grandchildren shall you now have? Ha, ha! How many? How many? Ha, ha, ha!'

Of course we all laughed with him; but the general hilarity admitted of a variety of constructions.

Then suddenly he seized my hand, and dragged me, *nolens volens*, my little Louis holding fast by my skirt, through several sombre passages, along which crouched duennas, shrivelled and grotesque, and many youthful women, covering their faces, as if blinded by the splendor of the passing Majesty. At length he stopped before one of the many-curtained recesses, and drawing aside the hangings, disclosed a lovely, childlike form. He stooped and took her hand (she naïvely hiding her face), and placing it in mine, said, 'This is my wife, the Lady Talap. She desires to be educated in English. She is as pleasing for her talents as for her beauty, and it is our pleasure to make her a good English scholar. You shall educate her for me.'

I replied that the office would give me much pleasure; for nothing could be more eloquently winning than the modest, timid bearing of that tender young creature in the presence of her lord. She laughed low and pleasantly as he translated my sympathetic words to her, and seemed so enraptured with the graciousness of his act that I took my leave of her with a sentiment of profound pity.

He led me back by the way we had come; and now we met many children, who put my patient boy to much childish torture for the gratification of their startled curiosity.

'I have sixty-seven children,' said his Majesty, when we had returned to the Audience Hall. 'You shall educate them, and as many of my wives, likewise, as may wish to learn English. And I have much correspondence in which you must assist me. And, moreover, I have much difficulty for reading and translating French letters; for French are fond of using gloomily deceiving terms. You must undertake; and you shall make all their murky sentences and gloomily deceiving propositions clear to me. And, furthermore, I have by every mail foreign letters whose writing is not easily read by me. You shall copy on round hand, for my readily perusal thereof.'

Nil desperandum; but I began by despairing of my ability to accomplish tasks so multifarious. I simply bowed, however, and so dismissed myself for that evening.

On the Thursday appointed for the opening of my classes in the palace, one of the king's barges conveyed us across the Meinam. At the landing I was met by slave-girls, who conducted me to the palace through the gate called Patoo Sap, 'Gate of Knowledge'. Here I was received by some Amazons,[1] who in turn gave notice to other slave-girls

[1]The common (foreign) term for female guards at the palace.

waiting to escort us to a pavilion—or, more correctly, temple—dedicated to the wives and daughters of Siam. The profound solitude of this refuge, embowered in its twilight grove of orange and palm trees, was strangely tranquillizing. The religion of the place seemed to overcome us, as we waited among the tall, gilded pillars of the temple. On one side was an altar, enriched with some of the most curious and precious offerings of art to be found in the East. There was a gilded rostrum also, from which the priests daily officiated; and near by, on the summit of a curiously carved trunk of an old Bho tree, the goddess of Mind presided.

The floor of this beautiful temple was a somewhat gaudy mosaic of variegated marble and precious stones; but the gilded pillars, the friezes that surmounted them, and the vaulted roof of gilded arabesques, seemed to tone down the whole to their own chaste harmony of design.

In the centre of the temple stood a long table, finely carved, and some gilt chairs. The king and most of the nobler ladies of the court were present, with a few of the chief priests, among whom I recognized, for the first time, his Lordship Chow Khoon Sah.

His Majesty received me and my little boy most kindly. After an interval of silence he clapped his hands lightly, and instantly the lower hall was filled with female slaves. A word or two, dropped from his lips, bowed every head and dispersed the attendants. But they presently returned laden, some with boxes containing books, slates, pens, pencils, and ink; others with lighted tapers and vases filled with the white lotos [*sic*], which they set down before the gilded chairs.

At a signal from the king, the priests chanted a hymn from the 'P'ra-jana Para-mita';[2] and then a burst of music announced the entrance of the princes and princesses, my future pupils. They advanced in the order of their ages. The Princess Ying You Wahlacks ('First-born among Women'), having precedence, approached and prostrated herself before her royal father, the others following her example. I admired the beauty of her skin, the delicacy of her form, and the subdued lustre of her dreamy eyes. The king took her gently by the hand, and presented me to her, saying simply, 'The

[2]'Accomplishment of Reason', or 'Transcendental Wisdom' [Author's note].

English teacher.' Her greeting was quiet and self-possessed. Taking both my hands, she bowed, and touched them with her forehead; then, at a word from the king, retired to her place on the right. One by one, in like manner, all the royal children were presented and saluted me; and the music ceased.

His Majesty then spoke briefly, to this effect: 'Dear children, as this is to be an English school, you will have to learn and observe the English modes of salutation, address, conversation, and etiquette; and each and every one of you shall be at liberty to sit in my presence, unless it be your own pleasure not to do so.' The children all bowed, and touched their foreheads with their folded palms, in acquiescence.

Then his Majesty departed with the priests; and the moment he was fairly out of sight, the ladies of the court began, with much noise and confusion, to ask questions, turn over the leaves of books, and chatter and giggle together. Of course, no teaching was possible in such a din; my young princes and princesses disappeared in the arms of their nurses and slaves, and I retired to my apartments in the prime minister's palace. But the serious business of my school began on the following Thursday.

On that day a crowd of half-naked children followed me and my Louis to the palace gates, where our guide gave us in charge to a consequential female slave, at whose request the ponderous portal was opened barely wide enough to admit one person at a time. On entering we were jealously scrutinized by the Amazonian guard, and a 'high private' questioned the propriety of admitting my boy; whereat a general tittering, and we passed on. We advanced through the noiseless oval door, and entered the dim, cool pavilion, in the centre of which the tables were arranged for school. Away flew several venerable dames who had awaited our arrival, and in about an hour returned, bringing with them twenty-one scions of Siamese royalty, to be initiated into the mysteries of reading, writing, and arithmetic, after the European, and especially the English manner.

It was not long before my scholars were ranged in chairs around the long table, with Webster's far-famed spelling-books before them, repeating audibly after me the letters of the alphabet. While I stood at one end of the table, my little Louis at the other, mounted on a chair, the better to command his division, mimicked me with a fidelity of tone and manner very quaint and charming. Patiently his small finger pointed out to his class the characters so strange to them, and not yet perfectly familiar to himself.

Anna Harriette Leonowens, *The English Governess at the Siamese Court, Being Recollections of Six Years in the Royal Palace at Bangkok*, London, and Cambridge, Mass., Trübner, 1870, pp. 57–9, 83–5.

38
Photographing the King and Visiting a Bangkok Prison

JOHN THOMSON

John Thomson was a Scottish photographer who spent a short time in Siam, and was called to photograph King Mongkut. Born in Edinburgh in 1837, he was one of two surviving sons of a successful tobacco trader. His elder brother William moved to Singapore in 1859 as a watchmaker and photographer, and John joined him within two years. John spent some time in Penang, and in September 1865 went to Siam, arriving in Bangkok on the Chao Phya *steamer (the same which took Anna Leonowens (Passage 37) to the Siamese capital four years earlier, and was to take the Marquis de Beauvoir two years later (Passage 39)). Thomson was away six months from Singapore, during which time he went to Angkor to photograph the ruins made famous by the publication, in 1864, of Mouhot's explorations and illustrations. He returned to Edinburgh in 1866 to write articles on photography in the tropics, and published a book of photographic prints,* The Antiquities of Cambodia *(1867).*

In 1867, he returned to Singapore, went to Vietnam, then moved to Hong Kong in 1868, to supply photographs of Chinese life and occupations to the China Magazine. *He married in 1868 in Hong Kong a lady met two years earlier in*

Edinburgh, but his brother, wife, and son returned to Britain in 1870, leaving Thomson in Hong Kong to photograph China, in which he travelled widely, and its people.

Returning again to Britain in 1872 and settling in London with his family, he started to produce a series of travel books on the Far East illustrated by his own photographs. He also collaborated with Adolphe Smith on the famous Street Life of London *(1877–8). Already a Fellow of the Royal Geographical Society, by 1878 he had six children and needed a steady income. He set up his own studio in the West End, and was appointed a photographer to the royal family by Queen Victoria. He continued to write papers, give lectures, exhibit his works, and follow events in China until his death in 1921 at the age of eighty-four.*

Several of Thomson's photographs of Siam were used by Anna Leonowens (without full acknowledgement, and getting his name and the captions wrong). He records his travails in trying to photograph a moving buffalo with the equipment of the time, which required a stationary object. Thomson in Siam saw the usual sights, and apart from going on the canals of Bangkok and overland to Cambodia also went, like Henri Mouhot before him (Passage 36), on a trip to Petchburi, but in the company of the 'venerable' Dr Bradley (Passage 33). He naturally penetrated the grand palace to photograph King Mongkut, and his impressions of the occasion are given below. As a reward he was invited to the royal tonsure ceremony. His visit to the public executioner, however, was out of the ordinary.

I applied, through the British Consul, for permission to photograph the first King's palace. This was at once conceded, and his majesty was pleased to appoint a day on which I should take his own portrait as well. The King requested me to visit his abode on Monday, October 6, in the company of the Krum-mun-alongkot, a nobleman holding the position of chief astronomer, that is, the head of the astrologers attached to the palace. His majesty's letter informed me, among other things, that his royal brother 'was well understanding of the work of taking photographs, and being with Mr Thomson will have good opportunity to do according to his pleasure in and about this palace'. Here was indeed a fine sample of 'Siamese king's English'....

In front of the entrance gates we found a guard of soldiers drawn up, who presented arms to the Prince as he passed through. Soon we reached an inner court, and there fell in with a group of nobles, who crouched upon the pavement before our royal guide, and seemed, many of them, as if vainly anxious to render their portly figures invisible to a personage of such exalted rank. After a pleasant refreshment of fruit, cake, and wine, we were informed that his majesty was engaged in his morning devotions, and that during his absence we could amuse ourselves by examining the objects of interest in the audience hall. This palace has been constructed partially in a foreign style. A flight of broad marble steps conducts us within the audience hall, and facing us, as we enter, is the throne of state, ablaze with gold and jewels, and erected in the centre of the back wall of the apartment. The furniture in the room made up a miscellaneous collection of Chinese, Siamese, and European wares; the pillars were covered with polished brass to the height of four feet above their bases. At one end of the hall were life-sized portraits of Napoleon III and the Empress of the French, while a well-executed picture of the late Siamese King adorned the opposite side of the apartment. A shrill blast of horns heralded the approach of the King, and caused us hastily to descend into the court. His majesty entered through a massive gateway, and I must confess that I felt much impressed by his appearance, as I had never been in the presence of an anointed sovereign before. He stood about five feet eight inches, and his figure was erect and commanding; but an expression of severe gravity was settled on his somewhat haggard face. His dress was a robe of spotless white, which reached right down to his feet; his head was bare. I was admiring the simplicity and purity of this attire, when his majesty beckoned to me to approach him, and informed me that he wished to have his portrait taken as he knelt in an attitude of prayer. I accordingly adjusted my instrument, but not without a feeling of some surprise, for I had thought, incorrectly, as I afterwards discovered, that a Buddhist had no need of prayer. All was prepared beneath a space in the court, which had been canopied and carpeted for this special purpose; when, just as I was about to take the

King Mongkut 'dressed in a sort of French Field Marshal's uniform', photograph by John Thomson, 1865.

photograph, his majesty changed his mind, and without a word to anyone passed suddenly out of sight. I thought this a strange proceeding, and fancied I must have given him some offence; but it was possibly only one of his practical jokes. I appealed to the Prince; but his reply was simply that 'the King does everything which is right, and if I were to accost him now he might conclude his morning's work by cutting off my head.'

As that would have been a result distasteful to his royal highness, we patiently waited, and at length the King re-appeared, dressed this time in a sort of French Field Marshal's uniform. There was no cotton stuff visible about his person now, not even stockings. The portrait was a great success, and his majesty afterwards sat in his court robes, requesting me to place him where and how I pleased. I consulted the Prince, who said—'Yes, place him, but do not for the life of you lay hands on him, more especially on his thrice sacred head.'

Here was a difficulty. How to pose an Oriental potentate who has ideas of his own as to propriety in attitude, and that, too, without touching a fold of his garments? I told the King, in plain English, what I wanted to do, and he said, 'Mr Town-shun, do what you require for the excellency of your photograph.' He enquired my nationality. I told him I was born in Edinburgh. 'Ah! you are Scotchman, and speak English I can understand; there are Englishmen here who have not understanding of their own language when I speak.'

I shall never forget the scene I witnessed inside a Bankok prison. The public executioner lived close by, so we paid him a visit before we entered the jail. He was a hideous-looking fellow, but proudly conscious of his brawny chest and sinewy arm, that with one fell swoop of the sword had closed many a luckless criminal's career. He readily produced his fatal weapon, bright with recent polishing, passed his fingers lightly, nay, almost lovingly along its sharp-edged blade, grinned, and disappeared. I meanwhile watched his retreating figure, and then took a long breath. I thought the fellow eyed me professionally; he certainly looked at my neck, which was thicker than the average of those with which he had commonly to deal. In one part of the prison grounds men heavily ironed, and covered, one or two of them, with old sores, were making bricks in a mud pool. Some had been in chains for years, and their condition reminded me of pictures of the Buddhist hells which I had seen on the walls of their temples. The air was filled with the wails of distress and the clank of fetters. Seated on a bench there was a condemned woman, who had been implicated in a murder. She seemed to be treated with mercy, and even indulgence, as she wore no chains but those which bound her to a pretty little child that lay smiling and crowing in her lap, and struggling to bring back the sunshine to its mother's worn and haggard brow. It was afterwards reported that she had been reprieved, partly for the sake of the child; and I can readily believe the rumour, as the King had a passionate affection for his own children, and devout Buddhist potentates deem it a merit rather to save life than to take it away.

J. Thomson, *The Straits of Malacca, Indo-China and China, or Ten Years' Travels, Adventures and Residence Abroad*, London, Sampson Low, Marston, Low, and Searle, 1875, pp. 88–9, 92–5, 102–3.

39
The River at Bangkok and a Farewell Visit to King Mongkut and His Wives

MARQUIS DE BEAUVOIR

The Marquis de Beauvoir is perhaps the first genuine tourist to leave an account of Bangkok as he found it in 1867, when he stayed for a week in January. He was only twenty at the time of his visit, and while he apparently carried no camera, he made use of early photographs in his published account of his visit.

He was brought up in England during the Second Empire, with the descendants of the deposed Oléanists, after the overthrow of Louis-Philippe. He accompanied the ex-king's grandson, the Duc de Penthièvre (son of the Prince de Joinville), on a tour of the world, leaving London in April 1866 and returning in September 1868, accompanied only by an aide-de-camp, Captain Fauvel. The first part of his Voyage autour du Monde *(1872) appeared as* Java–Siam–Canton *in 1869, and both went through many editions. The English translation appeared in 1870, without illustrations.*

Beauvoir and his party took the venerable Chao Phya *steamer to Bangkok from Singapore, stayed in the French Catholic Mission, and saw all there was to see: Wat Aroon, Wat Po, Wat Saket (for its exposed bodies and vultures; see Passage 47), the royal palace, where they were twice received by King Mongkut and even taken into the reserved female quarters, as well as being given the ritual tour of the royal elephant stables (during which they managed to obtain hairs of the white elephant). They also visited the palace of the late Second King, saw his funeral pyre, a* likay *performance, the royal barges, and visited the Prime Minister.*

They were young men out to have a good time. They were often convulsed with laughter at the incongruities they witnessed, and were less than reverent in respect of King Mongkut, who clearly they nevertheless loved for his eccentricities. The king was not at first sure how to receive them. He was on the worst of terms with the impossible French Consul, Aubaret (he eventually demanded his withdrawal), but the Duc de Penthièvre himself lived in exile from Napoléon III, whose agent was Captain Aubaret. The duke decided not to call on the consul, though Beauvoir and Fauvel did eventually, on their third day. Aubaret reported this on 18 January, lying on two counts to his Ministry of Foreign Affairs, saying that he had rendered the marquis and the captain 'chancellery services' and that they and the duke were staying at 'a nasty English hotel'.

Ludovic Hébert, Marquis de Beauvoir, was born in Brussels in 1846 where his father was King Louis-Philippe's chargé d'affaires. He was taken by his father into exile in England in 1848, but returned to France during the Franco-Prussian War of 1870–1. He served in the army during the seige of Paris, and was decorated. He joined the Ministry of Foreign Affairs in 1873, becoming deputy principal private secretary to the minister, the Duc Decazes, in 1876, but resigning in 1879 to work for the Duc d'Aumale, Louis-Philippe's fourth son, and then serve as head of the guard of honour to the Count of Paris, Louis Philippe's first son. He retired to Marseilles and died in 1929.

BEHIND a bend of the Me-Nam (the mother of the waters), the entire town of Bangkok appeared in sight. I do not believe that there is a sight in the world more magnificent or more striking. This Asiatic Venice displays all her wonders over an extent of eight miles. The river is broad and grand; in it more than sixty vessels lie at anchor. The shores are formed by thousands of floating houses, whose curiously formed roofs make an even line, while the inhabitants in brilliant-coloured dresses appear on the surface of the water. On the dry land which commands this first amphibious town, the royal city extends its battlemented walls and white towers. Hundreds of pagodas rear their gilded spires to the sky, their innumerable domes inlaid with porcelain and glittering crystals, and the embrasures polished and carved in open work. The horizon was bounded to right and left by sparkling roofs, raised some six or seven stories, enormous steeples of stone work, whose brilliant coating dazzled the eyes, and bold spires from 150 to 200 feet in height, indicating the palace of the king, which reflected all the rays of the sun like a gigantic prism. It seemed as though we had before us a panorama of porcelain cathedrals.

The first general view of the Oriental Venice surpassed all that we could have hoped for in our travellers' dreams. We longed to get into gondolas and go through the lively canals which are the streets of the floating town, and where the bustle, animation, and noise bewildered us. And then shall we be permitted to see these sacred pagodas, these royal palaces?

Going back along the river, we could not contain our admiration of the wonderful effect of the roofs, and the glittering spires and points of which I have spoken to you. But suddenly our oarsmen threw down their paddles and prostrated themselves flat on their stomachs on the benches. What was the matter? We were in sight of the King's palace, and of the quay where he embarks. When in front of it, all the Siamese must bow down, and worship the abode of their sovereign, while great nobles and princes of the blood shut up their umbrellas. If they infringe this law, the sentinels from a post which commands the river have orders to punish them by firing at them out of their air-guns. We landed and enjoyed walking round a great public square, upon which the chief door of the royal residence opens. It is of white stonework; groups of columns in pairs support immense capitals of nine crowns placed one above the other, from which rises a spire more than forty feet high, bold and tapering. The whole is studded with thousands of rose-shaped designs in red, green, yellow, and sky-blue porcelain, which the setting sun lights up like fairy-land. On each side

The city of Bangkok, engraving from a photograph by John Thomson, *Illustrated London News*, 25 May 1867.

'elephant wharfs' stand out, with white marble balconies, whose grand and severe style of architecture contrasts with the fanciful character of the other designs. When the King goes out, these are his steps, whether he mounts the colossal animals or gets into a palanquin. At the end appear the pointed roofs of the centre palace, whose polished tiles are dazzling. The beams of the roof, carved in sandal-wood, and cut in delicate lacework, overhang and protect glittering gables; all sorts of lights were thus reflected. It was an endless prism of splendid decorations....

But while we were watching two regiments of Siamese infantry, dressed in French uniforms, and playing at ball in the public square, round piles of air guns much bigger than themselves, suddenly the drum beat a salute, the soldiers ran to arms, though much inconvenienced by shoes, the population crouched down as if by a magic blow, and a procession

advanced, announced by whirlwinds of dust. It was the King. We were about seventy paces from the road he was coming to his palace. Drums, two detachments of infantry, and a whole swarm of mandarins dressed in brilliant silks jogged along before him. He was carried in a gilded palanquin inlaid with mother-of-pearl, by sixteen men dressed in blue silk; and two large white umbrellas, at the end of inconceivably long handles, sheltered him beneath their wavering and changing shadow. The king was bedizened all over with gold chains, and surmounted by a gilt crown, which looked like a high extinguisher. His suite consisted of some fifteen young princes, mounted on gaily decked ponies, and another palanquin in ivory and lacquer held a whole heap of his daughters. But the procession passed at a smart trot, with such a crowd of mandarins, female slaves, umbrella bearers, and halberdiers that we remained behind bewildered; the moment the King saw us, he signed graciously to us with his hand....

Soon it was our turn to go in; the king looked radiant. After having asked the identical same questions that we had answered the other day, about our age, where we lived, and the date of our leaving Europe, he began to talk with inconceivable volubility. He took the Duc de Penthièvre's arm, put on his fingers one of his own great rings of plaited gold, 'very very pure gold of Siam', and led him from the throne room to his private apartments; he was quite brisk and lively to-day, it was very evident he was no longer afraid of us. Mumble, mumble, mumble, a short period during which he munched a little pink fresh sugar-plum.[1] 'Me love' (then came a few words in Siamese); 'very, very' (again a pause, during which the ball passes from the royal mouth into a new golden vase), 'very much your high high highness, me will' (mastication becomes frantic); 'give Sieraklas my photograph to to to'—he misses the spittoon—'to you,' and so on. I wish I could speak Siamese as he speaks English, but I cannot tell you the quantity of Siamese, half Latin and half French words, which were quite unintelligible to us, with which he interspersed the few English words I quote. So he went on, holding the prince's hand affectionately between his, while as for us, we followed in silence through great halls sparkling with brilliancy, amongst a troop of laughing children, who seemed very much delighted with the Europeans. By some signal favour ... we were permitted to cross the threshold of the harem! Groups of fifteen or twenty women taken by surprise by this unexpected visit, instantly threw themselves down on the coloured mats which covered the floor, supporting themselves on their elbows and knees, and looking terribly frightened. There must have been 160 of them, some taking refuge on the steps of the winding staircases, on the projecting balconies, or in kiosques joined to the rooms by marble bridges; others again fled to the shady avenues in the garden. Through the chinks of half-open doors sparkled bright eyes, animated with the liveliest curiosity. Some of them were ancient matrons, with baggy, dried-up skins, who squatted down on one side in their short yellow skirts; then

[1]The young marquis did not apparently realize the king was chewing a betel quid.

there were gentle nymphs of a chocolate colour, languid young Sultanas, with a ribbon, narrower than the width of a hand, worn across the shoulder instead of a boddice, a little blue scarf, and diamonds on their necks, hands, and feet, who crowd together like bees in a hive.

Then this drone king stepped towards the group of the elder queens, and taking one of them by the hand, he dragged her, alarmed and trembling, towards us; he held the Sultana's arm in his right hand, and one of ours in his left, and thus we were permitted to touch her hand with the tips of our fingers. I do not wish to be disrespectful, but in any other part of the world this ancient houri would be called an old hag. 'Good woman,' said the king to us, as he dismissed her after this Asiatic mode of shaking hands, 'she has presented me with three children.' Then he went to fetch another, and the same joining of the first fingers was gone through with the second lady. 'Excellent woman,' he continued, 'she has given me ten!'....

Gradually our escort was increased by some thirty of Paramendr-Maha-Mongkut's sons, each one more lively than the other, and then the sacred portals of the chapel belonging to the harem were thrown open. It is, in miniature, as rich and beautiful a pagoda as any in the town; every one must go in bare-footed. The king made all the statuettes and precious stones shine out in the dimness by lighting with his own hand before us numbers of wax lights, and we especially remarked a god made of rock crystal, two feet high, with a ruby belt, and a pointed crown of diamonds.

The audience closed at about four in the afternoon, in the throne room, where, filled with delight and gratitude, we took leave of the worthy king Mongkut; we embraced the little princes, and saluted the harem....

The Marquis de Beauvoir, *Java–Siam–Canton*, London, John Murray, 1870; the section on Siam reprinted as *A Week in Siam, January 1867*, Bangkok, Siam Society, 1986, pp. 11–12, 20–2, 78–81.

Travellers and Residents in King Chulalongkorn's Reign (1868–1910)

40
New Roads in the Capital and an Old Road to Prachinburi

FRANK VINCENT

If the Marquis de Beauvoir (Passage 39) was the first tourist proper, he was soon followed by Frank Vincent, who was there neither on official mission, nor for business, nor to work, but simply to see the place. Vincent was a well-heeled New Englander, born in Brooklyn in 1848, son of a prosperous trader. He entered Yale in 1866, but because of poor health only completed two semesters. He decided to travel, and his first journey, begun in 1871, took him to Japan, China, South-East Asia, and India, the result of which was his first book, The Land of the White Elephant, *published in 1874.*

This secured him an honorary MA from Yale in 1875, and he went on to acquire membership of numerous scientific and literary societies, as well as to continue his travels, in Scandinavia, South America, and Africa, all of which he wrote about. He left a piece of sculpture acquired in Angkor to the Metropolitan Museum of Art, married his cousin when over sixty, and died, notwithstanding his earlier ill health, in 1916 at the relatively robust age of sixty-eight.

It cannot be said that his observations were always accurate (he maintained, for example, that 'an absurd custom prevails, which requires that at the close of each reign all the temples and most of the palace buildings shall be torn down and new ones erected in their place'). He is on safer ground when he quotes Sir John Bowring, which he does extensively. Through the American Consul, General Partridge, Vincent had an audience with the Second King (known sometimes by the name of George Washington) and the Regent, Chao Phraya Sri Suriwongse. He did not meet King Chulalongkorn, who was visiting India at the time, so he did not see the royal palace.

In fact, Vincent saw little of Siam outside the usual sights of Bangkok, where he stayed at 'Falcks' Hotel' in the company of German skippers, and the by then standard side trip to Petchburi (for the palace, the 'cave of idols', and the nearby Lao village). He travelled overland to Angkor though, passing through Prachin and Kabin en route *to Siem Reap, in the company of the American Consul and the missionary McFarland (he of lexicographic fame), together with two servants, an interpreter, and Deng, the Chinese cook formerly in the employ of Henri Mouhot.*

Extracted here are his comments on the 'new macadamised road' in the capital, and the beginning of his overland journey to Angkor, at first by boat to Prachinburi, and then on horseback.

HAVING pretty extensively traversed the city by water, one day some friends proposed a horse-back ride to the palace walls and back. We rode over a good, macadamised road, built by the late Supreme King, to the main entrance of the palace, where we saw a battalion of native troops exercising. Halting for a few moments, we observed that their drill and evolutions were performed with rapidity and exactness. Their uniform consisted of yellow coats and blue trousers, with white canvas caps (navy pattern); their feet were bare, and their weapons were muskets and swords of European design and manufacture. The palace walls, fifteen feet high by twelve in width, with a notched parapet, and the trees conceal most of the buildings within, though we noticed some such lofty structures as a clock-tower, also some *wats* [temples], pagodas, and 'sacred spires'. The native houses have been torn down and cleared away for some considerable distance around the walls, and it is intended that this space shall be neatly turfed or arranged in parks and flower gardens. At one corner of the palace enclosure we passed the royal (black) elephant stables—a dozen in number—the 'white' elephant being housed within the walls. The gates of the palace are built of simple teak wood, embossed with huge nails, but they are neither strong nor handsome.

Near this part of the city the late King has laid out several streets at right angles to each other, and built upon them compact blocks of two-storey brick houses, which are now rented by the Government (the King?) to the people. The present King has followed the example of his royal father in these civic improvements. He has built a good road around the city just within the walls, and also several blocks of houses next adjoining those erected by the late King. In several instances the intersection of two streets has been made or built into a circle, having a fountain or tower in the centre.... Having roads, the Siamese will next have ox-carts or carriages; indeed, some of the nobles have already imported the latter from Calcutta, and they may occasionally be seen taking a drive, at the fashionable hour of the afternoon, sitting gravely upright, and as they roll along the dusty streets looking upon their friends and neighbours with a very perceptible sense of new-found importance, illustrative of deep culture and nice refinement. The Supreme King himself is also accustomed to take the air in a barouche drawn by six horses, with liveried postillions, and attended by gorgeous outriders and a mounted escort of the royal guard.

The boats were anchored about midnight, and in the spacious cabins we slept soundly until morning. With daylight we saw the canal was lined with bamboo huts, and that passing us were many boats on their way to Bangkok with market stuffs. In the middle of the day we stopped for an hour to allow the men rest and time for eating their fish and rice. The canal continued very narrow during the remainder of the day; its sides were covered with a thin strip of cocoa palms and bamboos, but the country beyond was a vast plain of rank jungle grass, with an occasional hut in sight, or a small village of a dozen or more dwellings, and always a cock-pit, licensed by, and a source of great revenue to, the Government. The huts were very dilapidated. A rule with the Siamese is never to repair a building, but to live in it until it almost falls upon their heads. The people appeared poor, and were certainly shockingly dirty. The mosquitoes proved very troublesome, becoming towards evening almost unbearable. We noticed that all the natives slept within curtains, and that the huge buffalo-cows were coralled in small swampy enclosures, in which they wallowed, covering themselves with mud and water as a protection against the stinging pests. At night we entered the nettings we were so careful not to leave behind, but no such thing as 'balmy sleep' could be obtained; there seemed to be quite as many mosquitoes within as without the curtains. They made a buzzing as of a thousand bees; the air was literally thick and heavy with them. The only respite we had from their attacks was when completely enveloped in our blankets; but this was simply 'from the frying-pan into the fire', for the action nearly suffocated us. In the morning the General said he counted fifty of the merciless insects which were hanging on the *inner* side of his curtains, in a semi-torpid state, after the night's sanguinary foray; and my face was so red and swollen as scarcely to be recognisable by my companions.

On the morning of the second day from Bangkok we enter the Bang pa Kong river, which we propose to ascend about fifty miles to Pachim [Prachin], the residence of a governor; and then, if possible, we shall go on by water to Kabin [Krabinburi], thirty or forty miles farther. In an old *wat* where we breakfasted, thrown over a small image of Budha, was a piece of yellow cloth, about a foot in length and two inches in width, upon which was written in Siamese characters, 'This cloth I, Nang Yai, send to my aunt Sim; if anybody steals it, may he go to hell.' From which we understood that the cloth was consecrated to the memory of Nang's transmigrating aunt, and that he entertained pretty strong and precise feelings towards the person who should purloin the hallowed offering. The Bang pa Kong river is three or four hundred feet in width, deep, with strong tides and a very tortuous course; we did not pass a straight reach as much as an eighth of a mile in length. In the afternoon we observed an alligator about eight feet long, with open, cavernous mouth and sleepy, half-closed eyes, lying in the tall grass on the bank, enjoying the bright rays of the sun.

Arrived at Pachim, the Governor sent us an invitation to pass the night in a house which he had prepared for our reception (we had sent a messenger ahead to herald our approach), but we preferred sleeping on board the boats. The Governor's house we saw on the following morning. It is a large bamboo building, raised upon piles, and in the long room, having one side open, His Excellency received our party. Before us stood an old gentleman of short stature, intelligent and amiable countenance, with grey hair, and teeth much blackened by use of the betel. His dress was a silk coat and buff cloth waistcoat, with a simple *panoung* [sarong], and bare legs and feet; he wore besides a pair of immense spectacles. The room made a rather primitive 'audience chamber', containing as it did only a small sofa, beyond which were some emblems of authority—large umbrellas—a bamboo mat, chandeliers hanging from the beams, and two paroquets with rich plumage in cages at either end; and there were also two clocks, both of which insisted upon indicating that the hour (at seven in the morning) was half-past one. Lying upon their hips, prostrate upon the floor, were a dozen or more officers and attendants. We conversed about half an hour with the Governor, through the Missionary [McFarland] as interpreter. He promised to obtain three ponies for us, and four bullock-carts for our servants and baggage, and at taking leave he sent with us a present of meat and fish, asking what other provisions we were desirous of receiving. The Governor will send orders in advance to the sub-governors of the provinces between Pachim and Siamrap, who will have provisions and conveyance waiting, so that in future we may not be delayed.

The town of Pachim lies upon level ground on the north bank of the Bang pa Kong river, and contains, scattered over a large extent of country, some two or three thousand inhabitants. Anchored before the town were about fifty boats, some of them of large size, and owned by Chinamen; and back of the town the Government authorities were building a citadel and palace, the brick walls of which are to be six feet in breadth, and are to enclose a section of land about eight acres in extent. A saw-mill and brick-yard are in operation, preparing the materials of construction; we visited the latter. The work is mostly done by women. The bricks are made of clay and *paddy* husks, and are burnt: they sell for $2.40 a thousand, delivered in Bangkok. At the entrance of the new citadel we saw a remarkable natural gateway, formed by two trees (the *poh* [bo] species, the sacred tree of the Siamese, being that under which Budha is said to have expired when he left this world), about two feet in diameter at their bases, joining and growing together in the form of a perfect arch twenty feet from the ground, and towering up in a single trunk thirty feet higher, and spreading out in grand masses of bright green foliage. It seemed that formerly the gate of an old stockade stood there, which compelled the trees to either die or unite, and owing to the fertility of the soil and their inherent vigour, they chose the latter, and so are now living united, like the Siamese twins.

Frank Vincent, *The Land of the White Elephant: Sights and Scenes in South-Eastern Asia*, New York, Harper and Brothers, 1874, pp. 130–2, 175–80.

41
Petchburi Seen by a Resident

MARY LOVINA CORT

Petchburi (variously spelt) has several times from the middle of the nineteenth century been mentioned as a place visited by those coming to Siam. Sir John Bowring describes a 'gentleman's excursion to the city' in his book on Siam. Mouhot, Thomson, and Vincent all went there to see the palace built by King Mongkut, the temples, and the great cave (which was incorrectly held, following Mouhot, to be of volcanic origin).

Foreign residents came with the establishment, in 1861, of the Baptist Mission station by the Revd S. G. McFarland,

Dr Daniel McGilvary, and their wives. Two ladies joined the mission: Sarah Coffman, who was to write a chapter about Petchburi in Siam and Laos as Seen by Our American Missionaries *(Philadelphia, 1884), and Mary Lovina Cort, who in 1886 published in New York her* Siam, or the Heart of Further India. *Ms Cort wrote most extensively about Petchburi, devoting three chapters to its sights and smells, unfortunately employing a style more appropriate to the primary school teaching in which she was engaged than to literary greatness.*

Mary Cort went for a while 'in the field' in Chiangmai, where McGilvary also worked, and seems to have liked the Lao. She notes that physically Chiangmai recalled for her Petchburi. Carl Bock (Passage 42) during his visit to Petchburi in 1881 wrote rather tartly: 'I called on the American Mission, where Mr and Mrs McClelland [McFarland?], and two evidently disappointed ladies of middle age, were doing some good Christian work in the way of teaching a few young Siamese.' There can be no doubt that the 'two evidently disappointed ladies' were Misses Cort and Coffman. Ms Cort tells us how she left tracts in temples on her visits around the town, and refuses to give alms to an old woman beggar until she sweeps the bridge over which she has to pass.

Here follow two short extracts relating to the town and the cave.

OUR city was a favorite resort of the late king, Maha Mongkut, and on that account it boasts of some improvements which very few Siamese cities outside of Bangkok can show, such as the palace, temples, pagodas, and forts on *Kow Maha Sawan*, the Mountain of the Highest Heaven; the water-works, with pipes from the river to the foot of the mountain; the fine structure of solid masonry, called the Elephant Bridge, which spans the river; the two-storied brick buildings along Market Street, and the many and costly idols in the Royal Cave. The city is built on both sides of the Petchaburee River. Lying all about the city are wide-spreading plains, dotted with clusters of cocoa and sugar palms. These stately trees are so abundant that an eccentric lady once visiting us complained that she 'could not look out in any direction without seeing palms'. Toward the close of the rainy season the fields are clothed with verdure,

The great cave at Petchburi, from Henri Mouhot, *Travels in the Central Parts of Indo-China (Siam), Cambodia, and Laos* ..., London, John Murray, 1864.

and the heavy heads of rich, white rice are maturing for the harvest, which is gathered for the threshing by our Christmas time.

The sun comes up out of the sea every morning to shine on our beautiful home, and disappears at night behind the mountains in the west which stand guard between us and Burmah. There are lovely sunsets, with grand illuminations of Palace Mountain, when every roof, and spire, and pagoda is touched with fire reflected from the burnished heavens, and the palms on the plain below are bathed in the mellow glow....

At the mouth of the [Royal] cave we found some curious rocks, and succeeded in breaking off several good specimens. They show decided volcanic action, and appear to have been fused in a molten, bubbling state. In the cave are the greatest wonders. There are several chambers, but the first one, if you enter properly by the royal steps, is the largest, the longest, and the loftiest. It is perhaps one hundred and fifty feet long and sixty feet wide. The rocky walls arch over dome-like and solemn. At the apex there is an irregular opening through which the sun shines clear and bright, and looking up we could see the white clouds floating lazily by. Bushes and shrubs grow about the edges, vines clamber down the rough sides, and delicate mosses, ferns, and wild flowers cling to the overhanging rocks; while some great brown roots have scrambled down, down till they have reached the very foot of the cave. Pretty, bright-eyed doves have made their nests near by, and they sit pluming themselves on the ledges, and looking at us sidewise with eyes full of wonder, and then at a given signal they will all fly off together with a great whirr and rush that echoes and re-echoes through the dark, gloomy recesses.

There are many graceful stalactites depending from the vaulted roof, but the stalagmites which could climb up to meet them have all been removed, and the floor of the cave leveled and paved with large red tiles, and there is a wall of masonry with an arched doorway leading into a smaller room paved with ordinary bricks. All round about are arranged shelves and ledges that are set full of little images of Buddha, and in little niches and holes in the ceiling these vacant-looking, lifeless gods peer out at us. Not a sound is heard but the dropping of the water or the rustle of falling leaves. Now and then we hear the screeching of bats and are reminded of the old prophecy, and hope the time will soon come for its fulfilment.

There are many dark passages and winding ways leading off from these larger spaces, and the walls of the cave are full of little chambers and alcoves, and there are ledges of rock jutting out, and little pinnacles, each one crowned with an idol. The school-boys once counted one hundred and eighty-two, but I think there must be many more.

Mary Lovina Cort, *Siam, or the Heart of Further India*, New York, Anson Randolph and Co., 1886; reprinted in Michael Smithies (ed.), *Early Accounts of Phetchaburi*, Bangkok, Siam Society, 1987, pp. 42–3, 63–4.

42
The Lao of Chiangmai and Chiangrai

CARL BOCK

Carl Alfred Bock was a Norwegian explorer and naturalist who was born into a merchant family in Oslo, then Christiania, in 1849. He went to England in 1868 and took up a post with the Swedish–Norwegian Consul in the fishing port of Grimsby before moving to London where he married Mary Jane Absalon, daughter of a ship's captain, and determined to devote himself to a career in the natural sciences. After travelling through Lapland in 1877, he was commissioned by the Marquis of Tweeddale, Arthur Hay, to go to Sumatra to make a collection of specimens. Bock took the chance, and in 1878 arrived at Padang, at the height of the Aceh War. He sent two shipments to England (the second sank in the Red Sea) before learning of the death of his patron in 1878. Undaunted, he managed to get in contact with the Governor-General of the Netherlands East Indies, van Lansberge, who was persuaded to commission him to make an expedition into the almost unexplored south-eastern part of Borneo. This was not something to be undertaken lightly; numerous explorers had been killed in earlier attempts. He spent 1879–80 in Borneo (much energy was expended looking for the mythical Darwinian 'missing link': men with tails), and his report was translated into Dutch. The version for the general public appeared in London in 1881, with the eye-catching title, The Head-Hunters of Borneo: A Narrative of Travel Up the Mahakham and Down the Barito; also, Journeyings in Sumatra.

He then undertook a journey through northern Siam, and this was published in 1884 as Temples and Elephants: The Narrative of a Journey of Exploration through Upper Siam and Lao. *It was dedicated to King Chulalongkorn, whom he met, and who gave considerable assistance to Bock in his travels. His career after this was as a diplomat in the Swedish–Norwegian consular service; he was posted as Vice-Consul to Shanghai in 1886, was in Antwerp in 1899, and Consul-General in Lisbon 1900–3, before retiring to Brussels, dying in 1932. Although decorated, he is not shy of telling us, as early as 1883 by the Emperor of Austria and the Emperor of Brazil, awarded the gold medal of the Geographic Society of Lisbon, and made an honorary member of the Geographical Society of Rome and the Anthropological Society of Florence, he was awarded no honour by the Royal Geographical Society of London, though he does have a hawk-cuckoo, which he discovered in 1880 in Borneo, named after him.*

Here are some extracts from his travels in the north, in Chiangmai and Chiangrai, both of which have changed beyond all recognition since his time.

IN one corner of the room an old Chinaman tailor was busy making a coat of light blue cloth for the Chow, who himself shortly appeared, an old man, tall of stature, but slightly stooping beneath his load of sixty-four years, dressed in a black jacket with gold buttons, and a *palai*, but barefooted. He was smoking a buree, which went out as soon as he left off 'pulling' in order to speak to us, as these native cigars always do; upon which the slave who followed him took it from him, placed it between his own lips to relight it, and handed it back to his master. When I presented my letter from Bangkok, the Chow called in one of his secretaries to read it aloud, whereupon he said the natives were forbidden to shoot birds, but he would see if an exception could be made in my case, and sent for six Phyas, to consult with them on the point. The country, he said, was rich in flowers, especially orchids, many of which were scented, and especially reserved for the princes' use. One mountain, a few days' journey distant, was noted for certain varieties, which could be found nowhere else. Picking up a couple of specimens, he handed them to me; they were a species of scented *Dendrobium*. As I held them in my hand, the Chow told me to follow the Lao custom, and stick them in my ears; and when I pointed out that my ears were not pierced, he took one, and showed me how to make up for this deficiency by fixing it after the fashion of a quill in a clerk's ear.

The fashion of piercing the ears is universal among both sexes of all ages in Lao. The ears are bored when very young, and a wooden peg inserted, the hole being gradually enlarged by being stretched with pieces of wood, ivory, or metal, or with a leaf rolled up, or any other article that may be at hand, till it is capable of receiving the full-sized *lan*, or ear-ornament. This consists of a plate of unalloyed gold, a little over an inch wide, lightly twisted up until it forms a roll of cylindrical shape, about half an inch in diameter, which is simply held together by tying a string round it, and inserted into the enlarged ear-lobe. The poorest girls content themselves with a hollow cylinder formed of a single coil of plate, the cavity of which is filled up with lead, while the wealthy classes have a many-coiled roll, the edges of which are ornamented with diamonds or rubies. When a gold ear-ornament is not forthcoming, a flower takes its place. The men seldom wear ear-ornaments, but invariably carry a flower in the ear, or use the hole as a convenient receptacle for a buree.

This fashion of stretching the ear-lobes and the practice of carrying flowers, cigars, and other articles on the top of the ear, causing the upper part of the ear to project from the side of the head, makes the naturally large ears of the natives look still larger. But large ears are regarded as a sign of longevity, and are appreciated accordingly. The chief of Chengmai is especially remarkable for the large development of his aural appendages. The Siamese commissioner once remarked to him that he ought to live to a green old age, if the size of his ears was to be regarded as a sign, and the simple old chief seemed quite flattered by the remark.

As I explained to the Chow my intention of passing through Lao into Ngiou, and asked for his assistance, he listened very quietly—generally with his mouth wide open—nodding assent, but declining to commit himself by words. He looked—as he had the reputation of being—a kindly-disposed man, but weak. He was, it appeared, quite overruled by his wife, who seemed to be quite a sufficiently strong-minded individual to make up for his weakness. She was his third wife, and when he married her she compelled him not only to enter the priesthood, but to put away all his concubines. He did not wear the yellow cloth long—only seven days—but that was considered long enough to cleanse him.

Presently I went into the village [of Chiangrai], and called upon the Chow Hluang, who said the only accommodation he had for me was a small Sala, which, being out of repair, I declined. I then went, with the letter of introduction which the Chow Operat had given me, to his son-in-law, the Chow Radjasee, who very kindly offered me hospitality in his own house.

My host and hostess, who warmly shook hands with me, seemed friendly disposed, and were greatly delighted when I presented them with sixteen yards of blue silk cloth, interwoven with gold thread, and it was not long before they returned the compliment with the usual gift of rice and eggs, fruits and fowls.

My host was a man of about forty-five years of age, who, after being eighteen years in the priesthood, had married, two years previously, the Chow Operat's daughter, a very plain woman with a terrible squint, but a very good heart withal. They lived in a good-sized house, built in the ordinary style of teak and bamboo, where they did everything to make me comfortable.

I had not been here more than two or three days when I discovered that, although I was supposed to be the guest of the Chow Radjasee, I was practically living at the expense of the community at large; for the slaves of my host were sent round every morning to the people, collecting fowls, eggs, fruit, and other comestibles, which the common folk did not dare to refuse to deliver on demand. The whole social system here, indeed, seems to be based on a recognized round of begging or borrowing, so that the borrower of a fowl to-day is asked to lend a few eggs to-morrow, and so on, right round the circle. For myself, I endeavoured to set a good example by promptly paying for everything that I wanted, but I was continually besieged by applicants for needles, candles, skeins of thread, bottles of scent, and other articles, of which I had brought a small stock to give away, but any of which could be bought at Chengmai, and most of which I even found on sale in the small market here. I was a frequent visitor to the market, for, as soon as I discovered the conditions on which the Chow Radjasee supplied me with my 'board', I did not allow the system to continue, and went out every morning to lay in a daily stock of food. The young girls and old women do all the provisioning of the place, sitting half the day with their baskets of rice, fowls, and eggs, before them. There is very little downright buying and selling; hardly any money changes hands, everything being done by 'exchange and barter'.

Neither guest nor host, I think, regretted my determination to take into my own hands my commissariat arrangements. The chief's *menu* comprised rice, chillies, and dried putrid fish, diversified occasionally with an egg more or less nearly approaching a state of rottenness. I asked him one day if he did not eat poultry or fresh eggs, which were very cheap, fifteen eggs costing a 'fuang', or one-eighth of a rupee, and eight fowls a rupee. He laughed, and replied 'Sometimes'—'once a month,' I believe he added. This abstemiousness was purely the result of the native meanness of character, for, although the Chow had many fowls brought to the house as the result of the requisitioning expeditions of his slaves, he preferred to sell them whenever a buyer offered. He could, however, enjoy a dinner of roast chicken as much as anybody, and as I always passed on to my host and hostess whatever remained from my meals, after I had taken to provisioning myself, this accommodation was mutually advantageous, and the chief and his wife visibly improved in appearance under the more generous diet.

The Laosians take their meals twice daily, at about seven in the morning and towards sunset. They sit in a circle on the floor, or on mats, with a lacquer or brazen tray before them, on which are placed a number of saucers or small bowls containing dried or boiled fish, bits of buffalo-meat stewed, a salted egg, or a piece of the favourite pork: all these meats are invariably served with rice and curry. For vegetables they eat stewed bamboo shoots—not at all a bad substitute for asparagus—beans, plantains, tamarinds, and powdered capsicums. Pervading everything is the inevitable fishy flavour, which, like the garlic among the Spaniards, is never absent. This is imparted by adding to the dishes a small quantity of rotten fish—the *ngapee* of the Burmese—the preparation of which is as much an art among Laosians and Siamese, Burmese and Malays, as the anxious endeavour on the part of the European housewife to keep her fish fresh. The rice, simply boiled or steamed, is served separately to each person in a small basket; and coarse salt is also provided separately; many persons, indeed, carrying about a supply of salt with them. From the basket of dry rice a small quantity is taken with the fingers and rolled between the hands into a ball, which is then dipped into one or more of the various curries and flavouring dishes. Plates are as little known as knives and forks, and that is not at all. Among the very poor a plantain-leaf, always at hand, and easily thrown away, involving neither cost nor trouble in 'washing up', takes the place of the bowls or saucers which the better classes use. Strict silence is observed at mealtimes, and when the repast is finished a small quantity of water is drunk from the heavy clay decanters or goblets, which are passed round, each person rinsing out his or her mouth, and ejecting the contents into a spittoon, or, if this convenient receptacle be wanting, through an equally convenient hole in the floor.

Carl Bock, *Temples and Elephants: The Narrative of a Journey of Exploration through Upper Siam and Lao*, London, Sampson Low, Marston, Searle, and Rivington, 1884, pp. 224–6, 302–3, 310–13.

43
After Dinner with the King and Post-cremation Diversions

FLORENCE CADDY

Florence Caddy, née Tompson, born about 1837, was the only child of an army officer who died when she was very young. Her French mother, on his death, rejoined her family in southern France, taking Florence with her, but she too died and her daughter was sent to live with distant relations in England and educated, it would seem well, there. She then went to study art in France and in Athens, and married in London, in 1857, Dr John Caddy, a regular medical officer in the navy, almost twice her age. They had five children and lived in London and, for a time, when he had a shore post, in the west of England. In 1876, Dr Caddy retired to set up private practice in west London. Money was short, children had to be educated, and Florence turned to writing.

Her first book, published in 1877, Household Organisation, *was a practical guide to running a middle-class household. She then wrote a three-volume novel, partly autobiographical, about an art student who goes off on a tour of Europe to escape her guardians, and another novel about a young sculptor and his arty friends. A second volume of the 'Homes and Gardens' type,* Lares and Penates, *appeared in 1883, and then two quite carefully researched volumes, one following the routes in France of Jeanne d'Arc, published in 1886, the other following in the steps of Linnaeus in Sweden, published the following year.*

She had gone to Sweden on the Duke of Sutherland's yacht, presumably having met him in the course of her literary production, and was apparently invited to accompany him on the much longer journey to Asia, more as a companion in middle years to a relative of the Duke, also one of the party, the young widow, Lady Clare. Ostensibly, the Duke was taking a winter journey to recover from an illness; in fact, he was going to further railway construction, in which he had financial interest and which Siam wished to promote. Nothing came of this promotion drive, since the Siamese contract was eventually given to a group in which a former Governor of the Straits Settlements, Sir Andrew Clarke, had dealings.

Florence Caddy wrote no more after To Siam and Malaya in the Duke of Sutherland's Yacht 'Sans Peur', *probably because her husband's practice had now been established and the children were on the way to becoming self-supporting. Dr Caddy died in 1902, and two of their sons pursued successful medical careers. Florence continued to live in London and the west country until her death in 1923.*

Notwithstanding the lack of promotional success of the Siamese visit, the party was royally received, and Florence describes dinner with King Chulalongkorn in the palace, yet another royal cremation in detail, and visits to all the sights.

AFTER dinner we were conducted to a smaller saloon, richly furnished in European style. Here the king handed garlands of flowers to many of us, which we hung round our necks or arms. Mine was a chain of alternate white and yellow night-scented flowers (yellow the royal colour). Some of the wreaths were pink, some white, all various and all perfumed. When I got home I hung up my wreath to preserve it. The scent was so strong that I could hardly bear it even with three open windows and a draught right through the room. I noticed the incense smell of odorous night-scented flowers all over Siam, in those 'still, heavy, oppressive, fragrant nights'.

Though the king conversed with us through an interpreter, he fully understood what we said; indeed, I always addressed myself to him directly. Prince Premier told me the king knew and spoke English as well as the best of them, but he has a certain shyness in speaking lest he should make any mistakes. Some books say it is not etiquette for the king to speak in any but his own language, but this is not the case. Prince Premier, and indeed all the princes, spoke of the king with much affection, and a respect bordering on veneration. He seems a most amiable monarch.

We ladies and the Duke of Sutherland were taken to another part of the palace to be presented to the queen, a charming little woman dressed in black—she was in mourning for her children—wearing the panung (of black silk), which, like the men's costume, is arranged so as to have

King Çhulalongkorn, from Carl Bock, *Temples and Elephants* ..., London, Sampson Low, Marston, Searle, and Rivington, 1884.

the appearance of knee-breeches, showing her legs in open-worked black silk stockings to the knee. She has very small and pretty feet and ankles. She wore the national form of scarf across her shoulders, and several orders on her black jacket, which was sewn with seed pearl. Her hair is cut short like a boy's, and she wears nothing on her head. It is a comical, yet piquant costume. The queen is not handsome in face, but dignified, and very pleasing in manner; I was captivated by her. Her Majesty does not understand English, so we spoke through an interpreter. She spoke gravely, I thought nervously, as if unaccustomed to such public speaking. She said she was gratified to receive a visitor of such distinction as the Duke of Sutherland. We backed out in proper form. What must she have thought of our voluminous trained skirts!

Immediately after the cremation they all burst out into wildest rejoicings, their cherished dead having now arrived safely at a higher stage of existence, and having approached nearer to Nirvana, or the Ineffable. To us the transition was startling, as our pearl of chamberlains took us in hand again, and marshalled us through the crowd, which fell into line, leaving a pathway for us to pass, and led us to seats immediately facing the royal dais whither His Majesty went, after leaving the cremation-chapel, and where he presided over the numerous diversions which had been arranged in honour of the occasion. He came here shortly after our arrival, and was now surrounded by several of his children, dressed in white, as mourning for their little brothers, and wearing, as before, tiny wreaths of small white flowers round their top-knots of hair. We saw none of the ladies of the harem. We thus found ourselves seated nearest to the king, whose throne faced an open space, where games and the fireworks were to be exhibited.

Here began the wildest high jinks. The distribution of money to the natives took place as usual at cremations, when the custom is for the king to distribute money and presents to his people. The princes and relations of the king all give presents to add to the collection, and they each get a return present.

A grand scramble was made for the green limes enclosing silver coins, which limes the king took from large baskets placed by his feet. We all scrambled for them, and there were plenty for all. Several of the Duke's officers were present, and had good places provided for them. The 'Sanspures', as the sailors style themselves, were in the background, most active in the scrambling. The king seemed amused at seeing the sailors so eager after the limes, and shot plenty in their direction.

Then he flung hollow balls, like nuts, containing lottery tickets; many of these he fired pointedly at us, and, as His Majesty is a good shot, I had no less than seven of these mostly fired into my lap. He occasionally threw some limes and nuts among his children, and many among the courtiers near his throne. There was much laughter all round, even among the group of elder nobles and grandees of Siam, dressed in cloth of gold, kincobs from India, I believe, and gorgeous stuffs, who sat close by the king in a transept to his left. It was droll to see us, our great Duke and all, scrambling; all of us including the principal European ladies in the place, Lady Clare in pale peach-blossom moiré and white Maltese lace, and my more than middle-aged self. Our palace may verily be the Palace of Calm Delights, but I shall always think of Bangkok as the City of High Jinks.

The humming, whirring sound of distant music of the Siamese band was audible throughout.

Then the Duke's party were called up separately by name, and we each received two special nuts from the hand of His Majesty. The numbers enclosed in mine gave me a symbolic ring made of a gold and a silver sacred cobra entwined, set with diamonds, and emeralds for eyes; the second ticket gave me a blue-and-white tea-service on a small silver tray. It had now grown dusk, and the fireworks commenced by a simultaneous ignition of all the distant surrounding pieces, caused by the king setting fire to a dragon, which at once whizzed off from the throne, and set fire to the lofty pagoda standards of nine umbrellas tapering above each other, which all unfolded like fiery flowers as the light crept up their tall columns. This had an excellent effect. Many ingenious devices were exhibited, such as a beautiful fire fountain, figures of fiery monkeys darting out of the tops of high poles, &c. The lucigen light blazed in the centre, and lighted up two lines of men with lanterns, forming a colossal representation of dragons trying to swallow the moon, a reminiscence of the recent total eclipse. There were loud strains indicative of lamentation at the loss of the moon's light, and the clashing of cymbals represented their custom of striking on pots and pans when there is an eclipse, because they think this phenomenon is caused by the malignity of a dragon, which devours the two lights of the world: by making a great noise, they endeavour to frighten the animal that would deprive them of the light of day. It need scarcely be said that their efforts are always effectual.

Florence Caddy, *To Siam and Malaya in the Duke of Sutherland's Yacht 'Sans Peur'*, London, Hurst and Blackett, 1889, pp. 115–16, 162–4.

44
Muang Nan and Uttaradit in 1887

GEORGE YOUNGHUSBAND

Major-General Sir George John Younghusband, as he became in 1915, was born in 1859, the son of another major-general. He studied at Clifton and Sandhurst, and almost inevitably entered the army in 1878, serving in the Afghan War of 1878–80, during which he was decorated. He was in Sudan in 1885, on the North-West Frontier of India in 1886, and took part in the Burma War of 1886–7. In 1887, during six months' leave, according to his own account, he made a long journey through Burma, Siam, and the Shan States, most probably reconnoitering the largely unexplored territory for the British Government; an account of this was published in 1888. He was made captain in 1889, he married in 1891, and rose upwards: major in 1896, lieutenant-colonel in 1909, major-general in 1911, with campaigns along the way in the Philippines, South Africa, and India. He served in the First World War, during which he was knighted, and became Keeper of the Jewel House in the Tower of London in 1917. He died in 1944.

Younghusband was the author of three publications about the Tower of London, a history of the Guides, and a volume of memoirs, Forty Years a Soldier, *published in 1923. Of interest here is his first publication, which did 'not profess to any literary merit whatever', in which he called himself an 'ordinary British subaltern',* Eighteen Hundred Miles on a Burmese Tat *(a* tat *being a pony), giving an account of northern Siam, then generally, if loosely, called Laos. Written, like the other military author, Frederick Arthur Neale (Passage 32), in a very gung-ho style, confirming his lack of literary pretentions, he gives a similar picture, at about the same time, as Carl Bock (Passage 42) of the outposts of the north. Zimné (Chiangmai) 'is composed of two stockades; they contain about 8,000 inhabitants; a long street of shops runs through them. The market is held every morning.... There is a wooden bridge about 300 feet long spanning the River Me Ping....' Kiang Hai (Chiangrai) was of even less account, a fortified place without shops on the Me Khok River, 'in an extensive plain, with distant hills visible north and west. The houses are very thinly scattered amongst trees, and the population must be small for the size of the place.'*

Extracted here are accounts of some of the experiences of George Younghusband in Nan, to the east of northern Siam, and Uttaradit, further south, from where he took a boat back to Bangkok.

ON the 12th of April we reached Muang Nan, a walled town on the Me Nan River

There had been heavy rains, which made it cooler, otherwise it is hot and muggy. April is considered the hottest month in these parts. We seem to have pursued the 'hottest month' with much vigilance. At Kiang Tung we caught him, and now again. At Muang Nan there is no regular bazaar, only a daily market attended almost solely by women. Outside the north-east corner of the town are sheds, in which caravan men sell cheap cotton and silk goods. The whole trade at this season is done by bullocks, the river not being navigable above Muang Pak, about five miles south of this place. This is considered a very cheap country for buying elephants; I met several Burmans from Moulmein looking out for them. The only other means of transport are bullocks, and of these we met many hundreds on the road between this and Kiang Hai....

At Muang Nan the Prince's son came to see me, a pleasant, civil youth with one eye, who seemed delighted to meet me. I thought at first he mistook me for some one else, till it transpired that he had been to Bangkok and there imbibed a lasting admiration for Englishmen and all things English. This admiration extended even to the homely 'solah topee' of my nation, his costume consisting of a linen patrol jacket, a silk loin-cloth, lavender-coloured stockings, boots, and a very dirty pith hat; the whole turn-out making up a sort of cross between a poor Eurasian and a Bengali Babu in boots. I should certainly have taken him for something of that sort, if I had not noticed the people grovelling before him as he came along. We talked about roads and ways and means, and got on very well together.

The people of Nan look like and dress like the Zimméites, in fact they are merely a political division of the same race. The women wear their hair knotted rather higher up on their heads. The men are much addicted to drink, judging from the number of jolly fellows we saw being conveyed to the bosoms of their families at all hours of the night and day: 'kinloh'[1] they call it. There is the same lavish display of the female form divine here as elsewhere in the Laos States, but I don't know that their morals are any the worse for that.

The greater part of the male population, including a large sprinkling of priests, seem to spend their days in letting off huge rockets. The largest was a 30-ft bamboo as thick as my arm. This bit of timber was launched into the air by the agency of a whole cluster of bamboo powder-flasks lashed to its head. These firework parties start off in the morning for some open space, taking several rockets of all sizes, a band of music, and plenty of 'kinloh'. There they proceed to let off the rockets and drink the 'kinloh', to the accompaniment of the dulcet strains of their band. Towards evening they return to the town very noisy and happy. This noise and happiness they keep up the greater part of the night. The women are quiet and industrious, and do not participate at all in these jovial gatherings. Poungies (priests) here, as everywhere in Siam, abound, wearing the same yellow clothes as in Burmah. They have the character of being a dissolute lot, but we met with nothing but kindness from them....

We reached Muang Phang on the 24th of April; next day brought us to Utaradit, on the Me Nan River. The road for the last thirty miles had been very difficult, in many parts never having been used before for anything but passenger traffic and elephants. The path through the dense bush was so narrow that the ponies could scarcely push their way through it, and the ascent and descent out of the river and water-courses were often so steep and narrow that the ponies had to be unloaded, and their loads carried up and down.

Utaradit is a long straggling place, extending for more than a mile along the right bank of the river, the houses being dotted in a dense bush forest. Along the river are moored many hundred boats, in which a great portion of the popula-

[1]Kin lao = drinking, drink.

tion appear to live. These boats are large, with the dwelling part closed on every side. I saw one or two huts on rafts and piles. It was very difficult here to procure eatables, there being apparently no daily market.

Tobacco is cultivated here on an extensive scale along the low-lying bits of the river-bank, but little or no paddy is grown, owing to the difficulty in clearing the jungle....

On arrival at Utaradit we turned into the first empty shed available; this proved to be the Post Office, a rickety shanty with a large red letter-box lashed to a massive centre post by a wisp of bamboo. We were wondering why some one did not take the opportunity, when the box was full of money orders, to walk off boldy with his Majesty's mails, pillar-box and all. On examination, however, it proved that the lid of the aperture through which the weighty correspondence of Utaradit was supposed to enter, was so securely jammed down that it was impossible to prize it open with a penknife. On the other hand, the small door at the bottom of the box, which is usually used for taking out the letters, was left unlocked with the key in the lock—from both of which signs it was quite manifest that the confiding Siamese public had not yet learnt to entrust their letters to a Post Office. Several passers-by pointed out the red pillar to me with scarce concealed pride, and invited me to put my letters into it.

After breakfast I cleaned myself up and made ready to call on the Siamese Commissioner, to whom I had a letter of introduction. It turned out that I had not far to go, the Post Office being at his very gates. Moreover, we were more or less acquainted already, for, to my fearful horror, I found that we had been grazing our ponies in his compound all the morning, thereby moving a fat female slave to much wrath and indignation. The Commissioner, who seemed to bear no malice, was a tall, thin, fierce-looking gentleman, sadly afflicted with congestion of the liver. Of course he consulted me, and I as usual prescribed my only medicine, Vaseline. He ate a large chunk of this, and an hour or two afterwards came to me saying he felt much better. It had a good effect on his temper too, for he promised to help us to get boats and to dispose of our ponies—a feat he had declared impossible at our first interview. I gave him a shawl just to jog his memory, and in return I was besieged all day by his wives carrying presents of eggs, fruit, tobacco, etc.

For several days I noticed a youth loafing about in a wistful sort of way with a bundle of letters under his arm. I thought he had designs on my few remaining rags, and cautioned Judh Bir [his servant] to keep his weathermost eye on him. Things reached a crisis when, one morning whilst I was dozing with one eye open, I saw him stealthily enter my hut. I rose and rebuked him with considerable severity, pointing out to him the heinousness of his offence in trying to rob the stranger and foreigner of his little all. He received my verbal castigation with the greatest humility, and murmured in a deprecatory voice that he was very sorry to intrude, and that he did not want to steal, but that this was the Post Office and he was the Postmaster! Mutual apologies and a fair division of the Post Office immediately made.

A small Chinese boy aged about three years came one day with his Siamese nurse to see me. She was suckling him as they came in, but my young gentleman, easing off for a minute and scrambling down from her lap, strode up to me, and in a loud and imperious voice said, 'I am Chou Shesheen (Governor Shesheen); who are you?' A first-class little man, and likely to become an ornament to his race if he ever reaches maturity, the latter perhaps rather a problematical contingency, considering the mixed diet he indulged in. Whilst with me, in addition to the above-mentioned wholesome nutriment, he ate two plantains, and would have smoked half-a-dozen cigarettes if his nurse had not stopped him in his wild career. He probably chews betel-nut as well.

Lieutenant G. J. Younghusband, *Eighteen Hundred Miles on a Burmese Tat through Burmah, Siam and the Eastern Shan States*, London, W. H. Allen, 1888, pp. 91–2, 97–105.

45
Spirit Possession among Northerners

DR CHEEK

The name of Dr Cheek occurs with great regularity in connection with visitors to Chiangmai in the 1880s. He was a medical missionary doctor, but his commercial concerns seem to have occupied much of his time and energy. He was responsible for the teak bridge across the Ping in Chiangmai, he owned a paddle steamer doing the trip from Bangkok to Nakorn Sawan (up to Tak, then known as Raheng, when the depth of water was sufficient), and Louis Leonowens, Anna's son, records numerous commercial dealings with him. James McCarthy (Passage 50) refers to him in 1890, with justification, as 'an enterprising American, who had spent many years in Siam'.

By 1886 he is no longer listed as part of the missionary establishment of 'the Laos Church' (that is, the Chiangmai mission) by Mary Lovina Cort (Passage 41), but she does quote him in relation to spirit possession. This is interesting, because trances and possession of this kind remain common in the north and north-east of present-day Thailand, and are usually referred to as phi-pob. *Those held possessed are still required to move away from their homes and attempt to settle elsewhere; hence the suspicion of strangers new to villages.*

I had repeatedly … requested permission to witness an investigation of a case of witchcraft, and I was at last granted an opportunity. I found upon inquiry that the patient, a girl of about sixteen, had some months previously suffered from a protracted fever, probably typhoid, and that upon recovery had lost the power of speech, though in other respects she seemed quite well.

One day she went with a party of children to a temple, and while there she spoke a few words more or less distinctly. Immediately the children became alarmed and ran home. Supposing the case to be one of witchcraft the owner (for the patient was a slave) sent for the spirit-doctors. Three of these professionals were present when I reached the place, and one of them, who seemed to be considered more eminent than his fellows, assumed the *rôle* of chief inquisitor. After becoming thoroughly infused with the inspiration of a rather large bowl of *arrack*, this eminent doctor began muttering some gibberish, and, taking up a tiger's tooth, he drew it along the side and back of the patient, leaving deep scratches, while the patient of course writhed and struggled. At length a rather deeper and more skillful incision, which drew the blood, elicited a cry of pain, and this cry was interpreted by the ferocious, drunken spirit-doctor as indicating the seat of the spirit. Then, with a vigorous thrust between the ribs, while his assistant pressed a bluntly-pointed piece of wood against the unhappy patient, he, with foul and abusive language, ordered the spirit to leave. The exorcism was a failure, and the patient refused to speak, although pressingly flattered to do so by the combined efforts of these two drunken savages. The patient is in such cases, for the time, supposed to be the not altogether 'unconscious envelope' of the infesting spirit; and any injury inflicted by the spirit-doctor is directed against the spirit, and any answer given to the questions put by the spirit-doctor, or the friends of the patient, are from the spirit. So the witch-doctor asks its name and abode, and the names of relatives, and sundry questions concerning domestic relations, supposed to be known only to members of the family. If to all these questions the desired answers are given, the person whose spirit it is, is accused of witchcraft, and, together with all the members of the family, he must leave the neighborhood; nor can they settle anywhere in the vicinity of their home again. Everything belonging to them, except such articles as can be easily removed, is committed to the flames. They cannot sell their rice-fields, gardens, houses, or any other possession, since no one will risk the supposed contamination. Hundreds of families become outcasts yearly. We have attempted to aid individual victims by making our premises places of refuge, and enabling those who had been driven from home to find work and protection; but we are helpless before this wide-spread and degrading prostitution of the human intellect.

Quoted in Mary Lovina Cort, *Siam, or the Heart of Further India*, New York, Anson Randolph, 1886, pp. 351–2.

46
Ministries and Ministers

SIR HENRY NORMAN

Sir Henry Norman was a British Member of Parliament at the turn of the last century who concerned himself with Eastern affairs. He wrote a book, The Real Japan, *and visited Siam in 1894, a year after the French gunboat incident, and was very critical of much that he saw. In his long book,* The Peoples and Politics of the Far East *(1907), which comprised 'travels and studies in the British, French, Spanish and Portuguese Colonies, Siberia, China, Japan, Korea, Siam and Malaya', Chapters 26–30 deal with Siam, and his observations going back to his 1894 visit. The last two chapters, 'The true story of France and Siam' and 'England and the future of Siam', reflect more his interests in the struggle between two colonial powers. His conclusion was that 'The French have twice before tried to found an empire overseas to rival that of great Britain—once in India, and once in Canada. Indo-China represents their third attempt ... there is practically no ground whatever to hope that an independent and prosperous Siam will continue to exist under the present regime. And if not, then Siam will come under either British or French protection, and the only question is, which shall it be?'*

Norman was a false prophet; the regime adapted quite happily, and the Entente Cordiale put under the carpet Anglo-French rivalries. His comments on much of what he saw are not merely patronizing, but downright disdainful. He had little to say of good about the organization of Siamese government, with one notable exception: Prince Damrong, then effectively Minister of the Interior (though listed as being Minister of the North), is given full praise. His impressions of a visit to the Ministry of Foreign Affairs are in great contrast to what one could find now, but his observation that 'Bangkok is not Siam' remains more true than ever.

EVERY visit that I paid to the Royal Siamese Ministry of Foreign Affairs was an Oriental object-lesson. A lazy sentry lolling on an old oil-tin at the outer gate would insolently ask my errand, and lazily give a reluctant guttural assent to my doubting ingress. Another sentry, if my visit was late—as it generally was, for the Foreign Minister usually began his work at eleven o'clock at night—lying asleep within the entry, would sulkily respond to my shouts of inquiry with a hardly intelligible reply in colloquial Siamese that the Prince was in or was out,—*yu* or *mai yu*—as might suit his own particular humour, without any needless reference to the truth of the matter. As I thus necessarily carried on my own hesitating researches unheralded into the inner regions, my ears were met with the snores of attendants lying about the passages, or the yawns of sleepy clerks kept there the whole night in idleness; till at length one might come suddenly upon the Royal Prince Minister [Devawongse] himself, at supper with some favoured gossip, or intent upon a vigorous and exciting game of chess.... In the meantime suitors might wail, and Consuls rave at the needless delays, the perpetual procrastinations, which often continued from week to week and even from month to month; and usually wearied out, as they were intended to do, the unfortunate foreigners. Go where one would, and when one would, in this strange medley of departments, bureaus, and government offices, every passage and every room was all unswept and littered with the daily mess, the cast-off cigarettes, the decaying betel-nut, and all the indescribable *débris* of the countless hangers-on and ragged retainers who attend the footsteps of every official. In not a single office but that of Prince Damrong—a brilliant exception to the general slovenliness of Siamese ministers in this, as in many respects—did I observe the slightest desire for neatness and order, or even an idea of common cleanliness.

It is a pleasure to turn to the personality of Prince Damrong. One of the first surprises of my original visit to Siam was in finding a prince who had then never been outside his own country, and who yet spoke English with ease and accuracy, was a regular reader of the English newspapers, conversant with European politics and literature, and anxious to enter instantly into a discussion with me upon the details of the complicated situation in home politics at the time. At the age of twenty-one he was a mere subaltern in the King's bodyguard. The Education Department, which he afterwards founded, grew out of the King's approval of a small class he had formed for the instruction of his own men. He is one of the very few Siamese who have any sense of either punctuality or neatness. When Minister of Public Instruction he made a daily inspection in person of all the hospitals under him, visited one of his schools every afternoon, and was always to be found in his office from eleven to four. I can hardly attempt to explain how remarkable this is in Siam. I first learned to respect Prince Damrong from a trifling personal incident. In Siam every request of an accredited foreigner is instantly granted—in words. The promise bears no relation whatever to the performance, but nothing is ever frankly refused. When I was exploring the ruins of Ayuthia, the ancient capital of Siam, which was destroyed by the victorious Burmese in 1767, I discovered the broken-off and battered head of a Buddha lying buried among the almost impassable growth of tropical weeds. It had been there for half a century, and would, of course, remain untouched for ever. I marked the place, and inquired on my return under whose control this would be. On learning that Prince Damrong had charge of all matters of this kind, I asked his permission to send back for the head and take it away with me. He replied that he would consider the matter, and afterwards wrote me a very courteous letter, saying that although the head was broken and neglected, and nobody would ever pay any attention to it, nevertheless it was the head of Buddha, and therefore he did not think it would be decorous for a foreigner to take it away as a curiosity. The more I learned about Siam, the more I liked Prince Damrong for this refusal. His insight into the needs of his country is shown by his latest scheme for internal reform, namely, the proposal to bring under one responsible head in Bangkok the many clashing provincial authorities. That this is being bitterly opposed by all his rival Ministers is perhaps the best proof of its desirability....

Sir Henry Norman, MP, *The Peoples and Politics of the Far East*, London, T. Fisher Unwin, 1907, pp. 414–15, 447–8.

47
Wat Saket, the 'Burning Ghat of Bangkok'

MAXWELL SOMMERVILLE

The end of the nineteenth century not only saw a great increase in the number of foreign residents in Siam, many of whom went on to write their memoirs, but also the gentle beginning of what was, another eighty years on, a tourist invasion. Siam was exotic to a degree at the time, and illustrated accounts of its way of life and sights started to become popular.

Maxwell Sommerville was one such traveller. A professor of the recondite subject of glyptology (defined by Webster as 'the study or the art or process of carving or engraving, especially on gems') at the University of Pennsylvania, he and his party (presumably comprising his wife), were amused when the Chinese deck steward asked how he liked his lice. He put up at the Oriental Hotel (there follows a generous description), he visited (and photographed) the main temples, and he took a boat trip up to the ruins of Ayutthaya and back. To pad out this rather banal account, he threw in 'three romances illustrative of Siamese life and customs'.

One thing he saw, though, which modern tourists are deprived of, was the public burning of the bodies of the poor at Wat Saket, now better known as the Golden Mount, in Bangkok. His is by no means the first description of this open charnel house; the Marquis de Beauvoir (1867) and Carl Bock (1881) had both described it, with astonishment, before. It was indeed one of the tourist sights of the time.

THE principal pagoda is constructed on an abrupt hill, and stands at an elevation of about two hundred feet above the avenue that leads to it. For some eighty feet there is a thick grove of trees on the hillside, with an occasional rest pavilion. Throughout the interior of this hill, which serves as a pedestal for the superstructure, are a number of circuitous staircases. After mounting the exterior by one of the massive stone stairways, comprising one hundred and forty steps, we observe diverging passage-ways winding around and up to the summit space, which has a breadth of about fifty feet. This terrace is so high that the municipality has rigged up a mast and yard-arms, and employs it as a signal station. From it again rises the upper bell-shaped pagoda, which, with its narrow, tapering spire, reaches an additional altitude of about seventy feet. On its altar is a bronze Buddha and other decorations. This point commands an extended view. We also look down from here on one of the most offensive and horrible sights of Bangkok: it is the most grewsome public institution in all this land,—yes, in the world. Its records are fragments of bones, heaps of ashes, beasts and birds that gloat over the victims who daily become part of the dire history of the Burning Ghat which we are about to visit.

On coming down, we at once entered the Burning Ghat of Bangkok by a dilapidated gate-way and through an old stone building within a long wall, which here extends on the southern side of the avenue. As we turned our eyes from the skulls and bones which hung upon the wall, we were still in view of the lofty pagóda crowning the golden hill from which we had just descended. It was altogether a very dreadful sight; no matter how carefully we walked, we stood upon the ashes of human remains. Most of the flesh had been consumed, and dogs were there to gnaw their share from scattered bones,—fragments left on the joints by the rapacious birds. Fire had reduced the bones to splinters and to powder; as in Holy Writ it was prophesied, 'Him that dieth of Jeroboam in the city shall the dogs eat; and him that dieth in the field shall the fowls of the air eat.' In this enclosure, on account of the infrequency of winds, the cinders lie undisturbed; all else of mortality has been devoured by the vultures, the burning pyres, the dogs, and (by night) the stealthy rodents.

The disposition of the remains of the dead depends almost entirely on the amount of money the family or friends of the deceased are able to expend. If they can afford thorough cremation, a large pyre is constructed and the defunct is rapidly disposed of in that manner. Where any pretence at mourning is made by a family, they wrap themselves in white cotton cloth. The bodies of the poorer classes, the penniless, and particularly culprits, are subjected to the more revolting fate of destruction of the flesh, fibre, and tissues by the voracious birds of prey that congregate in the trees about the funereal pile....

The principal cluster of tall silk-cotton-trees [kapok], on which more than a hundred vultures were resting, has evidently been injured by the grip of the birds' claws and scorched by the hot cinders that rise from the public cremations. The floss of these trees is used for filling in mattresses, the fibre being too brittle for weaving into textures. The birds perched upon the trees are the reserve guard only; the more voracious vultures stand on the ground beneath the trees and near the funeral pyres, lazily swaying to and fro, waiting for the next cadaverous feast to commence.

The vultures first assert their right, and it is recognized by the appointed custodians, who often serve the more audacious birds with morsels of flesh from the newly arrived subject. The vultures are allowed to attack the bodies of the penniless and friendless, as they lie exposed on inexpensive pyres built of sunbaked cow-dung.

When friends of the deceased attend who are in moderate circumstances, they add fatty matters—oils, cocoanuts, and other substances—to hasten combustion.

The vultures are often called off from one victim by the arrival of a fresh subject, so that there is always a joint here and there for the dogs. The quick, penetrating eyes of these birds sometimes espy a dog with too large a portion, in which case they pounce upon him and tear away his prize. So eager are they for their prey that the attendants have difficulty, at times, in keeping them at bay until they can prepare and place the body on the pyre.

When we were about satiated with this terrible though interesting place, and had said to Banjore [their guide], 'Let us leave this. What shall we see next?' he replied, 'Oh, no; let us wait. The best part of it is coming now,' and he pointed to two men who had just raised from the ground an ordinary wooden bier,—simply a long box with two shafts or bars at either end and straps to pass over the shoulders of the carriers. Just then one of them smilingly threw a red bunting cloth over the box, and away they went, laughing and chatting, to the municipal prison near by, as the chief custodian of the ghat had been notified that a prisoner had just died in that jail.

Our guide urged us to remain, as we would then have an opportunity of witnessing the whole ceremony; but having seen so many cremations at Poonah, Bombay, Benares, and Calcutta in India, we declined. Before leaving, however, we again looked at several burning pyres, noticing particularly the hungry vultures, which were now flapping their wings and coming nearer and nearer to us under the trees, they having observed the two employees start for the prison. The men soon returned, and one of the custodians quickly raised the body of the prisoner up in the box and with a sharp knife cut a number of strips of flesh from the arms and thighs and callously threw piece after piece to the more greedy birds, who now eagerly crowded around; thus heartlessly did this custodian dispense portions of that deserted human tenement whose life had flown within the hour. He did it with a malicious satisfaction which seemed to imply that in his wretched occupation he had formed attachments for certain vultures, and therefore favored them with choice morsels in advance of the others. This revolting scene would not have been recorded, but for the fact that it is a deeply interesting feature in this picture of a country of which we know so little.

Maxwell Sommerville, *Siam on the Meinam from the Gulf to Ayuthia* ..., London, Sampson Low, Marston and Co., 1897, pp. 138–40, 142–4.

48
Nakorn Srithammaraj and the Korat Plateau

H. WARINGTON SMYTH

H. Warington Smyth was an employee of the Royal Siamese Government who was in the country from 1891 to 1896, and was associated with both the surveying and mining sections of the government. He knew James McCarthy (see Passage 50) well enough to provide some sketches for his Surveying and Exploring in Siam *(1902). His own book,* Five Years in Siam, from 1891–1896, *also contains many of his own sketches.*

Warington Smyth travelled across the countryside extensively, like McCarthy, but seems to have been less at ease than he with the land in which he was working. He scoffed at the idea of building a railway to Petchburi as a railway which 'leads to nowhere', little foreseeing it would become an essential link to the relatively rich south. However, he knew his geology better than many, and was the first to give the lie to Mouhot's view that the great cave at Petchburi was of volcanic formation (some visitors before Smyth had even gone so far as to say they could smell sulphur there).

Here are two extracts, one describing Nakorn Srithammaraj, in earlier times known as Ligor, and which he calls 'Lakawn City'. He correctly notes an indefinable Indian influence in this ancient, wealthy, isolated, and leisurely southern city. The other describes a journey by buffalo cart across the featureless Korat Plateau in the north-east, and conveys a feeling of deprivation which the visitor today can still find away from the excellent main roads.

HAVING cooked and disposed of breakfast before an admiring crowd, we walked up to call on the governor by the wide roadway which connects the *Muang* [city] with the Chinese market and landing-place. The approach to the town is lined with magnificent peepul-trees, and the ruins of pagodas and monasteries, walls and gateways, attest to its former importance in the days when it was a port for ships. Old Hamilton[1] says there were many 'Pagan temples in it which have steeples built very high in [the] form of very sharp pyramids'. The town itself was 'built of bamboos and thatched with reeds', as at this day, and it produced 'abundance of tin'. An uncommon aspect is given to the scene by the way in which the women carry on their heads basket piled on basket to a weight often of 75 lbs. In most parts of Siam the head is regarded as almost sacred, and you should never even stroke a youngster's hair; much less is it to be used for carrying burdens. Thus the contrast here is striking, and the general effect of the grouping and colouring and the wide shaded spaces, with the dark complexions and comely

[1]See Passage 20.

stature of the women folk, both Malay and Siamese, was much more like a bit of India than of Siam.

Around the great brick wall of the city runs a deep moat, some fifty yards wide and thirteen or fourteen feet deep. The wall itself is about four miles round, and is mainly of red brick, and more massive and lofty than those either at Nan or Korat; but, unlike those places, there are no handsome gateways, and the only entrances which appear to be of ancient date are at the north and south ends of the city, and these were evidently more for defence than ornament, being pierced with embrasures for big guns and protected by curtains. It is now much grown over, and especially on the west side many ways have been broken through it. The town, inside the wall is like some big garden of palm and fruit plantations, with jungle houses scattered among them.

The remains of many *Wats* [temples], bowled over by the Burmans, are seen crumbling to ruin. The unhappy Buddhas inside, under the temporary *attap* [nipa palm] roofs, blink sadly in the gloom, with streaks of damp streaming down their faces, as though they wept for the glory that is departed. The great *Wat* of the place, Wat Pratat [Mahathat], is of great antiquity. Its chief feature is the pagoda, which stands nearly a hundred feet high. Its gilded point is one of the marks used by vessels coming in from the sea; but its reputation in the province depends on the fact that it casts no shadow. On two occasions when the skipper visited the *Wat*, sure enough there was no shadow to be seen, although the sun shone brightly—the unorthodox Nai Suk said the reason was that it was noon. In shape it is unlike most of the *Prachadis* in Siam, for the lower part is bell-like and high-shouldered, resembling some of the *zaydis* of Lower Burma. Around the base stand numbers of smaller pagodas, ten to twenty feet in height and of the same general character, said to be 189 in number.

The entrance into the area they occupy is through low-walled, high-roofed cloisters, and the ascent to the great pagoda is on the north[2] side, by a long low building, the roofs of which rise as they approach it. Inside, a flight of steep steps leads up, guarded at the base by weird dragon men, and above on the doors are seven-headed snakes and figures

[2]The east is the most usual [Author's note].

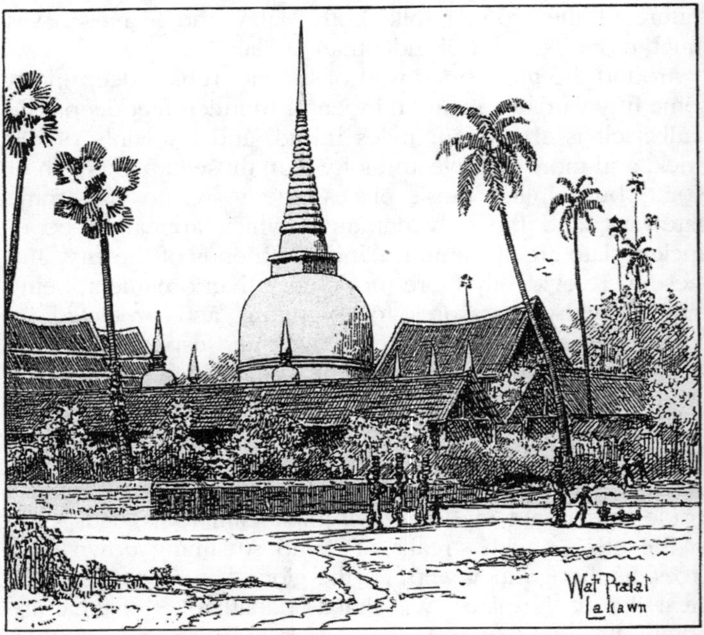

Wat Pratat [Mahathat] at 'Lakawn City' [Nakorn Srithammaraj] from H. Warington Smyth, *Five Years in Siam, from 1891 to 1896*, London, John Murray, 1898.

with many hands and faces, relics of the Brahmin influence for which Ligor was famous, and which extended at one time over the whole of this portion of the peninsula.

A fire destroyed part of the roof last year, and it was being renovated by 'merit-makers', not in the handsome red and gold of the old work, but with common white paint, which we warned the good people could bring but little merit. Below were some really good pictures worked in gold relief of Siddhartha leaving his sleeping wife and household and riding off with the *Tewadas* [heavenly assistants] assisting him. The town itself teems with elephants and goats, which are always having rows, to the great delectation of the market folk. The effect of Malay tradition is gratefully apparent in the absence of pigs and pariahs. There are some 5,000 people in the town and of these probably 400 are in the monasteries, and such others as are not the governor's slaves are agriculturists.

The chief himself was polite even to friendliness, and there was nothing to suggest the cruel outbursts of temper for which he is famed among his people, except the line of the mouth when he had ceased speaking, and the occasional somewhat irritable manner of addressing his attendants. During our visit his manner was less loud and ostentatious than that of many of his class, and his knowledge of the mining affairs in his province was in marked contrast to that of the governor of Langsuan. Still, the fact remains, that torture is practised to obtain evidence, and, although the easy-going people seldom take the trouble to hate any one, he is cordially feared and hated for his arbitrary ways throughout the province.

The *kwien*, the cart of Siam, the ship of the jungle lowlands, is a most admirably adapted contrivance. There is ne'er a nail or metal fastening used in the construction, for the jolting and straining are too great for any metal to stand. The body of the carriage, like a cariole in shape, is light and shallow, and ribbed somewhat like a boat; the intervening spaces are filled in with plaiting, and the pole which spreads below it forms a double backbone to the whole concern.... A plaited roof, which varies in shape according to the part of the country, is a necessary adjunct, and keeps the rain out very well, making the cart, if it is not full, a very good sleeping berth....

The country [near Korat] was not interesting, and we had no work to do in it but to cross it; the rains were in full blast, the streams rising rapidly, and the *nawngs*, or wide open swamps, were becoming impassable morasses, defended by hosts of elephant flies, mosquitoes, ticks and leeches, which drew blood at a rate to have delighted the souls of the practitioners of sixty years ago. We twice obtained new relays of oxen, but our speed was melancholy. Sometimes three hours crossing a stream thirty yards in width, carrying the carts high upon our shoulders; sometimes floundering in mud and water to our knees, across a vast plain of tall grasses, to the next firm ground two miles away; at others trying in vain to catch the oxen, who seemed to know what they were in for—such was our nine days' pastime....

The drivers were good fellows, and cut the firewood for camp, and were always ready to go on at any time of night, when the blurred moon came out a bit; but the heroes of the hour were those patient-eyed little oxen, who toiled so silently, while the great blood-sucking flies settled black upon their humps, and the leeches left them bleeding copiously below. In the heaviest rain we had to stop, because in rain the oxen lose their pluck and gall their necks; then they would be turned loose to get a hurried feed, and we lay down to get a sleep beneath the carts....

On favourable situations near the streams, and as a rule some way from the main trail, the villages will be found among the padi fields and gardens. To these places it is necessary to go to buy food, and get the headmen out to help the carts across the stream, if it be deep. There are seldom a hundred houses in any of them, there is little to be bought, and generally the Lao Pung Kao [north-easterners] seem far inferior to their western brothers in the refinement and comforts of life....

At one time of the year without water for thirty miles, at another drowned to a depth of several feet, the Korat plateau is a territory of such extremes that irrigation and cultivation generally are carried on under much greater difficulties than in any other part of Siam I have seen....

The amount of salt in many parts of the soil of the plateau makes it inferior for padi growing, and large numbers of villages are thus made desperately poor. The beautiful villages which are here and there to be met with on better land have no extended market to grow for, and consequently cultivate but sparingly. As long as there is no outlet for the Korat plateau, these villages, when a few caravans from the salt areas are supplied, have no incentives to energy beyond their own simple wants. Cut off from the outside world by the belt of the Dawng Praya Yen,[3] a little barter and interchange among themselves is not unnaturally all they understand. Their rice and salt, their cattle and their hardwoods, silks, and jungle spices, sticklac, cardamoms, tobacco, hides, and horns are exchanged among themselves, or sold to the few Chinese

[3]Mouhot's 'Forest of the King of Fire' separating Korat from the Chao Phraya valley.

traders who care to risk the laborious cross-country journeys and the caravan trail through the forest belt.

H. Warington Smyth, *Five Years in Siam, from 1891 to 1896*, London, John Murray, 1898, Vol. II, pp. 124–9; Vol. I, pp. 227–33.

49
Rice Planting and Rice Harvesting Ceremonies

ERNEST YOUNG

By the end of the nineteenth century, Siam was a far more open country than at the beginning, when the only non-Asians in residence were a few mixed-race descendants of Portuguese and their consul. Under King Chulalongkorn's reforms, large numbers of Europeans were employed in the administration, particularly in the Education Department. Many took advantage of their opportunity to write up their experiences of their stay in the country once they retired on usually fairly generous pensions.

Ernest Young was one such employee, and is remarkably discreet about his teaching occupations and professional activities. He does, at the end of his chapter on children, give a summary of the existing situation in the Education Department, which had established a training college for teachers, four 'Anglo-Vernacular Schools' for boys, a boarding-school for girls, and a practising vernacular school attached to the training college run by a succession of Englishmen. Most of the vernacular schools still preserved 'their antiquated methods'. They were without furniture or registers or records, and though usually in the grounds of a temple, the teachers were not priests.

Young, an upright Victorian, rather gave up on the older children, since they became 'early tainted with the national vices, vices that flourish more particularly in hot climates and luxurious soils', so he preferred to concentrate on 'the younger children at a time of life preceding the period when sensual enjoyments begin to enchain both mind and body'.

Based in Bangkok, Young only mentions by name Petchburi, the pilgrimage spot of Phra Phutthabat, and Anghin (Angsila, near Chonburi) as places visited outside the capital. However, he appeared to be well acquainted with some other coastal places and with the then-forested north, describing the felling there, noting that 'no replanting goes on, and great waste of timber is caused by the servants of the lessees', and prophetically observed, 'The loss that the world will experience from the loss of the wood, will be infinitesimal compared with the injury that is likely to fall upon the country itself in the changed climate conditions that invariably attend such wholesale deforestation.'

Young gives details of two ceremonies observed in Bangkok to mark the rice-planting and rice-harvesting calendar. The former has recently been revived, though the minister's attendant maidens are more likely to be less than young civil servants who have little acquaintance with ricefields. The swinging ceremony still took place in 1928, but has since fallen into disuse, though the Giant Swing outside Wat Suthat remains.

TWO curious ceremonies take place each year in connection with the agricultural operations. One is held in connection with the opening of the field season, while the other is an Oriental form of 'harvest-thanksgiving'. The first ceremony is known as 'Raakna' and is generally held about the middle of May. Until the 'Ploughing Festival' is over, no one is supposed to plough or sow. On a certain day foretold by the Brahmin astrologers of the court, the Minister for Agriculture, who is always a prince, or a nobleman of high rank, goes in procession to a piece of ground some distance from the city walls. He is for the time being the King's proxy, and on that day many shopkeepers, and holders of stalls in the markets, pay their taxes to him as the representative of their sovereign. Formerly his followers were in the habit of seizing the goods of any shopkeeper which were exposed for sale along the route of the procession, but this arbitrary manner of collecting dues has, like many other harmful customs, completely disappeared during the reign of the present enlightened monarch.

On reaching the scene of the festival ceremonies, the

Minister finds there a new plough with a pair of exceptionally fine buffaloes yoked to it. Both plough and buffaloes are gaily decorated with flowers and leaves. The Minister takes the plough, and for about an hour he guides it over the field, closely watched by the assembled spectators. They do not, however, concentrate their attention upon his skill as a ploughman, but on the length of the piece of silk which forms his lower garment. If, in the course of his amateur agricultural operations, the Minister should pull this garment above his knee, it is believed that excessive and therefore disastrous rains will occur during the wet season. On the other hand, should he allow it to fall to the ankle a great scarcity of rain is anticipated. A prosperous season is foretold when the folds of the garment reach midway between knee and ankle.

When a certain portion of the field has been ploughed, several old women in the King's service, strew grain of different kinds over the recently ploughed land. The animals are unyoked and led up to the scattered grain and allowed to feed upon it. Once more the crowd are on the alert, as they seek for yet other omens. That kind of grain of which the buffaloes most freely partake, will, it is expected, be scarce at the next harvest; the kind they disdain will be reaped in abundance. The ceremony over, the minister returns in procession, accompanied by soldiers and military bands; while the brightly dressed, chattering crowds return to their homes to prepare for the ploughing and the sowing, hoping for abundant rain and sunshine, and looking for a fruitful harvest, that thereby they may escape the terrible and remorseless hand of famine.

The harvest-festival ceremonies are of Brahminical origin and are known to the people under the name of 'Lo Ching Cha'. The first word 'Lo' means 'to pull'—'ching cha' is 'a swing'. The place where the 'Swinging Festival' is held is inside the city walls. It is a small green lawn situated opposite to a very large temple [Wat Suthat], and on the edge of a very busy thoroughfare. For three hundred and sixty three days in each year, there is nothing, except the huge pillars of the swing, to draw one's attention to the spot. A few boys playing football or flying kites, a few old women squatting down for a little gossip, or a few Malay grooms with their masters' ponies are the usual everyday occupants of the spot. On the other two days of the year, when the harvest festival is held, every inch of available space is occupied. The native children, unable to see over the heads of the men and women when they are upon the ground, quickly mount the neighbouring walls, and perch themselves in the branches of the trees, or cling, like monkeys, to every lamp-post and telegraph pole within sight of the proceedings. The thoroughfares leading to the place are blocked with innumerable carriages and rickshaws. The crowd is an exceedingly good-tempered one, and brawling of any kind is very unusual. The distant sound of a military band heralds the approach of another of those processions so dear to the heart of the Siamese. The procession passes through the dense crowd without any trouble, for the people willingly fall back so as not to impede its progress. Strangely coloured banners bearing quaint devices, flutter above the heads of the crowd.... Decorated buffaloes dragging decorated carts, bundles of rice, offerings of fruit and flowers, are all evidences of the thankfulness of the people for the safe ingathering of their harvests.

In the centre of the procession, carried in a chair of state on the shoulders of a number of strong well-built men, and shielded from the sun by a huge state umbrella, sits the Master of the Ceremonies resplendent in cloth of gold and jewelled ornaments. At one time the Minister for Agriculture officiated on these occasions, but now a different nobleman is selected each year, whose business it is to organise and superintend all the arrangements for the festival. All eyes turn towards the seated figure in his tall conical hat and jewelled robes. He is carried to a small brick platform, which is draped with the national flag and covered with flowers. He takes his seat, with two Brahmin priests on his right hand and two on his left. He places his right foot on his left knee, the left foot resting upon the ground. After having once seated himself in this position he is not allowed to remove his foot off his knee until the whole ceremony is finished. As this lasts about two hours, the presiding nobleman must be fairly uncomfortable by the time it is over. The penalty for moving the foot was, formerly, the confiscation of the culprit's property and the loss of his rank, in addition to any immediate ill-usage the

The Giant Swing at Bangkok, from Henri Mouhot, *Travels in the Central Parts of Indo-China (Siam), Cambodia, and Laos* ..., London, John Murray, 1864.

attendant priests might think fit to bestow upon him; but this is now all done away with, and the only deterrent influence brought to bear upon the temporary sufferer is the opinion of the people, who would feel deeply hurt and disappointed should any detail of their well-beloved ceremony be omitted.

The attention of the crowd is next directed to the performance of the swinging games. The swing itself is like any ordinary child's swing except for its enormous size. The side pillars are about ninety feet high, and the seat of the swing is about half-way between the ornamented cross-bar and the ground. A few feet in front of the seat, on the side towards the Palace, a long bamboo-stem is fixed in the ground, and from the top is suspended a small bag of silver coins. The men who take part in the games are usually Brahmins. They are dressed in white, and wear conical hats. They swing towards the bag of money and endeavour to catch it with their teeth. There are generally three competitors; the prizes for the first being worth about fifteen shillings, while for the second and third they are worth about ten and five shillings respectively. When the winners have received their rewards they pass amongst the crowd, sprinkling the spectators with consecrated water contained in bullocks' horns. Soon afterwards the Minister returns to his home, the crowd disperses, and thus this very ancient ceremony is brought to a close.

Ernest Young, *The Kingdom of the Yellow Robe: Being Sketches of the Domestic and Religious Rites and Ceremonies of the Siamese*, London, Archibald Constable and Co., 1898, pp. 210–17.

50
A Surveyor in Songkhla and Chiangsaen

JAMES McCARTHY

James McCarthy was a Fellow of the Royal Geographical Society and for many years Director-General of the Siamese Government Surveys. For twelve years, from 1881 to 1893, he was, in his own words, 'engaged in collecting material for the compilation of a map of Siam which might form the foundation of a national survey system'. By 1898, from London, he could write that the Survey Department had 'settled down to regular cadastral work'. The result was his Surveying and Exploring in Siam, *published in London and bearing the imprint of the Royal Geographical Society, which was sufficiently popular to run to a second impression by 1902. His successor, in 1901, as Director-General of the Royal Survey Department was R. W. Giblin.*

McCarthy makes little of the very difficult conditions of his work, and the constant fevers which wracked him during it. He was one of the many foreign specialists brought to serve the Siamese Government under the reforms initiated by King Chulalongkorn, with whom he seems to have been on the best of terms. Florence Caddy (Passage 43) mentioned his presence in 1882 at a dinner hosted by the king in the Grand Palace in honour of the Duke of Sutherland, and says she frequently met him during her short stay. She referred to him as an explorer rather than a surveyor, and went one Sunday afternoon along some Bangkok canals with him: 'Mr M'Carthy, lately the hero of the Royal Geographical Society, took me out in his gondola, towed by his steam-launch, cruising in a canal lined with busy shops, set among tall elm-trees and palms and plantations, that I had not previously explored. . . . I enjoyed the trip so much that I was sorry I had to rush home to dress for Mr Michell's dinner party' (given at the Oriental Hotel; Michell was the king's legal advisor).

McCarthy was no stylist, but a solid workman, and he covered the country, as well as a great deal of what is today Laos, setting up triangulation points and attempting to define the hitherto somewhat vague Siamese frontiers. Excerpts here give his impressions of Chumporn and Songkhla in the south, and of Chiangsaen in the north.

I had barely recovered from my fever when I started on an expedition to the Malay peninsula. A dispute had arisen about the correct boundary-line between the British Protected State of Perak and Patani, but it was difficult to locate the disputed territory....

The preliminaries being settled ... we went on board the *Narrow Beam*, where we met the Siamese commissioner, P'ia Pichai Sawng Kram. The captain of the steamer was a Cambodian Malay who had been refused leave to go on a pilgrimage to Mecca.

He was not in the best of temper, and pleaded that he was totally ignorant of the west coast of the Gulf of Siam. To make up for the want of local knowledge, he had an Admiralty chart of the coast of Nova Scotia.

We found no access could be had to the cabins of the steamer, as the keys were said to be in the palace; so we did the best we could on deck, not too well protected from wind and rain. The Malay captain having explained to the Siamese commissioner that he knew nothing of the route along the west coast of the Gulf, it was arranged to strike west from the lighthouse, and, anchoring at night, to steam closely along the coast during the day.

A bold coast-line is always grand, but feelings of admiration for the coast-line of the Gulf of Siam are somewhat modified by a knowledge of the loneliness of the forest-clad mountains and the fever that lurks there. The Sam Roi Yawt, or 'three hundred pinnacles' of limestone, form a beautiful picture, but do not possess a human inhabitant, and the voyager is always reminded that it was on this coast that the late King of Siam contracted a fatal fever when he accompanied a party of European astronomers, whom he had invited to make observations of a total eclipse of the sun in 1868.

We cast anchor off Champawn [Chumporn], where, it may be said, the Malay peninsula begins. The little harbour was full of rocks covered with oysters. The usual cocoa-nut palms and grass shanties marked the position of the village.

A few months before my arrival some French engineers

had visited the place with a view to making it one of the entrances to a ship-canal designed to pierce the [Kra] peninsula, the highest point of the intended route being 250 feet above sea-level.

On June 15 we anchored off Sungkla, or Singora, and remained there a few days, waiting for the acting governor, who had been appointed a boundary commissioner. We landed in the midst of holiday-making in connection with the cremation of the late P'ia Santara, and there was a great display of bunting in every direction. Sports were also the order of the day, and included boxing competitions in the native style. Kicking was permitted, and freely indulged in; and it was surprising to see with what force and dexterity a man would land a foot on his antagonist's jaw. There were also some buffalo fights. The horns of the combatants were highly polished, and the animals were goaded on by their keepers, to the intense delight of the crowd, who yelled frantically whenever one was gored to earth.

Covering one side of the reception-hall of the governor's house was a beautiful work of art in brass relief, representing 'The taking of Singora'. The grandfather of the present governor came from Amoy about the time of the founding of Bangkok, and, attacking Singora, captured it from the Malays. The Malay coast offered an easy prey to the venturesome Chinese in their junks, and both the east and west coasts of the northern part of the peninsula were brought under their influence.

From [Ban Pawm] we passed over the plain of Chieng Sen, which, owing to great floods, was almost bare of trees, the few that did exist being very stunted. As we approached the town of Chieng Sen, we observed a great number of bogs. The town was surrounded by low hills, all famous in local history, and the old governor, who was a nervous and excitable man, and hated the second governor, had extraordinary and very wild legends about them.

To the south, and beyond the low hills, about 6 miles off, is a large swamp teeming with fish; on the east is the noble Me Kawng [Mekong], and, as the soil is very productive, the people gain an easy livelihood. Every man in Siam is an excellent farmer, and the cultivation of fruit trees is a favourite employment of wealthy men, who take a delight in making the soil disclose its riches.

Chieng Sen is remarkable for its excellent cast figures of Gautama. Some are very large and very beautiful. At one time there were hundreds of those known as *Khatamapet*, regarded by the Siamese as being very ancient. As they were of a convenient size, they were carried off to Bangkok, where they would be better cared for. It was looked upon as desecration that they should be allowed to moulder away in ruins. The inhabitants of the city are nearly all officials, for the settlers, chiefly from Lampun, live in villages scattered over the plain. The settlers pay no taxes; their life is free and easy, and it is very difficult to induce them to work....

I returned to Chieng Sen on June 7, and felt great relief in taking up my quarters in a comfortable house. I had passed through much trouble, which would have been a great deal worse but for the assistance given me by P'ia Srisdi.

The triangulation round Siam had been started with great difficulty, but still a beginning had been made. To prevent delays in taking the field, I resolved to remain in Chieng Sen during the rainy season.

After seeing my things in the house, I went off to complete some work on a small hill about 2 miles to the south. While taking a round of angles, I was horrified to see my quarters in flames. I was too far off to think of hastening to the rescue, so I finished my work, and then descended to find my place burnt to the ground. Most of my things were saved, but P'ia Srisdi lost everything except the clothes he had on.

James McCarthy, *Surveying and Exploring in Siam*, London, John Murray, 1902, pp. 8–9, 137–8, 143.

51
Drainage, Latrines, and Pawnshops

A. CECIL CARTER

The Crown Prince of Siam, later King Vachiravudh, during a visit to the United States in 1902 was entertained by the Louisiana Purchase Exposition Company in St Louis, and the commitment was made for the Siamese Ministry of Agriculture to assemble an exhibition as part of the Louisiana Purchase Exposition in St Louis, in 1904. This was a grand affair commemorating the purchase of territory from France a hundred years earlier. According to the official report presented to the US Senate in 1906, 'On the occasion of the exposition there was published by the Commission a richly illustrated book entitled "The Kingdom of Siam". This work was presented to the educational institutions of this country, to public libraries, and to all persons who were known to be interested in Siam.'

This volume was edited by A. Cecil Carter, Secretary-General of the Siamese commission for the exposition. He worked in the Department of Education, and appears to have contributed six chapters to the book, three of which carried his position, and three which were anonymous, presumably because they covered sensitive topics (respectively, the royal family, the government, and the naval and military forces). Other named contributors included the eminent Dr Frankfurter, Colonel Gerini, and W. A. Graham.

All these persons were to be involved in the setting up of the scholarly Siam Society in the same year as the publication of the book. Carter was appointed its Honorary Treasurer at the first meeting of the Society's Council.

Being an official publication, there is no personal reflection, and no adverse comment. The book sets out the authorized viewpoint of the country as it existed in 1903, when the different chapters were compiled. As such, it gives a clear, detailed, and impersonal account of Siam at the beginning of the twentieth century, when the effects of King Chulalongkorn's modernizations were beginning to be felt.

Extracts here come from the chapters which Carter himself

wrote, giving some unexpected practical information about drainage, public latrines, and pawnshops.

IN Bangkok there is no system of drainage by closed pipes such as one sees in European countries. The numerous canals which intersect the city, as well as the deep and quickly flowing rivers, are the main sewers of Bangkok. These are flushed daily by the rise and fall of the tide, the influence of which is felt for many miles above the city. In addition to these natural drains, side drains have been constructed by the Sanitary Department alongside most of the streets. Into these flow the flood water after rainfall, as well as the soiled water from the neighboring dwelling-houses. Many of the drains have now been provided with sluice-gates where they join canals; the gates are opened at low water, and thus the drains are effectually flushed, the cleansing being assisted by sweepers. These drains are solidly built brick culverts lined with cement, and with man-holes every four metres apart to enable the coolies to cleanse the drains more easily.

As the pail system of conservancy is employed, nothing but bath, kitchen, and surface water enters these drains, so that complaints of their being offensive are not so frequent as might be imagined by those unaccustomed to such an open system of drainage.

[The removal of house refuse] is done entirely by the Sanitary Department. Seven bullock carts and metal hand-carts are used for this purpose, and by aid of these some fourteen tons of refuse are carted away daily. In the meantime this refuse is utilized for the purpose of filling up marshy holes in and about the city. When enough refuse has been deposited, a layer of good soil is scattered upon the surface as a deodorant, and in a year, so rapid is the disintegration of all vegetable refuse in this climate, it is found that what was once a rubbish heap has become transformed into innocuous soil.

It is proposed to erect refuse incinerators, not only to destroy the ordinary refuse, but also to desiccate the night soil so that it may be sold as a fertilizer.

Within the city of Bangkok there are now seventy-nine public latrines with a total of 361 rooms. The bucket system is employed and the daily changing of these is given out to contractors. An average of three thousand buckets of one gallon capacity are removed daily from these public latrines and from private houses. The night soil is taken first to a central depot, it is there emptied into barges specially built for the purpose, and is then taken away some miles beyond the limits of the city where it is buried.

Until the year 1901 there was no supervision of pawnshops. Before that time there were 432 shops, all of which habitually acted as receivers of stolen property. As there were no regulations of any sort and as the owners were under very many different jurisdictions, it was practically impossible to suppress crime.

In April, 1901, the pawnshop regulations became law, and there are now ninety-five pawnshops which are under strict laws.

Under the regulations, all forfeited pledges in pawnshops are examined by the police before any can be sold, and are compared by them with the lists of stolen property. For facility of reference, all property is divided into certain classes, and the description of each kind is entered in the appropriate volume, each inspector being provided with a complete set of volumes. Every morning at 8 a.m., the description of all property stolen during the previous twenty-four hours is sent to the Special Branch, the descriptions are entered in the volumes of stolen property, and the lists are then printed off and one copy sent to every pawnshop. In the event of any pawnbroker being already in possession of any of the property described or subsequently receiving it, he is obliged under heavy penalties to report the fact to the nearest station. To ensure his doing so, the examination of forfeited pledges already described is made. Another of the duties of the Special Branch is the identification of previously convicted offenders. The method in use on the Bangkok police is the finger-print method, the prints being classified by Henery's system. The bureau is maintained by the jail department. The fingerprints of every man arrested for serious crime are despatched each morning to the bureau. They are there examined, and in those cases where the offender has been previously convicted his former convictions are entered on a form which is taken to the court and attached to the case papers before the court opens for the day.

The finger-print is also utilized for the detection of crime, every person who pawns an article being required to place the print of his right thumb on the pawn-ticket counterfoil.

In those cases in which suspicion has fallen on several persons, and there is no clear proof against any one of them, this affords a very valuable clue to the police as an inspection of the fingers reveals who, if any of them, was the person who pawned the recovered stolen property.

A. Cecil Carter, *The Kingdom of Siam*, New York, G. P. Putnam's Sons, 1904, pp. 117–19, 124–5.

52
Religion and Death

OSCAR FRANKFURTER

Dr Oscar Frankfurter was an employee of the Royal Siamese Government who became a considerable scholar in its history, language, and religion, in which three areas he contributed chapters, under his own name, to Carter's Kingdom of Siam, *1904 (see Passage 51). He seems to have moved between several ministries, and in 1903 was attached to the Siamese Foreign Office.*

Frankfurter was the first Honorary Secretary of the Siam Society, founded in 1904, and one of its longest-serving presidents, holding the office from 1906 to 1918.

So many visitors to Siam gave often rather curious accounts of Buddhism as practised in the country, that it seems fair to let Frankfurter have his say here, giving an authorized account with the imprimatur of the Siamese Commission, headed by the then Crown Prince Vachiravudh, established for the St Louis exposition and Carter's related book.

THE religion of the state is Buddhism, while all other religious creeds are granted full liberty of worship, nor are their followers, by virtue of their creed, prevented from occupying any secular office under the administration or disabled in any other way.

The king is the highest 'supporter of the doctrine', and stands at the head of the religion, and in consequence of this position a spiritual hierarchy has developed which corresponds in many ways to the position of the temporal hierarchy. The king appoints all ecclesiastical dignitaries, and they as well as all other priests and monks are, with regard to their temporal affairs, under the Ministry of Public Worship....[1]

The term 'monk' may be applied to the large class of persons living in the temples without any official rank and engaged more or less earnestly in the study of the sacred writings or in meditation. It is, moreover, an essential part of the education of a Siamese, when he has completed his twentieth year, to enter a temple for a time. Many of the Siamese while still boys of fourteen or fifteen also enter as novices (*Samaneras*) for a short period, in the upper classes usually from six months to a year. This custom, however, is not so universal as their entering as priests when grown up. There is no restriction placed on a priest as to the duration of his stay in the priesthood, but while a monk he has strictly to obey the rules of the order.

The initiation generally takes place at the commencement of the rainy season (full moon of the eighth month, i.e. July), and is always accompanied by a festival. It forms the conclusion of the education.

This initiation and service in the priesthood is of special importance to the princes of the reigning house, and most particularly to those princes in the direct line of succession, for the king as temporal head of the religion must have shared in the common lot of the followers of Buddha in order that he may be in full sympathy with their feelings and ideas, and the great reverence in which the priesthood is held forms a firm bond between the highest and the lowest in the land....

[1]The functions of this have now been subsumed by the Religious Affairs Department of the Ministry of Education.

With regard to the tenets of Buddhism as practised in this country, it can only be said that it is the Buddhism of the southern school. The sacred books contained in the *Tripitaka*, known in Ceylon and Burmah, are likewise known in Siam, and it was from this country that the *editio princeps* was issued a few years ago. Amongst the educated classes, Buddhism is practised in its pristine purity, while of course, just as elsewhere, superstitious practices have crept into the popular belief. Buddhism in Siam has kept clear, however, of esoteric influence, as it was prevalent a few years ago in Ceylon under European influence; it has thus kept the command forbidding to claim or to aspire to supernatural power, whilst Nirvana is rightly explained as the extinction of the three fires of lust, hatred, and delusion. A more realistic view is taken, however, among the people, who believe in future substantial states, and in a migration of souls which enter new bodies according to the good or evil deeds performed in this world, though according to the pristine teaching it is only the deeds, as such, that survive.

This may perhaps be due to the birth stories which, although they do not form part of the sacred writings, are well known in Siam as in other Buddhist countries. These birth stories are in many cases old folklore tales which were used to illustrate a verse in the sacred writings.

With regard to the whole doctrine of life and death as presented in Buddhism, we will quote from the sermon preached by Somdet Pra Vanarat at the memorial service of the late Crown Prince, in whose words is found a solution of the whole question both with regard to the dead and the living.

'In the life of sentient beings there is no certainty. We know not when or for what reasons life will be extinguished. No one is able to guarantee existence; short is our life and swiftly are we extinguished, and our sorrow never ceases. As the potter's work will be broken, so our life will come to an end, and whether children, young or old, whether foolish or wise, all fall under sway of death. We may speak of days, months, and years; but we cannot say when our existence will come to an end. No one is spared, whether of kingly origin or a Brahmana, whether a Vaisaya or a Sudra, whether of the lowest caste or a slave; all fall under the sway of death.

When we depart from one existence to another, the parents cannot protect their child, nor will the love of the kinsman avail aught to his kin; the lamentations and grief over the departed do not benefit him. Death is the natural consequence of existence, and our life is like that of the cow which the Brahmana leads to the altar for sacrifice. Knowing this, what will lamenting over the departed benefit us? The dead are not supported by our grief. The dead have no consciousness of our acts, and they have prepared their existence by their own deeds. Everything is subject to change, although we may think it permanent; this is the law of the universe.

'Thus having listened to the words of the Fully Enlightened One, we know that the dead cannot come to life again; therefore let us cease lamenting and turn our attention to the living, so that the country may prosper; work for the living. For such is the work of the living, when death has not yet reached them. We are born and die, this is the way of the world; but the good works we do in this world, they will bear fruit in future, they will last.'

Oscar Frankfurter, 'Religion of Siam', in A. Cecil Carter, *The Kingdom of Siam*, New York, G. P. Putnam's Sons, 1904, pp. 95, 98–102.

53
Practical Aspects of Rice Cultivation

W. A. GRAHAM

W. A. Graham was, like Oscar Frankfurter, another contributor to the official government publication, The Kingdom of Siam, *edited by A. Cecil Carter (Passage 52). In that volume, he was listed as 'formerly Assistant to the Ministry of Agriculture'; again, like Frankfurter, he seems to have moved between several ministries during his time working for the Royal Siamese Government. He wrote an extensive compendium of information about the country,* Siam: A Handbook of Practical, Commercial and Political Information *(London, Alexander*

Moring, 1912). An expanded second edition, with the shorter title Siam, *appeared with the same publisher in London in 1924.*

Again, like Frankfurter, Graham was closely associated with the scholarly Siam Society in its early days, and was its President from 1921 to 1925.

As little has appeared so far in this volume on the practical aspects of rice cultivation, the extracts from Graham's piece relate to this.

THE Siamese are, before all things, an agricultural nation. From time immemorial, the valley of the Menam has been one vast rice-field, and the present inhabitants of the country continue to plough, sow, and reap in it after the same methods, and with the same kind of implements, as were employed by their predecessors a thousand years ago.

The Siamese man does not take kindly to most forms of labor, and is quite content to see such trades and manufactures as there are in his country in the hands of Chinese and other foreigners. The pursuit of agriculture, however, he reserves to himself, and, while nine tenths of the people of the country follow the calling, it is very rarely that foreigners [i.e Chinese] are found taking an active part in any form of agriculture except market-gardening.

The principal product of the country is rice. Indeed, so much is this the case, that thus baldly to state the fact is to convey but a feeble and inadequate impression of the supreme position of this cereal in the land. It might almost be said that rice is the only agricultural product, for though Siam exports timber and grows maize, millet, sugar, tobacco, and fruit, yet her rice production preponderates so entirely, and her commerce, politics, and social conditions are now, and have always been, so profoundly influenced by rice, that all these lesser products amount, by comparison, almost to nothing. The European, whose idea of a staple food is formed from a knowledge of the part played in the economy of his own country, can only vaguely imagine the importance of rice to the Siamese. It constitutes not merely the principal, but almost the sole food of every one, from the highest noble to the lowliest plebeian: horses, cattle, dogs, cats, and all other domestic animals live on it; it is used for making beer and spirits; it enters largely into all ceremonials, and the superstitious observances in connection with it provide the people with their most frequent occasions for holiday-making. The only recognized means of investing money is, or was until the recent introduction of European banking, the purchase of rice-fields; the nobility is graded according to the (now purely nominal) grants of rice-land conferred by the king; dealings in rice and the ownership of rice-land are the causes of most of the civil litigation in the law courts, and the result of the last, or prospects of the next, rice harvest, make the most absorbing topic of conversation at all times. It is rice which forms the cargoes of the thousands of boats ever passing up and down the river Menam; which supplies the grist of the numerous mills of modern Bangkok (the furnaces of which are fed with rice-husk), and which is carried away in the ocean-going steamers always to be seen loading in the port; finally it is from rice that the Government derives, directly, almost the whole of its revenue....[1]

The practice of 'Na Dum' [planting rice] is an art. The seedlings, when the fields are ready for them, are taken from the nurseries in bundles of a hundred or so and neatly tied together, the mud being shaken from their roots by a deft kick administered to the bundle at the moment of drawing it from the soil. This work falls to the men and the planting usually to the women, and as skill in planting vastly enhances a girl's chances in the marriage market, so a young man who should hand to the women, to plant, bundles clumsily tied or with muddy roots would stand small chance of getting a bride in his own village.

Buffaloes are used for ploughing in the lower plains, where the atmosphere is humid, but the buffalo, in spite of his great strength, is useless in a hot, dry climate, and therefore, in the higher and drier parts, bullocks are used, a pair of these doing the work of one buffalo.

While the paddy, as it is called until the grain is husked, is growing, it demands no labor, and until it is reaped nothing is done beyond a little spasmodic bird-scaring by the children. With the reaping time all are busy again: the crop is cut with

[1]This is, of course, no longer true, especially since the abolition of the premium, effectively an export tax on rice.

small sickles loaded on sleds and drawn to the winnowing-ground, a small spot either in the fields or near the village, on which the earth is beaten down hard and smooth. There, after the spirits have been duly propitiated, the sheaves are strewn out and are trampled upon by the cattle until the grain is all detached from the straw. Winnowing then takes place, after which the golden yellow grain is stored in specially constructed huts and the year's work is over.

W. A. Graham, in A. Cecil Carter, *The Kingdom of Siam*, New York, G. P. Putnam's Sons, 1904, pp. 153–5, 158–9.

54
A Public Execution

P. A. THOMPSON

P. A. Thompson was a painter (he was elected to the Royal Academy) who was very interested in the archaeology of the country. His general book on Siam, which had an American edition in 1910 with a different title, Siam: An Account of the Country and the People, *is a carefully documented work with footnote references to experts like Gerini and Aymonier. Thompson often writes in the first person, but does not make clear if he was working in Siam to gather his varied impressions. The assumption must be that he was, since he gives generous coverage to the roles of the European advisors and officials in the government.*

Thompson trots out all the sweeping generalities of character relating to the Siamese which Westerners of the time loved to indulge in. He comments unfavourably on the paper strength of the army, and so on, but does at least admit, 'We must not judge them by our standards.' He was one of the earliest to note the assimilation of the Chinese though, agrees that the Siamese are 'an artistic people' and travelled fairly widely in the country to visit its antiquities.

Here he gives an account of a public execution he witnessed by chance while travelling in the provinces.

THOUGH murder and dacoity are not uncommon forms of crime, the death sentence is rarely passed in Siam, and still less often carried out. Executions are public, but not very many, even amongst the Siamese themselves, have ever seen one; for the place of execution is known only to a few, and in Bangkok it always takes place at the first streak of dawn. It was quite by chance that once, as I was travelling far up the Bangpakong River, beyond Pachin, I passed a boat full of soldiers with a prisoner in their midst, and found that the man was to be beheaded that day at the next *wat* [temple] upon the river bank. No secrecy seemed to have been observed here, for there were more than a hundred people assembled when I landed, and amongst them the Governor of the district. When the condemned man arrived he was handed over to the monks, who spent the morning in preaching to him, but he appeared to derive little comfort from their words. When this was over he was allowed to ask for anything that he wanted, but he only desired a little rice. It is said that condemned men are often given opium, but this man had none. It seems that he had been lying in prison under sentence of death for two years, and this delay, which is perhaps the most objectionable feature of the whole business, is not uncommon.

During the morning the executioners built for themselves a little room of leafy boughs. It was to be the 'green-room' for the succeeding tragedy, and in the centre of the stage they had planted a bamboo, with a cross-piece about two feet from the ground. To this the condemned man was led. He sat cross-legged on the ground with his back to the bamboo, and his arms, closely pressed against his sides, were tied at the elbows to the cross-piece; but with this exception he was left free to move. Then one of the executioners, kneeling beside him, filled his ears with clay and gave him lighted joss-sticks to hold. At times, also, he appeared to stroke the condemned man's face, almost as though he were trying to mesmerise him, but if such were his object it was of no avail, for the poor wretch was quite unnerved and the joss-sticks fell unheeded to the ground. Now the second executioner came out, dressed in red with a red band bound round his forehead, and carrying a sword. He advanced until the condemned man could see him out of the tail of his eye, and there, some twenty yards away on the man's right hand, he sat upon his heels, and appeared to await the moment when he should strike. Thereafter the condemned man kept his head turned towards him, looking over his right shoulder.

Meanwhile the first executioner had swiftly run back and donned the red dress. He now entered the wide ring of spectators almost directly behind the condemned man, but during his stealthy advance he kept always on his left hand. *Wai-ing* once to the Governor, and then raising his joined hands to heaven, he took his sword—a long slightly curved blade broadening towards the point, with thick heavy back and edge keen as a razor. Then he danced out with half-a-dozen prancing steps on tiptoe, and stopped with one foot in the air. His sword was held above his head, one hand grasping the handle and the other fingering the point. So, in a series of little rushes, varied by extraordinary posturing and twirling his sword, he crept nearer and nearer to his unsuspecting victim, amidst a silence that was painful. At the end his movements were so rapid that we could scarcely follow them. He was well out of striking distance when there came a quick rush, a circle of light in the air, and a sudden jet of crimson. He had not paused for the fraction of a second to take aim, but the head was severed with that single blow.

When all was over the monks came out again, and chanted over the dead man. They held a strip of cotton stuff, and allowed one end to hang down and rest upon the body. Then the body was laid in a grave already dug near by, while the head was stuck upon a pole and left as a warning to evil-doers.

P. A. Thompson, *Lotus Land: Being an Account of the Country and People of Southern Siam*, London, 1906, pp. 284–7.

55
Kampengpetch and Srisachanalai in 1904

E. LUNET DE LAJONQUIÈRE

Captain E. Lunet de Lajonquière (c.1850–1933) lived in colonial French Indo-China from 1883, and met by chance Louis Finot, the first Director of the Ecole Française d'Extrême Orient, when travelling by boat after a leave in France. Finot resolved to make use of Lajonquière's knowledge of the region, and bring him into the newly founded school. The two soon published together an inventory of Cham monuments (1900), and Lajonquière subsequently published, from 1901 to 1914, a stream of volumes relating to the archaeology, geography, and history of the region, before retiring to Malaysia.

In Le Siam et les Siamois, *Lajonquière describes a journey from Bangkok up the river to Tak (Raheng), into Mulmein and Rangoon, and back into Siam, taking in Sukhothai, before returning to Bangkok. The journey of 1800 kilometres took two months at the end of 1904, and he recommended it to 'tourists seeking new paths', which were not without difficulties. He gave detailed descriptions of the ruins of Sukhothai, embellished with photographs and drawings. Here are parts of his descriptions of Kampengpetch (where he missed the most important remains outside the old town) and the kiln sites at Srisachanalai, in which he produces the saw about the potters being of Chinese origin, but points to the need for investigation, which has very recently been done.*

TOWARDS 10 o'clock, we reached Kampeng Pet, at least the new town, for the old one is still another kilometre further away.

It is a sort of hamlet where the huts are arranged along two roads parallel to the river [Ping]; it is a district centre. The government offices, built opposite the boat landing, occupied a huge wooden building, and as it is open for the most part, we could see inside a number of pen-pushers, dressed in European fashion, industriously turning their papers. Close by is the market to which some twenty Chinese shops give some animation. A little to the rear is the dwelling of the

Governor, horribly touched up in gaudy colours by some Chinese artist, who devised, when carving the gables, the essentially national motif of a bat hanging by its teeth from a ring.

Upstream, the two roads led to a temple, the chapels of which were in part built with material taken from the nearby ruins. A new *bot* [prayer hall] was being built there with typical oriental sloth; it will not be finished for a year, maybe two. Already, though, the old one was disappearing under a thick layer of dust; it had not been swept for months and the rags which covered the statues and statuettes cluttering its altars were in part rotting away.

In one of the shady avenues leading to the temple, a police officer was taking his men through shooting practice with much zeal. Their stiff bearing, the harsh and piercing sound of his orders, contrasted sharply with the indifference and nonchalant appearance of the monks. What would the gentle Gautama have said of this warlike invasion of one of his peaceful monasteries?

The Governor ran to greet us. He was dressed in European fashion, topped by a ridiculously small cap on his huge head, and visibly uncomfortable in clothes which he was not used to wearing. He told us he had received orders, he was going to prepare the horses and would come back to take us right away. With that, he abandoned us, leaving us to do what we would, without even thinking of offering us some shelter other than the low and stifling roof of our boats. A little later, however, he came himself to find us and take us to the ruins. He had, to mount horse, put on khaki trousers over his white pants, which protruded at least a hand below the others, and that completed the comical look already given by his tiny head-dress.

Kampeng Pet (the Diamond Fortress) was already cited in inscriptions dating from the twelfth century of our era. In spite of its imposing name, it was never a capital, but most probably merely a vassal fortress of the kingdom of Sukhothai, the centre of which was more to the east, on the central Menam. Almost nothing except the irregular earth walls exist, enclosing a rough trapezium with rounded sides, oriented north-east–south-west on its long axis, along with three or four very ruined temples. The thick bush, almost velvety, covers everything with a uniform green mantle. We crossed the enclosure at one of the corners, and, following poorly marked paths, were taken to see the miserable remains of what was formerly the pride of this city with the resounding name. The only durable materials used in the construction of its monuments were limonite [laterite], a hard but rough stone, and brick, which the sculptors of these lands never knew how to carve like the artists who decorated the monuments of Cambodia.

The statues, first built of limonite blocks, then trimmed with a knife and covered with stucco, the massive monolithic overturned columns, stretches of thin walls, the irregular pyramids [spires], gave the impression they were the work of a newly arrived civilization without any artistic tradition. It is true two fine bronze statues were found there which are now in the Bangkok Museum, and on the foundation of an old palace can still be seen the remains of some statuettes which, in some elements, show a fairly advanced knowledge of modelling, but it seems likely they were not cast here. They seem to have come rather from some Cambodian temple and to have been transported here, as divinities snatched from their altars by some army chief returning from a victorious raid, from whom protection was sought which the statues were unable to give their former devotees. Now everything conspires to destroy these miserable remains, the luxurious tropical vegetation, the monks from the nearby temple, who come to take materials they need for their new buildings, and the treasure hunters, who, in the belief of some more or less accurate legends, have disembowelled every statue and pyramid.

Returning to our landing, I received the complaints of our cook, who maintains he paid two sous of our money for eggs, more or less the same price as in Paris, and assures me he was not able to buy even one chicken. I had to seek the help of our police lieutenant; then, stocked thanks to his intervention, we went to moor for the night by an islet in the middle of the river, to profit by the breeze and escape at the same time the mosquitoes, the noise, and the importunately curious.

When we arrived there, as we were taking our daily bath, a boat came up with a young Siamese lady and her three children, the eldest of which was hardly ten. Quite unperturbed by our presence, she began to make, there and then, some holes in the banks from which the waters have recently receded and were still covered by a layer of silt; her children behind her planted shoots of those sweet potatoes which grow in bunches, and very quickly the harvest will be ready; she will not give them any attention until they are gathered. Are they not excusable for being so totally lazy, and has not nature so contrived that they should be so?

Everything [in Srisachanalai] that was formerly enclosed in the walls of the old capital is now abandoned to the dense vegetation of the thick forest. Thick undergrowth, full of thorny lianas, conceals from everyone the remains of buildings, so sumptuous at the period they were constructed, and which King Ramkamhaeng and his ancestors built. Around these ramparts, lost beneath the greenery, the simple and easy life of the people has not been extinguished in this favoured region, one of the most agreeable I know in Indo-China; only the kings have departed thence. Centuries-old rice-fields, fertilized annually by the floods, give the peasants their ever abundant harvests, nature makes for them an existence devoid of hard labour and travail. The past has only left them with vague souvenirs on which they have spun a thousand ingenious tales and the discoveries they make when ploughing the earth of their fields or digging in the mud of their pools, are pretexts for new tales. I was shown today two life-size hands, coming from a bronze Buddha statue, which must have been very fine to judge by these fragments which are all that have come to light, at an interval of several months, in the 'rose pool' by a frog hunter. This crafty chap nearly made a small fortune. He spread the tale that you only had to touch these hands to be cured of the most serious maladies. Many are those who at all times and in all countries who, in their despair, give credence to such miraculous inventions. So they came, from everywhere in the surrounding region, to seek health in the hut of a fisherman who had already abandoned his harpoons and nets, when the Governor intervened and requisitioned the healing hands for the archaeological collection of the state. So evaporated the golden dream of the poor frog hunter.

The Thao Thurien (durian kilns) are situated on the right bank of the river Yom about five kilometres upstream from Srisachanalai. Nothing now appears to justify their name and I found there none of the trees whose fruits, according to certain gourmets, have so repugnant a stench. Below the track some twenty abandoned porcelain kilns are still in part filled with pieces that are partly fired and surrounded by rubble and wasters.

To judge by the shape of some of these pieces, it was a colony of Chinese workers who, probably under the auspices of the kings of Sukhothai–Srisachanalai, established themselves here. Above all, they made vases, dishes decorated with a celadon glaze, crackled or decorated with darker designs before firing; little remains, to tell the truth, of what they produced, and in this pile of rubble, which is very far from being completely excavated, nothing has been found, as far as I know, which is worth keeping, except as documentary evidence. I believe, though, that you have to beware of the so-called Sawankaloke porcelain which can be bought in Bangkok for a song. The date when these kilns were producing would make them, if they were authentic, far more precious. They were without any doubt made contemporaneously with the two capitals, since among the wasters have been found the remains of pottery statuettes representing lions, glazed white, similar to those which can be seen in the nearby ruins. One should therefore date them to the thirteenth century, a fine age for glazed porcelains which were still unknown in Europe at this time. Perhaps, by carefully clearing the area, which has not been done to date, some whole pieces will come to light which will establish more thoroughly the artistic value of the potters of Thao Thurien.

Capt. E. Lunet de Lajonquière, *Le Siam et les Siamois*, Paris, 1906, pp. 149–53, 333–6.

Into the Twentieth Century (1910 to the Present)

56
Travelling to Chiangmai in 1913

REGINALD LE MAY

Reginald Le May (1885–1972) studied at King's College, London University, and in 1906 passed the entrance examination for student interpretership in His Britannic Majesty's Far East Consular Service, joining the British Legation in Bangkok in 1908. He went to Chiangmai in 1913 to serve as Vice-Consul, and later the same year went to Lampang in the same position. After sick leave in England, he returned to Bangkok as Vice-Consul in 1916. He resigned from the Far East Consular Service in 1922, and joined the Royal Siamese Government service as advisor to the Minister of Commerce. With the overthrow of the absolute monarchy in 1932, he was prematurely retired, and thereafter lived mainly on his Siamese Government pension. He went to Pembroke College, Cambridge and obtained his Ph.D degree in 1937 at the age of fifty-two.

He published extensively from 1920, and was an authority on Siamese stamps, coins, ceramics, and South-East Asian culture. Back in England, he retired to his native Kent, retaining nostalgic memories of his time in northern Siam. Given here are extracts from his first journey to reach Chiangmai (at a time when the train only reached Denchai), through the north of the country, then largely inhabited by ethnic Lao.

At Pitsanulok it was necessary to find quarters for the night in the station rest-house, and to continue the journey the following morning.

The scenery from Pitsanulok to Den Chai was entirely different in character from that of the previous day, and was a source of unalloyed delight to one coming from the flat and uninteresting south.

As far as Utaradit the gradient is small, but after leaving that garrison town, the train goes up and up, winding slowly round the hillsides; on the one side are deep ravines, densely covered with jungle, and on the other, towering above in sharp contrast, a mass of sheer rock. All the while one is drinking a draught of the fresh mountain air, and breathing the scent of the jungle flowers. Innumerable butterflies of every hue and size swarm on the permanent way, to an extent that, standing on the steps of the carriage, it is possible to catch them with one's hand; and the dense undergrowth of the jungle around conjures up visions of tiger, deer and elephant—visions, however, which do not materialise, as those animals have long since overcome their resentment to the railway and now maintain a dignified seclusion.

At Ban Tan, just above Utaradit, we reached the lowest outposts of the Lao people, and I was filled with admiration at a bevy of Lao beauties who had come down from their village to the station to see the 'wonderful' train. They were dressed in the Lao 'Sin', or skirt (of red and black bands, as worn by the women of Phre), with a close-fitting bodice above, and had their hair dressed in layers, rather like the coils of a snake, with a red flower gracefully worn at the side. They laughed and chattered naturally and gaily, and seemed to possess a temperament different from that of the ordinary southern peasant, who is as a rule reserved and shy.

The journey came to an end all too soon, and we descended at Den Chai punctually at noon. Here, by previous agreement, I found awaiting me a travelling companion, Mr Wood, the British Vice-Consul at Lampang (now Consul-General at Chiengmai), who had been visiting Muang Thon, a small village in the neighbourhood, and was then staying at Phre on his return to Lampang. As my way to Chiengmai lay through Lampang, we agreed to travel that part of the journey together....

Laotian girls, from Henri Mouhot, *Travels in the Central Parts of Indo-China (Siam), Cambodia, and Laos* . . ., London, John Murray, 1864.

We stayed at Phre for two nights, just time enough to engage sufficient mules and carriers to take my baggage through to Chiengmai. These, to the number of ten carriers and four mules, were obtained without much difficulty, the carriers being Lao, while the mule men were Ho, a tribe from the Chinese province of Yunnan, who enjoy a monopoly of the mule caravan trade. They are hardy fellows, of good physique and of independent, though pleasant character. They rather amused me by showing considerable contempt for the carriers, with whom they declined to hold any converse whatever.

As regards porterage in the north of Siam, all heavy goods, especially those which are not required on the actual journey, are as a rule packed into elephant howdahs, each elephant carrying up to 600 lbs in weight, or, if these are wanting, on to Yunnanese mules which can always be hired at reasonable rates. The porters themselves each carry two round baskets, some eighteen inches high, one at either end of a long bamboo pole, which they put over their shoulders; into these baskets are thrown, haphazard, tins of provisions, kitchen utensils, in fact, everything which one will want on the march, but the load is never a heavy one, as the men are not of strong physique, and are moreover more inclined to peace and sleep than to hard work in a hot sun. They have, however, a good standard of honesty, and seldom will anything be lost from the 'hap', as the basket is called; moreover, although possessed of no great degree of intelligence, they have a certain sense of humour, and willingly respond to kindliness and a cheerful spirit....

We walked ahead for an hour or more, and then, coming to the Hue Kamin, crossed the stream and plunged into the forest. Knowing that generations of Shan and Ho with their caravans had travelled between Lampang and Phre on constant trading expeditions, I had expected to traverse a well-beaten track, but was pleasurably surprised to find that none such existed, and that we were to pick our way, now along the bed of the stream itself, clambering over rocks and boulders, now climbing steep rocky ascents, and now walking through forest glades. Overhead the branches of the giant trees met, shading us from the rays of the sun and keeping the air delightfully cool. The rippling stream, the small cascades tumbling over the rocks, and the song of the birds all combined to make us feel the joy of life, and our spirits respond to the brightness of the scene. Many have sung their hymns in praise of the forest life, but it is only those who have actually come under its spell that can realise the peculiar fascination and beauty of a tropical forest....

We had agreed to breakfast the next day in the forest on our way, but the fates conspired against us, and the carrier who had gone on ahead with the food failed to stop at the appointed time; consequently, by ten o'clock, after nearly four hours' walking in a vain effort to catch him, we had to call a halt and wait for the main party to come up. Fortunately for us, another carrier soon appeared, bearing a basket with spare provisions, and we had our breakfast after all, of sausages cooked in their tin and fresh pineapple, washed down by Pilsener beer. Seldom has a meal seemed so satisfying, or beer such a draught of nectar.

Our way again lay through the forest, but the hills were much steeper and there were no streams to charm the eye. We rode for some time after breakfast, and it was a matter of wonder to note how sure-footed the ponies were in climbing the rocky hills, and how they picked their way down the sharpest descents with the utmost care and precision. They are not very small either, like the Siamese 'rats', but stand on the average at least twelve hands high.

The second stage of the journey proved a light one, as we reached the 'Sala' [rest-house] at Pang Bue shortly after noon, and the elephants were not far behind. At Pang Bue we heard of a tiger scare. It seemed that a short time previously a man-eater had actually been bold enough to enter the compound of the rest-house and had carried off a pony belonging to the Governor of Phre, who was staying in the 'Sala'; and now came a story of how the same tiger had climbed a tree fifty feet high, dragged down a man who was hiding there for safety, and had eaten him. There appeared to be no doubt that the man had been eaten, but that the tiger had climbed fifty feet to fetch him was difficult for us to accept. Possibly the tiger had made a spring at the tree and the man had fallen into his jaws through sheer fright. We had thought of making preparations for sitting up that night over a kill, but from further enquiries it was clear that the tiger had changed his beat, and so we decided to go quietly to bed. That night we heard the 'bang', or flying squirrel, hooting in the forest, and our servants looked at one another in distress, as it is said to be an omen of disaster to the peasant mind.

In the morning, 'Phu Sido', the only male elephant of the four, as soon as he was unhobbled, refused to be caught and, when he finally allowed his mahout to scramble up on to his neck, trotted gaily off into the forest. We looked forward to several hours' delay hunting for him, but my companion sent 'Me Wak', his favourite amongst the females, after the wayward fellow, whereupon he came back like a lamb and gave his mahout no more trouble. Such is the influence of the woman, even among the elephant family.

We left Pang Bue rather late, but the day's journey was fortunately again a short one. The jungle on either side was not so dense as it had been on the previous days, and the trees were more scattered than usual; it seemed, in fact, more akin to a European than to a tropical forest; still the shade was sufficient to keep off the heat of the sun, and a light shower of rain which fell during the morning added to the coolness. Several times we heard the crisp sound of barking deer, or it might have been the barking of wild dogs, which are sometimes to be found in the forests, but of jungle life we saw no sign, except a purely silver-white snake which glided across our path, gazed at us with silent contempt, and with a swish of its tail was gone. We reached the 'Sala' at Me Moh about mid-day, but had a disagreeable surprise during the afternoon, for the roof proved to be badly in need of repair, and a storm which passed over our heads almost flooded us out. Fortunately the rain passed away, and that evening we saw a sight which gave us food for conversation during the remainder of the day.

Just outside the rest-house there was a tall tree and, while we were discussing the effects of the storm, we suddenly saw a Lao come and kneel before it, and place offerings at its foot, apparently to some 'spirit' which dwelt in the tree and which he desired to appease. Flowers, candles and fruits were reverently laid; the candles were lit, and the man disappeared. This was evidently a form of the worship of spirits, or 'Phi', as they are called in Siamese.

The thought of 'Phi' did not, however, keep us awake that night at Me Moh, and we rose early next morning, ready for the last stage of the journey to Lampang. At no great distance from the rest-house, the road broadened out and the jungle became very sparse, giving way to bracken and thinly-wooded forest. Throughout the day there was no shade from the sun, and a feeling of relief shone on the faces of the entire party when we emerged on to the plain below us and saw the walls of the city looming in the distance. High, and of red brick, they made an imposing appearance, yet would obviously be capable of offering but little resistance under modern conditions of attack. As we approached the town, to right and left we could just catch a glimpse of temples, mostly in the Burmese style, nestling outside the walls among the trees.

Reginald Le May, *An Asian Arcady: The Land and Peoples of Northern Siam*, Cambridge, W. Heffer and Sons, 1926, pp. 69–74.

57
Bang Pa-in and Queen Saowapa

MALCOLM SMITH

Malcolm Smith was born in 1875. Soon after qualifying as a doctor in London, he joined a practice in Singapore and then moved to Bangkok in 1901, where he remained in practice until 1924. He became at first an unofficial medical advisor to Queen Saowapa, a daughter of King Mongkut and one of King Chulalongkorn's queens, and then for five years served as her official doctor until her death in 1919. He was also the preferred Western doctor for many at court, and moved freely about the palace buildings. He returned to England in 1924, and devoted the rest of his life to research into reptiles. He also completed writing his memoirs of the queen's anecdotes and court life in Putney, London, in 1946, and these were published in 1957, the year before his death. Dr Smith also published, in 1944, an article on 'The Families of the Kings of Siam of the House of Chakri' in the Annals of Eugenics *(Vol. 12, pp. 151–7).*

His picture of the Queen Mother, as she had become when he was her doctor, is of a delightfully eccentric old lady, who treated day as night (palace guards were used to frighten away birds with blowpipes so that her sleep during the day was not disturbed), stayed by choice confined to her bed, and received relatives at all hours during the night. Though speaking no English, she still took a keen interest in world affairs. She could be generous and dismissive in turn, and disapproved of the failure of her son, King Vachiravudh, to marry and produce an heir.

She was brought up in the enclosed world of the women's quarters, 'The Inside', of the Grand Palace. Trips outside were few until King Chulalongkorn's time, and one of the favourite places to visit was Bang Pa-in, which she continued to return to annually almost until her death.

IT was in her [Queen Saowapa's] time that the emancipation of the harem from the rigid seclusion of the Palace took place, and it came about very largely through the King's love of travel. Nothing pleased him more in the days of his early manhood than to explore his own country and to take his large and growing family with him. Where the King went there went his Queens, his favourite wives, and all that vast human paraphernalia without which the Court could never move.

For the women of 'The Inside' his fondness for travel meant liberation, not indeed in their relations with other men—that would have been too much to expect—but from the four walls of the Palace. For the first time in their lives they saw—and saw frequently—something of the outside world. The river picnics, the trips at sea in the Royal Yacht, the annual hegira to Bang-pa-in, the building of the new palace at Dusit Park where many of them went to live during its construction, meant actual contact for them with places that before had been only travellers' tales.

The river picnics were not little, one-day affairs; they were lengthy and elaborate excursions into the country round about the Capital.

The great central plain in which Bangkok lies is a flat expanse of open land used mainly for the cultivation of rice. Here and there stand clumps of trees and bamboos where the peasants live, but except for these there is nothing to break the view as far as the eye can reach. The plain is intersected by many rivers and canals; upon their banks the people lived and upon their waters they journeyed from one place to another. They were the highways for traffic. Throughout the rainy season, when the country was more or less under water, transport was entirely by boat. There were no roads, and until the last years of Chulalongkorn's reign, no railway.

To travel through that region by boat in the months of December, January and February was a delightful experience. The climate was ideal. The north-east monsoon was blowing; the days were cool. There was freshness in the air that came at no other time of the year; the skies were cloudless and could be expected to remain so.

Into that land in those halcyon days the King took his Court, and a *picnic*—the word was borrowed for the occasion—might last for many weeks. To the country people it was an imposing spectacle. Across the open plain they could see it approaching from miles away, an endless procession of boats moving slowly across the landscape. The King and his party led the way. Many of the royal houseboats were really beautiful craft, roomy inside yet with graceful lines, and so highly polished that they seemed to blaze in the sun. They were rowed by 8 or 12 men standing gondolier-like to their oars. Behind the King came the princes and their families, and then, in boats of all sorts and sizes, the royal pages, the officials, the soldiers and the army of cooks with their kitchens that were required to feed them. A big picnic party might number between three and four thousand people....

For the King it was far from a holiday. For him the trip was a chance to make personal contact with the people, and at every stop he took it. As his boat drew up at the landing place he found the officials waiting for him; with them were priests from the temple, and in the background children with flowers for the Queen. He spent some time chatting with them and then moved off to see the place and talk with the inhabitants.

Once or twice a year, and always in the dry season, [Queen Saowapa] went away from Bangkok for a few weeks. It was called going for a change of air (*plien akart*), but except that it was a change in that respect, it made none in her way

Queen Saowapa, from Malcolm Smith, *A Physician at the Court of Siam*, London, Country Life Ltd., 1957.

of living. As soon as she had settled in her new bedroom, life went on exactly as it did at Pya Tai Palace. The seaside resorts of Hua Hin and Ta Chin, where large and commodious buildings of wood and attap had been erected for her convenience, were delightful spots for those who loved the sea. But the sea for her had no longer any attraction. Bang-pa-in Palace, from its long associations with the past, was regarded differently.

Some of the happiest days of her life had been spent there. She remembered with particular delight (*sanuk*) the outings by launch, when she and the King, her children and a few chosen friends—a family affair entirely—had gone off for the day into the surrounding country. They travelled without ceremony, exploring new waterways, stopping at wayside temples to have alfresco meals. The King would do the cooking while the ladies prepared the table and such dishes as they had brought ready with them. It was often long after dark when they got back.

One of King Chulalongkorn's greatest gifts was his ability to make himself at home in any company. His simplicity of manner and infectious gaiety charmed everyone and put them at their ease. On these trips into the country he often took advantage of the opportunity to mix with the people incognito, entering their houses and even sitting down to meals with them.

While the King was alive she had been to Bang-pa-in Palace every year, and after his death the custom was continued. She travelled there by water, and with a canal at the very gates of the Palace this was an easy matter. One of the great house-boats that had been used for picnic tours in the past was taken from its shelter and cleaned and polished and made ready for the trip. Like some old friend returning to greet her after long absence it drew up at her landing, shining and resplendent as it had been in the days when she was a young and active woman. Only one thing was missing. The gondoliers in their scarlet costumes were not there. Their place had been taken by the steam launch and tow rope, a swifter and smoother means of transport. The journey that would have required two days before could now be made in a few hours.

The Palace of Bang-pa-in lies some 40 miles north of Bangkok, at a spot where the river divides into a network of streams. The Palace itself stands on an island formed by these channels. It was commenced about the year 1640 and was used regularly by the Kings at Ayuthia, from which it lay distant only ten miles. When the Capital was transferred to Bangkok it was too remote and for more than 80 years it lay derelict. Many of its buildings went to ruin. With the coming of the steam-launch as a means of transport in the days of King Mongkut, it became again a royal country seat. King Chulalongkorn was particularly fond of the place and went there regularly. Most of the buildings that stand there today were constructed to his orders. Some of them are European in style, others typically native. The Chinese Hall was built originally in China and was taken to pieces, shipped and reconstructed at Bang-pa-in. A small pavilion, the *Pratinang Aisawantipat* which stands in the middle of an artificial lake, is one of the finest examples of Siamese architecture of its kind in existence. From its small size and its position, surrounded by water, it was evidently intended as an ornament and not for use.

While the Queen was in residence at Bang-pa-in Palace it was a busy place. Something of the gaiety it had known in the days of King Chulalongkorn was recaptured. Parties went up by launch and train—not to see the Queen, there was no hope of that for she never left her room—but to meet their acquaintances, to see the shows, to have a picnic. To all her friends and relatives she kept open house, and they came and went as they pleased. Troops of dancers were sent up from Bangkok to perform, theatrical shows were arranged. They took place out of doors. Under a moon riding high in a cloudless sky it was a picturesque scene. The stage was set up on one side of a large lawn and some rows of chairs were placed in front of it, but they were not much used. The audience for the most part preferred to sit on the ground or stand about. Some came to watch for a bit; others found it a convenient place for conversation; some as the night wore on fell asleep. No one ever thought of seeing a performance through.

The theatre in Siam, which provides several and entirely different forms of entertainment, has always played a large part in the life of the people; but its productions had become stereotyped in character. For years they had hardly changed, and they were of interminable length. At Bang-pa-in they began about nine o'clock in the evening and went on until two or three in the morning, five or six hours of elaborate and graceful posturing, of high-pitched nasal singing, of buffooning, and of plots that never seem to develop. The country people could sit and watch these shows for hours, but the educated classes were beginning to ask for something better, something more alive, something of greater human interest. The 'pictures' [cinema] had come to their knowledge, and bad and unreal as they usually were in those early days, they had awakened them to a new and entirely different outlook on entertainment. The new King, also, by translating European plays and having them performed by amateurs, had contributed to this change of ideas. And in consequence their own shows were beginning to bore them. When they went to see them, an authority on the Siamese theatre has told us, it was not to see a new play, for it seldom came, but to see the acting of their favourite stories.

I never saw the end of a performance at Bang-pa-in; I was in bed and asleep. But I was told they went on until there was no audience left to play to.

Malcolm Smith, *A Physician at the Court of Siam*, London, Country Life Ltd., 1957, pp. 81–2, 84, 129–31.

58
A View from the Golden Mount in 1928

ERIK SEIDENFADEN

Major Erik Seidenfaden was a Dane who, for a period in the early part of the twentieth century, worked with His Siamese Majesty's Provincial Gendarmerie. He was a scholar in his own right, contributing several learned articles to the Journal of the Siam Society. *In the 1920s, he was asked by the administration of the Royal State Railways of Siam, concerned at the need to supply 'the growing number of tourists who visit the City of Bangkok' with concise information about the country and its capital, to assemble a guidebook, his credentials being 'a resident of this country for a long time past and a real lover of Siam and things Siamese'.*

Seidenfaden, like most of us, was not the best of futurologists. He wrote in 1928: 'The future will see Bangkok as a vast well laid out, park-like town intersected with a network of broad shady roads running in all directions and it will then have become much more even than now "the city of great distances", by which name it is already known.' Certainly, the distances are there, but he could hardly have foreseen the frenzied development of the capital since the 1970s, which destroyed his hopes of a well-planned park-like city.

His description of the view from the Golden Mount is also interesting for the changes since 1928. Even in the 1960s, the view was much as he gives it, but the subsequent appearance of skyscrapers and elevated motorways was to change the scene dramatically.

LET us then direct our steps towards the Golden Mount which is one of the most conspicuous and picturesque landmarks of Bangkok. Where the present brick mountain stands there stood formerly a huge phra chedi, the building of which was commenced by King Phra Nang Klao or Rama III. He, however, had to give up the construction for the reason that the ground was too soft to stand the weight of the enormous brick mass. Later on King Maha Mongkut took up his predecessor's work and succeeded in constructing the present huge edifice which now rises over the crumbling mass of the old chedi. The slopes of the mount are adorned with a number of small caves, chedi, images and sala, and are planted with trees, which give it the look of a real mountain. Two winding staircases with low easy steps lead to the summit which is crowned with a phra chedi enclosed by a covered gallery. Access to the phra chedi can only be had during the annual Pu Khao Tong fair in the month of November when thousands of the faithful come to adore the relic enshrined in the base of the chedi. This relic is a genuine piece of bone of Buddha and was, together with other pieces, discovered in 1898 in a huge earth covered ruin of a stupa at Piprahwa near the Nepalese border in India. After the discovery the Indian Government divided the precious relics between the foremost Buddhist countries, viz: Ceylon, Burma, Siam and Japan. Siam sent a special envoy to receive its part of the relic and on its arrival in Bangkok it was borne in solemn procession to the top of the Golden Mount and deposited in the chedi there. From the platform on both sides of the chedi one can always enjoy a unique view over the capital. Looking down one sees at the foot of the mount the temple buildings of Wat Sraket [Saket] with their shimmering roofs and gilt carvings and the extensive monks' quarters, all set in a frame of big shady trees. Near to the mount runs the city moat called Klong Sapan Han, from which Klong Mahanak branches off, running in an easterly direction, and at high water this klong offers a most interesting and lively picture with its teeming life in all kinds of coming and going boats. Along the city moat we see the city wall with its embrasures, and just where the broad Rajadamnoen Boulevard crosses the moat there still remains one of the old picturesque forts. Looking westwards one can see the tall roofs of Wat Sudat [Suthat] and the top of the red painted swing while farther away over a labyrinth of house tops and big administrative buildings are seen the grand palace with the glittering spires of the Chakri Palace, the Dusit Maha Prasad and the shimmering fabric of the golden chedi inside Wat Phra Keo. To the south of the palace flash the gilt gables of Wat Po and further away again, on the other side of the river, the slender prang of Wat Arun soars upward and in this direction, too, a glimpse of the broad bosom of 'the Mother of the Waters' may be had. Looking to the south the horizon is closed as by a mighty forest, the vast and idyllic garden-land on the west bank of the river, from which here and there, some white prang [spire] or pointed chedi peep up out of all the greenery. On this side of the river, towards the south and south-east, the newer part to the capital extends with its throng of streets and houses, presenting a view which however, is not that of a desert of stones like so many American or European cities because here in Bangkok the trees and the verdure dominate. Seen from a high position, the town resembles one huge park though here and there tall chimneys belonging to rice mills or factories belch forth their smoke indicating that this is really a living and prospering town. Continuing, our eyes travel towards the east where among other buildings we can just discern the tall arched roof of Bangkok's Railway Terminus and furthermost east a glimpse is seen of the red towers of the Phya Thai Palace and then turning to the north we see the tree tops the Dusit Park and the white marble structure of the Throne Hall with its cupola. From the Throne Hall our eyes can now follow the broad and stately avenue of Rajadamnoen up to its end at the precincts of the Grand Palace; between this avenue and the river stretches the northern suburb called Samsen with its extensive gardens and palm groves. We have now made the round trip. To get a good idea of how Bangkok spreads, however, one must see it from an aeroplane. The clearest view over the city is obtained during the early morning hours but to see the sun setting over this town of palaces and flashing temple spires is also well worth a climb to the top of the Golden Mount. Before we leave Pu Khao Tong, a short explanation of the origin of such structures may interest the enquiring visitor. According to the Brahmanic religion the gods live on the top of the mountain called Meru, the god Shiva living apart on the top of Kailasa. The Cambodian kings, themselves of Hindu origin and fervent Shivaists, therefore excelled in building temples to the honour of the gods on the tops of the hills, especially Shiva temples, which always contained the linga, the symbol of this god. The Thai kings of Ayudhya followed in the steps of their Cambodian teachers and had also a golden mount built there ... but this mount was crowned, not with the linga, but with the chaste symbol of the chedi so when Phra Nang Klao started to build a golden mount in Bangkok he merely followed the examples given by his Royal predecessors.

Erik Seidenfaden, *Guide to Bangkok with Notes on Siam*, 2nd edn., Bangkok, Royal State Railways of Siam, 1928, pp. 241–6.

59
Amusements Old and New

W. A. R. WOOD

W. A. R. Wood was born near Liverpool in 1878, and joined the British Consular Service for the Far East at the age of eighteen. He was posted to Bangkok, and much of his work was as a magistrate in the extraterritorial British Consular court. He was first posted up-country to Nan in 1905, and subsequently served in Chiangrai, Bangkok, Songkhla, and

Lampang, before being sent to Chiangmai in 1913, where he stayed until and after his retirement in 1931. He married a local lady, Boon, and died in 1970, two days before his ninety-second birthday. In retirement he wrote and gave English lessons. During the war he was interned in Bangkok, and afterwards continued to write under the pen-name 'Lotus', and tend his garden at Nong Hoi, a little to the south of Chiangmai. He was fluent in Thai, and drawing on early chronicles, he compiled his History of Siam *(1924), which was reissued many times. His rose-tinted souvenirs,* Land of Smiles, *was written in 1935 and reissued in 1965 as* Consul in Paradise, *from which some recollections of amusements in Siam are taken.*

SIAMESE and Lao boxing differs quite a lot from ours. The feet may be used, and are used by some boxers to excess, and there is a certain amount of semi-wrestling, semi-jujutsu work. I am told that eighty-four different varieties of punch, grab, shove and kick are recognised; if a boxer tries to introduce an eighty-fifth kind, he is guilty of a foul. For instance, it is a foul to hold your opponent's head under your arm and thump it, or to jump on his face after knocking him down....

A Siamese or Lao boxer, before beginning to fight, often goes through various genuflections, kneeling on the ground and raising his hands in honour of his 'teacher'. After that he may do a little dancing. Sometimes the two opponents dance round each other for quite a long time before they get down to business. Some of them dance very well, and when knocked down will get up again not only smiling, but dancing. They almost always show the greatest good humour throughout the fight, and will smile and joke as long as they are able to stand up....

In the Siamese Peninsular States the people are very fond of bull-fighting. Bull against bull, be it understood. To us these fights seem rather tame affairs. In nine cases out of ten the fight consists merely in a trial of strength, one bull pushing against the other with its head, until the weaker of the combatants is forced back, when it turns and runs. The victor rarely pursues the vanquished for more than a few yards, and it is unusual for either of them to suffer very severe injuries. Sometimes their heads are a bit gory, but that is about all....

Some fighting bulls are very fierce, so to speak, in private life. When we lived at Singora [Songkhla], a neighbour's fighting bull broke into our compound and severely gored one of our ponies. But he got as good as he gave, for a tiny little pet pony of my wife's, about eight hands high, joined in the fray, seized the bull by the tail, and would not let go until he had almost chewed it off. After that, the owner of the bull wanted to sue me for damages.

Siamese fighting fish are well known. They are very beautiful little creatures, with long, lacy fins, and their scales show all the colours of a sunset sky. Their pugnacity is remarkable; not infrequently both combatants succumb to their injuries, their fins being so torn that they cannot swim. A great deal of money is often staked on fish fights, but to foreigners they are more or less slow and unexciting performances. Sometimes the two fishes will hold on to one another's mouths for almost an hour; the spectators wait in a state of rapt attention, but I must admit that I have often longed to poke the performers with a stick to liven them up a bit. I have often felt the same at a cricket match.

Cock-fighting is very popular, but this is, of course, nothing peculiar to Siam. Cricket fighting I have never seen, but I claim to be an expert at beetle fighting, having once kept a stable of five rhinoceros beetles, all tethered to sticks of sugar cane. To tether a beetle, all you have to do is to drive a post—a match will serve—into your sugar cane, and attach the beetle's horn to the post by a piece of string, leaving it to graze contentedly on the cane....

This is how beetles are made to fight. A long stick is prepared, in the middle of which there is a little, scooped-out prison chamber, shut by a tiny door, and containing an even tinier window. In this little prison a lady beetle is placed, unapproachable, yet partly visible, and presumably smellable. The two fighters are put on to the stick, and they fight for the lady. They are not always very keen, and have to be led on by the use of little tin buzzers on sticks, which are twiddled near them in order to excite them. They rarely, if ever, inflict any visible wounds on one another, but when their bodies are well pinched they give forth a curious hissing noise, which rather gives one the idea that they are feeling uncomfortable. Their owners revive them, between the rounds, by spitting sugar-cane juice on to them, and sometimes by fanning them. If one of the beetles runs away, and will not come back, he is adjudged the loser. Sometimes, too, one of the beetles will seize the other with his horns, drag him by force off the stick, and heave him bodily forth into the wide world.

The lady beetle has, I always think, a very thin time, cooped up in her tiny cell, while her rival lovers fight above her skylight window. Neither victor nor vanquished is for her, anyhow, for love-making is held to be extremely bad for fighting beetles. A lot of money is staked on these fights, and the owner of a first class beetle may make quite large sums out of it. But the poor beetle, after all its fighting, is not even allowed to snatch a hasty kiss. I call this unjust....

In former times, people used to race tortoises, urging them on to unnatural rates of speed by kindling fires on their backs. The Siamese Government long ago prohibited this cruel sport, but nevertheless I once saw such a race. It was in a distant jungle village near Pailin, and the promoters, I blush to say, were British [Shan] subjects. I came on them unexpectedly, late at night, and remember the scene well. A couple of dozen excited men, brandishing torches in a bamboo thicket, and in their midst two wretched tortoises, running frantically with some horrible resinous substance flaring on their backs. It was a most devilish thing, and yet I do not think anyone there realised how cruel it was. I rushed in, seized one of the tortoises and threw mud and sand on its shell, and the meeting broke up in confusion. The tortoise I dealt with was not much damaged, but the other one, which I caught later on, had to be killed....

The Siamese are extremely fond of the theatre. Of late years all kinds of Western innovations have been introduced on to the Siamese stage, and it is fashionable to regret this, and to bewail the decay of the old 'classical' traditions; but I, for one, much prefer the more lively methods of modern days, for I must admit that I found the old style of Siamese classical drama almost insufferably boring. I could only bear it at all if I was allowed to doze through the performance, but I was seldom left to slumber, kindly disposed friends always insisting on waking me up and explaining the plot to me. On one occasion I had changed my seat three times, so as to escape from plot-explainers, and at last came to anchor between two American Reverends, feeling confident that I would be safe there. Not a bit of it! Hardly had I dozed off when they jointly woke me up and started to explain the plot to me. I may add that the play was one which no clergyman ought to have attended without first stuffing his ears with sterilised cotton wool.

In the classical dramas, or *Lakhons*, all the players, except a few comic characters, were women, and the acting tended to be conventional, and made no attempt to 'hold the mirror up to Nature'. The comic plays, or *Yike* [likay], were much more amusing. All the performers were men, and there was a good deal of slap-stick farce, and a good deal of extremely broad humour. At the present time there are many *Yike* theatres in which both men and women take part. The actors and actresses are often remarkably clever at improvising verses, one capping the other, and trying to outdo him or her in audacity....

No film [in Chiangmai] less than ten years old was ever shown, and most of the films had come to pieces and been stuck together again—all wrong. There was a famous film called the *Hypnotic Detective,* in which the sleuth started by hauling the criminal off to jail for a murder which one saw being committed an hour later. Some of the films would have failed to pass the Censor at home. One of these, called *Father's Purge,* was extremely popular.

A curious thing about the Chiengmai cinemas was, and still is, that a number of young fellows derive great satisfaction from standing, night after night, *outside* a cinema hall. Many of them never go in to see the show, and so far as I can make out they are not usually in search of amorous adventures—I mean to say, not more than everybody always is. They themselves seem unable to explain why they go there beyond saying that it is *muan* (jolly). We formerly had a chauffeur who, when not on duty, stood in front of a cinema hall as regular as clockwork, from eight till eleven every night, wearing a saxe blue blazer with brass buttons. I daresay he is standing there now.

W. A. R. Wood, *Consul in Paradise*, London, Souvenir Press, 1965, pp. 75–83.

60
The Floating Market

JAMES KIRKUP

James Kirkup, a poet and lecturer in English literature in Malaya and Japan, wrote in the 1960s and 1970s a series of travel books dealing with East Asia which are often whimsical but show a keen sense of observation. His book on Bangkok has a passage on the life by the canals which has changed relatively little since the foundation of the city, and indeed reflects the waterside life of Ayutthaya before.

One thing, though, has changed: the floating market, which was the sight all tourists had to get up at dawn to see, is no longer to be found in the capital. Modernity, office life, and traffic jams have consigned it to the bin of one's memories, though this does not prevent its continued appearance on tourist posters, since, for the benefit of overseas visitors, it has been transferred to Dao Kanong to the west of the capital.

Kirkup now lives in Andorra.

THE floating markets on the *klongs* [canals] of Bangkok are certainly one of the city's most unusual features, but one which is perfectly natural and appropriate, considering the vast network of waterways, pea-green and muddy brown, that irrigate the capital with coolness and light. The floating markets are held every morning from about six-thirty to eight-thirty, except on Buddhist holy days.

The Bangkok people use their rivers and canals for bathing, washing clothes and dishes, and for transport. The smaller waterways are often smelly: the word 'Pong' comes, very appropriately, into the names of many of the canals.

Houses built of wood stand on piles and stilts along most canals, and this has made Thai domesticity very water-conscious. The water cannot be drunk of course: drinking water comes from communal taps, or rain water is used after being collected in the large earthenware jars that stand under the thatched *nipa* roofs. When one is floating along the canals one often sees men and women and children taking a dip in the scummy water: a pretty young girl descends the steps of her house, decently clad in a sarong tied tightly above her breasts instead of around the waist. Those little Thai breasts—how firm, fresh, silken they are! She takes her morning dip conveniently on her own doorstep, submerging herself right up to the neck. The air caught in the sarong makes it swell all round her like a big, flowery balloon.

The canals running beside main roads are usually very still and narrow, covered with brilliant green scum and clusters of acid-pink water-lilies, bordered by clumps of pink, orange, yellow and scarlet cannas.

But they are sometimes wide as rivers, fringed with water-palms standing deep in the reflection of their own green fans, with hanging webs of creeper and the floppy, translucent green-ribboned flags of banana trees. They are bordered also by house after house, shop after shop, all built out over the edge of the water on the same stilt principle, but all different, all hung with radiant rags and glorious banners of washing, overflowing with displays or rather haphazard collections of kitchen utensils, swarmed over by naked babies and little boys and girls, loaded with every conceivable kind of merchandise, from well-polished and gilded coffins to cascades of fluorescent plastic toys, from wide baskets of onions, bananas, fish, melons, meat, shellfish and herbs to sacks of charcoal, bales of cloth, tins of evaporated milk and small mountains of fresh laid eggs. Inside huge, dim warehouses are softly-glowing hills of golden rice.

The broader *klongs* have smaller ones branching off them, and these too are densely lined with packed houses; sometimes these canals are so narrow that the tropic trees on either bank arch right over, creating long tunnel vistas of deep green shade with one tiny speck of light, golden day, sparkling at the end like a high-flown kite or a star. These narrow tunnels of foliage, with their deep-rooted trees and *lianas*, reminded me of pictures I had seen of the Florida Everglades in that great film by Robert Flaherty, *The Louisiana Story*.

But most of the floating markets are held on the broader canals, open to sun and air, where there is more room to manœuvre the hundreds of small craft. It is best to go in the early morning hours, between six and ten o'clock. Sunrise on the canals is often remarkably dramatic, especially at the brief moment when, lighting the house fronts with dusky pink, the sun still leaves the water in shadow, dark and cold looking, agitated by the warmer reflections of the waking houses and the coming day. And as one drifts down the broad Chao Phraya River that runs through Bangkok, the immense three-decked roofs of temples and the tapering towers of the wats are for a moment silhouetted like cut-out scenery against a sky shading upwards from deep orange to palest blue, the colour of the milky zenith where a last white star dangles.

As I passed down the broad river on my way to the floating markets I saw all kinds of craft—junks, dhows, rowboats (rowed with a single long oar by a man or woman standing on a platform at the stern and working the rudder with one foot), skiffs with outboard motors, motor boats, motor launches with scallop-edged, fluttering white canvas canopies and long strings and convoys of low, heavy black rice barges roofed over with curved sheets of corrugated iron beaten flat. In these barges whole families live, and often more than one family. They transport massive, steeply piled loads of rice, rice husks, timber, sawdust, charcoal dust, coal, green bananas, mountains of papaya and vegetables and salad greens....

At enormous granaries and warehouses along the river there were endless processions of labouring men and women transporting sacks of rice and flour, basket-hods of charcoal, whole stems of bananas, trudging listlessly from barge to warehouse and back again in dumb monotony. Many, carrying a shoulder-pole, were earning a little extra by carrying double burdens of rice husks or red sawdust slung in baskets at either end of their waving poles. (These two last commodities are much in demand for the preservation of blocks of ice in Chinese coffee-shops.)

Outside big ice factories the heavy oblong chunks of crystal ice with their snowy, frost-flawed hearts were trundling down wooden inclines, and in the rising sun were shot, like formal icebergs, with splintering red and green fires. Men were sawing up the giant blocks into smaller slabs with long, flashing, deep-toothed saws that spurted fountains of ice dust, glittering like rainbows of frosted sperm against the black caverns of ice-ghosted factory hangars.

Everywhere men, women and children smiled dazzlingly and waved greetings from passing craft. Men and boys, after first modestly wrapping a towel or brief sarong round their loins, would pull their shorts or trousers from underneath this improvised bathing attire and lower themselves, the long ends of the sarong carefully tucked between their golden thighs, over the sides of boats for a morning bathe. Their wet bodies were gleaming like warm, dark honey, their work-hardened muscles rippling like clouded, melting amber, their smiles suddenly flashing from lovely brown faces like the glancing white light struck from the brown waves of our wake. How happy and carefree they seemed, how healthy, normal and strong! Yet they live on the border of poverty and destitution. But however poor they are always clean, for they have an enviable self-respect; they are hard working, and glad just to be alive.

These fine river folk seemed to me the epitome of the Thai race, a race that is in every way a beautiful one. It has a limpid, easy soul, a graceful body and the blessed gift of non-attachment to earthly things, to passion and persons. Their deep Buddhist faith is proof of this, and it is the reason for their special spiritual grace. Yet though their worldly possessions are few they know how to appreciate the true qualities of a simple life, and at the same time, like everyone else, love money (which they squander immediately, quite rightly), good clothes, pretty sights and any novelty. They are both attached and non-attached to the world, which they look upon gaily as a passing shadow occasionally pierced by shafts of lucky sun; themselves they regard as dust, as ephemeral as the swarms of insects that only live an hour in the dancing dazzle of heat and light. They have none of the neurotic despair and nagging doubts of the Japanese, nor the enervating melancholia of the Malays. If the Malays may truly be called 'nature's gentlemen', the Thais are nature's children, warm-hearted and untroubled by doubts and dreams; and, I am sure, they are smiled on with especial favour by the great Lord Buddha.

At a crowded water turning the broad river with its lovely vistas gave way to a large, broad canal, magnificent in the rising sun with the sight of a string of three monumental barges, their boards almost over-flowing with packed tons of golden yellow, unhusked rice, being solemnly and grandly hauled along by a fussy, brightly painted diesel tug, its smiling captain accompanied at the wheel by a three-year-old waving and wondering daughter. In each of the three barges were families in various stages of undress, engaged in all kinds of occupations: scrubbing clothes over the edge of the deck, scouring dishes, bathing, combing long dark hair in gleaming hanks over the stern, cooking in a large shallow metal dish over a small brazier, hanging out clothes and bits of cloth, washing vegetables in the sluggish wake, taking a dip clinging to the side of the barge, tidying and cleaning and endlessly rinsing and rubbing. A clean, crowded tidiness was the impression I gained from glimpses of the interiors under long tunnels of beaten corrugated iron which forms the only roof—bakingly hot even under the just-risen sun—of those aquatic homes. A naked male baby was having his beam end dunked in the canal. A boy, after a swim, clambered on board again, his wet loincloth perfectly moulding perfect thighs and hips.

On the landing-stage of a small house a group of naked little boys squealed and giggled and shouted 'Good night' as we chugged past, then merrily, squirmingly concealed themselves behind a large pink umbrella, each rib trimmed at its tip with a soft white cock's feather. Then there was the extraordinary sight of scores of small flowerpots, each flourishing its leaves and blooms, hanging on long cords like suspended gardens from the overhead framework of a house's combined veranda and landing-stage. A wisteria, growing from a vast, deep pot, was trained over the roof. It was at this house, embowered in banana leaves and bits of coloured laundry like demented bunting, that I noticed for the first time an old granny, crouching over a steaming, fragrant bowl of tea, and whose white hair was cropped like a boy's. All the old women I was to see on the *klongs*, whether their hair was grey, white or still unfaded, always had Eton crops.... Many of them were hard at work in granaries, in sons' or daughters' houses, or rowing their own narrow, canoe-like boats, laden lightly with a few eggs and bananas, papayas, mangosteens, coconuts, mangoes and the curious 'rose-apples', a pale, tomato-like fruit, not very nice. These old women guided their craft skilfully, with gnarled, strong, sinewy brown hands and arms, among the swarming water traffic of the canals....

But one or two old women are still wearing their iron-dark

grey hair piled on top of their heads in a horn-like bun. A little girl had her hair scraped upwards into a posy-like topknot tightly bound with a red elastic band. Little boys all had pudding basin crops; older youths had black, glistening wings of thick hair sweeping back from noble brows. Other young males left their hair quite dry, and the fine silken quality of the male Thai's hair was illustrated very prettily by the way their mop heads stirred languorously in the breeze of motion like feathery black sea anemones caressed by a drifting current in a warm tropic lagoon. As in Malaya and Japan there were endless groomings and combings and anointings, for, though he may have very little else, every Thai boy has a comb which he carries everywhere with him. To a Thai the top of the head is sacred, and should not be touched or caressed, either in public or in private, by another person. But such is their good nature, they never objected to my doing this while I was still ignorant of the prohibition....

Along another canal there were a number of water craft garages and 'parking spaces'; in the former, boats were being repaired and built with slow and patient craftsmanship. All along the *klongs* craft were being converted and adapted, sometimes producing curious cross-breeds of nautical styles, their mixed origin carefully concealed by a fresh pedigree of white or more usually crude red, blue and green paint that gives a boat a really magnificent appearance as it rounds a palm-leafed bend. Farther on was a large water garage crowded with powerful, glittering, bright red fire engine boats which firemen dressed in the pale khaki of the navy were scrubbing and polishing.

Then my boat turned into a narrower canal, the surface of whose water was almost entirely covered with small skiffs selling every kind of fruit and vegetable, fish and meat. The floating butchers' boats always had a pig's head stuck up in the prow, while the rest of the carcass was distributed in anatomically correct order down the entire length of the skiff, with the curled tail nailed to the stern. There were old women like witches—their evil eyes seemed to pierce my sun-glasses, but in vain—cooking rice and soup in their canoes over small charcoal braziers, or ladling out tea and coffee and coconut juice to passing ship-shoppers or fellow floating marketeers. I refused to drink the brews these rather sinister little floating coffee-shops and snack bars ladled out into chipped enamel mugs.

A postman was slowly delivering letters from a boat rowed by himself; letter-boxes are placed on verandas over the water.

The shape of the pale golden reed hats is that of Mount Fuji, or like the truncated mouth of a trumpet, very becoming, and very cool and shady. It is fixed on the head by a light, crown-like woven bamboo framework. I tried one on; they are very light, airy and clean. Sometimes they are lacquered with a light-coloured, transparent varnish, waterproof, that makes their pale eaves glitter in the sun. But even at the hottest time of the day in Thailand I never wore a hat: it is not necessary unless, like labourers in padi-fields and on canals, one is exposed to the direct rays of the scorching sun all day long. Some women carry sunshades; a Western lady could buy one here, in native silk, as a pretty and useful addition to her wardrobe. Children—both boys and girls—sometimes carry sunshades or oiled paper and bamboo umbrellas, but I do not recollect ever having seen a man using one.

When my boat entered again the broad river that divides the double cities of Bangkok and Dhonburi, as the Danube divides Buda and Pesth, I was conscious of the sky's vastness, my lowness on the water, the dwarfish look of even the highest buildings, both modern and ancient, on either bank.

Among these was the Temple of the Dawn, Wat Arun, an immense phallus roughly glazed with a riotously pretty crackle of broken crockery. Whole dishes had been artfully split into five segments like the petals of a flower and the inside of a yellow or pink cup stuck in the centre, like a corolla and stamens. Millions of cheap dinner services—blue or sepia willow pattern—or tea-sets of bold primary colours had been systematically smashed to ornament the vast, steep steps and stairways, the domes and tower. The whole effect is of overwhelming charm and prettiness; of all-inclusive, ravishing miniature detail of decoration on a colossal scale, its splendid vulgarity both monumental and gay, earnest and frivolous, matter-of-fact and artificial—combinations of all the qualities I most revere.

The three-headed elephant Erawan was ensconced in a chip-china niche half way up the main tower. Gilded Buddhas, rampant, couchant and cross-legged, were concealed in small glass and mosaic and china-encrusted chambers in the four side towers, where there were notices in Thai script and in English saying, inscrutably, 'To well discern the Buddhas'. Friezes of crackle-glazed, brilliant figures with joined hands, apparently dancing round the flanks of the main tower's buttresses.

A flurry of little stalls, all a-flutter with flags and bunting, selling niello ware, bamboo objects, reed hats, postcards, all kinds of goodies and colour transparencies.

Wat Arun is certainly a most extraordinary piece of religious architecture, unlike anything else I have seen. Its five tall towers are called, very suitably somehow, *prang*; the central and tallest one is 260 feet high. The four smaller towers, decorated with porcelain and broken pottery, are actually pagodas built in the ancient Khmer style. The main chapel at Wat Arun (known as the *bot*) once contained the Emerald Buddha before it was taken to the Grand Palace.

I sailed back down (or is it *up?*) the river, passing the horned and tilted roofs of the old royal palace and of the Temple of the Emerald Buddha, and cruising alongside a few small grey warships, very inoffensive looking, with khaki-clad Thai sailors lounging, waving and smiling at the white-painted rails, their pale khaki sailor collars lifted by the breeze ... to the covered dock where repose the seven immense royal and state barges with their huge golden and polychrome figureheads of giant birds, monkey gods and fierce, seven-faced dragons. It was a place of cool, shadowy peace, lit by the gold of those long boats with their crimson-painted seats that can accommodate hundreds of brawny young rowers, all in ceremonial dress. The boats are brought out only on ceremonial occasions, for example, at the festival known as Kathin, which takes place towards the end of October, the time when annual offerings of new saffron robes and other equipment are made to the monks. During this period long processions of people make their way to the various monasteries with their gifts. Though it is a religious festival, as so often in the East it is celebrated with great verve, with dancing, music and singing. Processions are often made along the river and the canal in gaily decorated boats.

The sight of these huge, wonderfully elegant gilded rowboats bearing their shrines and sacred red and golden ceremonial umbrellas down the river past purple, green and orange tiled temple roofs is an unforgettable spectacle.

James Kirkup, *Cities of the World: Bangkok*, London, Phoenix House, 1968, pp. 38–45.